Performances of Research

Studies in the Postmodern Theory of Education

Shirley R. Steinberg
General Editor

Vol. 440

The Counterpoints series is part of the Peter Lang Education list.
Every volume is peer reviewed and meets
the highest quality standards for content and production.

PETER LANG
New York • Washington, D.C./Baltimore • Bern
Frankfurt • Berlin • Brussels • Vienna • Oxford

Performances of Research

Critical Issues in K-12 Education

Edited by
Rachael Gabriel
Jessica Nina Lester

Foreword by Norman Denzin

PETER LANG
New York • Washington, D.C./Baltimore • Bern
Frankfurt • Berlin • Brussels • Vienna • Oxford

Library of Congress Cataloging-in-Publication Data
Performances of research: critical issues in K–12 education /
edited by Rachael Gabriel, Jessica Nina Lester.
p. cm. — (Counterpoints: studies in the postmodern theory of education; v. 440)
Includes bibliographical references.
1. Education—United States. 2. Multicultural education—United States.
3. Educational equalization—United States.
I. Gabriel, Rachael E. II. Lester, Jessica Nina.
LC196.5.U6P47   370.11'5—dc23   2012024299
ISBN 978-1-4331-1963-7 (hardcover)
ISBN 978-1-4331-1962-0 (paperback)
ISBN 978-1-4539-0863-1 (e-book)
ISSN 1058-1634

Bibliographic information published by **Die Deutsche Nationalbibliothek**.
Die Deutsche Nationalbibliothek lists this publication in the "Deutsche
Nationalbibliografie"; detailed bibliographic data is available
on the Internet at http://dnb.d-nb.de/.

Cover art by Ashley Addair

© 2013 Peter Lang Publishing, Inc., New York
29 Broadway, 18th floor, New York, NY 10006
www.peterlang.com

All rights reserved.
Reprint or reproduction, even partially, in all forms such as microfilm,
xerography, microfiche, microcard, and offset strictly prohibited.

Foreword

Norman K. Denzin

This book is a performance text about the performance turn in the human disciplines. For at least a decade interpretive ethnographers have been staging reflexive ethnographic performances, using their fieldnotes and autoethnographic observations to shape performance narratives, an anthropology and sociology of performance. Educational ethnographers are in a critical interpretive phase, performing culture as they write it. It is time to take stock, as editors Rachael Gabriel and Jessica Lester do in their Introduction. It is time to review, as they do, where reflexive performance and [auto]ethnography have come, to imagine where we may go next.

This book is about rethinking performance [auto]ethnography, about the formation of a critical performative cultural politics, about what happens when everything is already performative, when the dividing line between performativity and performance disappears.

The contributions in this new book reflect a desire to contribute to a critical discourse that addresses central issues confronting schooling, democracy and racism in a postmodern America. The authors understand that we inhabit a performance-based, dramaturgical culture. The dividing line between performer and audience blurs, and culture itself becomes a dramatic performance. Performance ethnographers create and enact moral texts that move from the personal to the political, the local to the historical and the cultural. These dialogical works create spaces for give and take, doing more than turning the other into the object of a voyeuristic, fetishistic, custodial, or paternalistic gaze.

A performance based social science is a minimalist social science. It attempts to stay close to how people experience everyday life. A performative discourse simultaneously writes and criticizes performances. In showing how people enact cultural meanings in their daily lives, the focus is on how these meanings and performances shape experiences of injustice, prejudice and stereotype.

Shaped by the critical sociological imagination this version of doing social science attempts to do more than just show how terms like biography, history, gender, race, ethnicity, family and history interact and shape one another in concrete social situations. The desire is to show how the histories and the performances that persons live are shaped by forces that go on behind their backs.

A critical sociological imagination responds in three ways to the successive crises of education, democracy and capitalism that shape daily life. It criticizes those formations, by showing how they repressively enter into and shape the stories, and performances persons share with one another. At the same time, it shows how people bring dignity and meaning to their lives through these self-same performances. In so doing, it also offers kernels of utopian hope, suggestions for how things might be different, and better.

This is what the chapters in this book do. They map new utopian spaces. They offer new visions, new scripts, new stories. We are in their debt for doing so.

Table of Contents

Introduction 1
Rachael Gabriel and Jessica Nina Lester

Chapter 1: "I Am Proud to Be African": Countering Deficit
Discourses in a U.S. School 7
Katharine Sprecher

Chapter 2: I Live in a Curled World…: Stories from
Immigrant Students and Their Teacher 33
Irina S. Okhremtchouk and Rosa M. Jimenez

Chapter 3: The Naming of the Dis/abled within
U.S. Special Education 71
Jessica Nina Lester and Rachael Gabriel

Chapter 4: Needing Intensive Remediation: How a
Reading Identity is Negotiated, Interpreted, and Lived 95
Anne McGill-Franzen and Renee Moran

Chapter 5: Doing Time in ISS: A Performance
of School Discipline 123
Katherine Evans

Chapter 6: Education Is a Small Part of the Life
I Have to Live 155
Allison Daniel Anders, Kafele Jahi Khalfani, and Amy E. Swain

Chapter 7: We Hear What We Know: Racial Messages
in a Southern School 195
Kimberly J. Howard

Chapter 8: *Our School*: College-Going Scripts of Students
in an Early College High School 217
James A. Brooks

Chapter 9: Queerer Than Queer! 245
Mark Vicars

About the Contributors 273

Introduction

Rachael Gabriel and Jessica Nina Lester

This book, a collection of nine performative texts, was written with three primary audiences in mind: (a) teacher educators, pre-service teachers, and practicing teachers who seek to develop an understanding of what are commonly referred to as "trends and issues" in education, especially those related to equity of educational opportunity; (b) scholars engaged in the study of qualitative inquiry, particularly those who seek to develop an understanding of performance as a method, practice, and theory; and (c) community organizers and advocates who engage in work that aims to question and complicate understandings of the everyday lived experiences of those who are targeted, marginalized, or otherwise oppressed in educational settings. While there are texts used in education courses that speak to broad trends and issues related to (in)equities within education, no volume has been produced that aims to engage students and course instructors in reperforming and reliving the experiences of youth and adults engaged in K–12 education settings.

The primary purpose of the book is to invite readers to engage with alternative representations of those institutionalized practices that generate and sustain educational inequities. Participatory performances have long been used to invite audiences to embody, voice, and imagine the perspective of different characters, values, and perspectives. In settings as diverse as prisons (Kelto, 2011; Winn, 2010) and Broadway (Ensler, 2001), texts which examine issues of power and social (in)justice are explored, read aloud, and represented over and over again by different communities. Performative texts, and more broadly, performance ethnographies, are the staged remembering, retelling, and re-enacting of "ethnographically derived notes" and/or data points (Alexander, 2005, p. 411). As an alternative format for disseminating research, performance ethnography creates a space for stories to be told and retold while providing readers and audiences a chance to participate in the retelling. Further, many scholars and artists have used performative approaches to offer a radical critique of normative, taken-for-granted practices. As Denzin (2003) has written, "performance approaches to knowing insist on immediacy and involvement" (p. 8), rather than analytic distance or detachment on the part of the researcher or the audience/readership of that research. While "addressing the gaps in the literature and contributing knowledge and information" is important, it may "miss the emotional, the ethical, the moral, and the performative provocation that sharing narratives can be, even when they come from humble beginnings such as data" (Chenail, 2010, p. 1288). Thus, we have come to view the sharing of research within performative texts as a powerful and meaningful way for wide audiences to interact with the words of the participants and all that gets named "findings of research."

We came to this work as former classroom teachers, current teacher educators, and educational researchers, with our research focused on the lived experiences of students and teachers around issues of disability, identity, educational policy, and equity. As such, we remain committed to carrying and sharing the stories of our former and current students, as well as the participants who have invited us into their classrooms, shared their experiences, and allowed us to learn from their successes and challenges, their hurts, desires, and disappointments. However, early on in our work, we realized that the very process of disseminating research in academic circles is fraught with actions that we do not always find helpful, such as analysis that involves "data reduction," the common call for "generalizability," and the calculation of an "impact factor" that is measured solely within academia. We found ourselves wanting to present some stories as we came to know them: complex, conflicting, particular, and, at times, compelling us to action and revision in our own work and day-to-day lives. Though we are aware that all (re)tellings are partial and all analyses positioned, we went in search of ways to interact with the research findings that honored complexity and increased accessibility, while engaging an audience outside of academia (Vannini, 2012).

We first turned to Ensler's *The Vagina Monologues* as an example of a performative text based on interviews with 200 women about their memories and experiences with sexuality; this is work that has been published and also performed in community theaters and on college campuses regularly as part of a global, grassroots campaign to end violence against women. We interviewed actors and directors involved with *The Vagina Monologues*, giving particular attention to the common idea that they were "taking a script and making it real." We were intrigued by the possibilities of pushing the boundaries of how and where findings are disseminated, and when and how the stories of participants are experienced and "made real." It was in and through performance that we saw possibilities for audience members—often cast as passive recipients—to embody and re-imagine the experiences of others.

Alongside our study of Ensler's work, in our research surrounding the discursive construction of learning disabilities in teacher-education programs (Lester & Gabriel, 2012), we realized that one of the popular methods for teaching pre-service teachers how to conduct planning meetings within special education was to have them role-play a meeting based on fake or anonymized data. We were intrigued by the idea of role-play as a way to encourage perspective-taking and introduce pre-service teachers to lived experiences of the roles, rules, and procedures they would come to know in academic settings. We recognized in our interviews that role-plays were most often used to develop a procedural knowledge of the paperwork and processes, rather than an embodied knowledge of what is at stake for the various "stakeholders" in such spaces. We therefore fused the notion of role-playing as a "hands-on" approach for learning and understanding with the transformative power of storytelling that comes from embodying the story and speaking the words of others. In performance studies, ethnodrama, and performance ethnography (e.g., Madison, 2008; Saldaña, 2005) we found examples of ways to move from research to performance. Like Denzin (2003), we recognized that "performance-based human disciplines" have the potential to contribute to social and political change at a local level (p. 3). Over the next two years, we constructed and performed a performance text about the naming of an individual as disabled during a routine educational planning meeting (Lester & Gabriel, 2012). We held public performances in a community arts space, at conference sessions, and in undergraduate and graduate-level courses in teacher education and qualitative research. With every performance, we became more convinced that performance is an important way for us to share the stories of others in ways that invite engagement, critique, conversation, and (re)imagining of everyday practices that we so often take for granted.

Having observed the potential of the performative, we invited scholars, some working in the academy, others working as educators in various school contexts, to contribute performative texts based on their qualitative research in educational settings. Each text (re)presents the lived experiences of children, youth, and schools staff involved in education, providing readers with an opportunity to participate in each retelling through performance. The authors invite the reader/audience to examine issues that pervade day-to-day school spaces in taken-for-granted ways. Specifically, the authors engage with a range of issues including testing practices, sexuality, student-inmates' educational experiences, the practice of naming students as abled and disabled, teachers' racial messages, identity construction among children with refugee status and those learning English, practices of school discipline, and first-generation college students. The performative texts in the chapters that follow were performed in multiple settings as part of the review process and, we hope, will continue to be taken up and performed many times over as a result of their inclusion in this volume. We have collected these texts into a single volume in order to provide a tool for readers to engage with research findings that challenge often ignored assumptions about schooling while engaging with moral and political matters (Conquergood, 1985). Each of the performative texts included here are dialogical in nature, inviting and engaging the reader to be critical of the structures and discourses that sustain and preserve unjust educational systems.

Organization of the Book

The collection represents a range of approaches to and uses of performance. Nonetheless, each chapter includes an introduction in which the author details the theoretical and methodological underpinnings of the process of creating a performative representation of research findings. This introduction is followed by a full-text version of a performative text that can be read both aloud and silently, alone or in groups, as a performance or as readers' theater—with or without props and staging. The texts are followed by discussion questions meant for use in both academic and social settings, to spark informal discussions or structure formal reflections. Many of the questions were generated as the texts were performed in various educational and community contexts.

As you read and perform each script, we invite you to consider the similarities and differences in the chapters' approaches to representation. We encourage you to note each author's decision to represent data as performative. For instance, the authors of Chapter 4 designed their study with the explicit and single goal of creating a performative text using the data they gathered, whereas other authors present performative texts that are one of two or many existing representations of data from the same investigation. Further, although all the chapters have some level of organizational similarity, variation exists. For example, in Chapter 6, the authors present the performative text after only a brief note to the reader, with method and context provided at the end of the chapter. We encourage you to consider the merit and consequences of the authors' methodological decisions, comparing chapters across the book.

How to Use This Book

This book does not need to be read from cover to cover in one sitting, and it especially does not need to be read alone. Rather, we invite you to read chapters and sections within chapters out of order, according to your interests. Take up the texts and perform them in a variety of settings, and then take time to reflect, discuss, and engage in imagining alternatives and new possibilities, both alone and in groups. In the context of a teacher-education course, we encourage you to read independently the introductions to the scripts, which explore each individual chapter's theme. Then, during a class session, you might participate in a live reading or even a rehearsed performance of the individual texts. The discussion questions at the end of each chapter can serve as a starting point for discussions of the connections and disconnections made between the script, personal experiences, and other course resources/readings. In the context of a qualitative methods class, this book might be used to provide scripts for use in a "readers' theater" format, with discussion perhaps also focused on examining the methodological choices made and the consequences of those choices. In community and other settings, either rehearsed or informal readings of the performative texts could involve audience members or volunteers. The chapter introductions might be used as a tool to welcome and focus engagement. In all cases, we encourage you to embrace multiple modalities when inviting response, such that participants and audience members might respond with and without the use of their voices, their hands, their bodies, written language, motions, or images. In our experiences with performances in varied academic and community spaces, we are humbled by the power of responses that come when we create space for more than an oral discussion (Lester & Gabriel, 2012). There are different ways to experience, interpret, and "speak back" to the world around us. In many ways, the time for response is as much a time for learning and building as the performance itself.

As you perform and reperform the scripts, we ask you to consider the connections and indices across chapters, and the ways in which presumably separate issues, examined by independent researchers, inevitably and terrifyingly intersect. It is no accident that chapters about reading tests, discipline, special education, and prison are in such close proximity. Nor is it happenstance that chapters detailing identity construction for students learning English and students with refugee status and students engaging with issues of sexuality are accommodated in the same text. We hope that this collection inspires both a sense of possibility for the methods used and a call to action for the substantive connections between issues of discipline, disability, identity, language, refugee status, testing, sexuality, and incarceration. We acknowledge that each (re)presentation is partial and positional, and that future readers and performers will perceive and interpret things that we cannot. So, we invite you to take up these performative texts as ways of knowing and embodying real lives, real everyday stories that call us to respond, to stand up and say something, and to imagine utopian alternatives.

References

Alexander, B. K. (2005). Performance ethnography: The reenacting and inciting of culture. In N. K. Denzin & Y. S. Lincoln (Eds.), *The Sage handbook of qualitative research* (3rd ed., pp. 411–441). Thousand Oaks, CA: Sage.

Chenail, R. J. (2010). Playbuilding as qualitative research: The play. *The Qualitative Report, 15*(5), 1285–1289.

Conquergood, D. (1985). Performing as a moral act: Ethical dimensions of the ethnography of performance. *Literature in Performance, 5*, 1–13.

Denzin, N. (2003). *Performance ethnography: Critical pedagogy and the politics of culture.* Thousand Oaks, CA: Sage.

Ensler, E. (2001). *The vagina monologues: The V-Day edition.* New York: Random House.

Kelto, A. (2011). Bringing the bard behind bars in South Africa. Retrieved from http://www.npr.org/2011/01/04/132650791/bringing-the-bard-behind-bars-in-south-africa

Lester, J., & Gabriel, R. (2012). Performance ethnography of IEP meetings: A theatre of the absurd. In P. Vannini (Ed.), *Popularizing research: Engaging new media, genres, and audiences* (pp. 173–178). New York: Peter Lang.

Madison, D. S. (2008). Narrative poetics and performative interventions. In N. K. Denzin & Y. S. Lincoln (Eds.), *Handbook of critical and indigenous methodologies* (pp. 391–405). Thousand Oaks, CA: Sage.

Saldaña, J. (Ed.). (2005). *Ethnodrama: An anthology of reality theatre.* Walnut Creek, CA: AltaMira Press.

Vannini, P. (Ed.). (2012). *Popularizing research: Engaging new media, genres, and audiences.* New York: Peter Lang.

Winn, M. (2010). Our side of the story: Moving incarcerated youth voices from the margins to center. *Race Ethnicity and Education, 13*(3), 313–325.

Chapter 1

"I Am Proud to Be African": Countering Deficit Discourses in a U.S. School[1]

Katharine Sprecher

Introduction

Throughout the United States, children from other places in the world—children who have been labeled *refugees*[2] by the United Nations—have been and will continue to be resettled with their families (Office of Refugee Resettlement, 2012; United Nations High Commissioner for Refugees, 2012). The resettlements often occur after years of living through war, persecution, and/or internment in "refugee camps" (Hamilton & Moore, 2004; Lustig et al., 2003). Children who have been subjected to such conditions often bring rich and diverse experiences of culture, language, and geography to their new schools and communities. They may also possess the strength of spirit and will to survive that characterize individuals who have endured extreme life events (American Psychological Association, 2010). Yet, too often, children whose documented status is "refugee" are perceived as problems that need to be fixed in U.S. public schools. Schools that adopt a problem orientation may exoticize and impose labels of deficiency on refugee children regarding their English-language capabilities, cultures and countries of origin, and emotions and behaviors (Keddie, 2011; Sarroub, 2008; Sleeter & Grant, 2003; Sprecher, 2011).

This performance ethnography critically examines the matriculation of Burundian children with refugee status into a predominantly white public school in the southeastern United States. Using multiple aesthetic methods based on different data and information sources—staff interviews, literature, and participant observations with the children—I contrast voices that *Talk About* against those that *Talk With* (Denzin, 2003) the Burundian students. My goal is twofold: (a) to demonstrate the power of language and research to shape how we view people who have been othered, and (b) to provide a direct counternarrative that privileges the voices and experiences of the Burundian children.

Theoretical Context and Epistemological Orientation

U.S. public schools frequently operate within a framework of Eurocentric neocolonialism (De Lissovoy, 2009, 2010; Tejeda, Espinoza, & Gutierrez, 2003) in which teachers of the white culture work to "civilize" children of diverse backgrounds by teaching them to assimilate (Kincheloe & Steinberg, 1997; McLaren, 1995). This requires conforming to rigid behaviors that reproduce the business model efficiencies and hierarchies needed to support capitalist economies. The efficiency model that predominates in public education is designed to prepare workers who will make profits for owners and investors or help run the infrastructures that support such profit-making environments (Apple, 2001; Anyon, 1980; Bowles & Gintis, 2002; Tyack, 1974). In such environments, movements and interactions are dictated by rules and directives from authorities, such as teachers and principals, regarding exactly when and how to speak, be silent, sit, stand, and walk (Tyack, 1974, 2003). Children who do not or will not conform to such behavior standards are usually categorized as problems or deviants, labels that are disproportionately applied to minoritized children (Roey, Fergus, & Noguera, 2011; Tyack, 1974, 2003).

Most public schools provide few (if any) supports for children who are struggling with emotional life events that induce trauma or extreme stress, even though many children have such experiences at some point in their lives (U.S. Department of Education Mentoring Resource Center, 2009). Rather, the standard school environment is more likely to impose even greater behavioral restraints, along with labels of deficiency, on children's expressions of suffering. This is despite the fact that children who experience grief, loss, and/or trauma commonly exhibit emotions and behaviors such as anger, depression, meltdowns, withdrawal, or a lack of focus—consistently or intermittently—over a period of months or even years (Doka, 1995; Frater-Mathieson, 2004; Haasl & Marnocha, 2000; Wolfelt, 1983; Worden, 1996). What is treated as deviant misbehavior in the school environment is actually quite normal under numerous life circumstances.

Moreover, expected behavior and intellectual norms are dictated by white, middle-class values. Eurocentric education rejects other/ed ways of being, knowing, and communicating. In the Eurocentric classroom, the sociocultural perspectives, values, and ways of interacting with the world of people from nondominant groups are treated as nonexistent, marginal, or inferior (De Lissovoy, 2009, 2010; Kincheloe & Steinberg, 1997; McLaren,

1995; Nieto, 1996; Tejeda et al., 2003). Processes of forced assimilation, in this paradigm, operate within a framework of deficiency in which mainstream educators seek to "save" othered children from their own cultures and communities (Titone, 1998). Imbued in this framework are myriad subtle and not-so-subtle racisms that include the assumed supremacy of the English language (McLaren, 1995) and the naturalness of social and economic stratification, both locally and globally (Bigelow & Peterson, 2002).

Attitudes of school staff and locally born students toward students from other countries may be influenced by mainstream assumptions about global hierarchies. In the U.S., common assumptions about extreme social and economic disparities around the world are devoid of context regarding the devastating consequences of colonialism, imperialism, and predatory global capitalism for peoples of so-called developing nations (Bigelow & Peterson, 2002; De Lissovoy, 2009, 2010; Tejeda et al., 2003). Rather, this global chauvinism accepts the assertion that societies that are more technologically and economically centered are superior to those that are less so (though the "inferior" societies may be more centered in other ways—socially, spiritually, or ecologically, for example). This worldview normalizes world divisions according to a racialized dichotomy of *developed* and *developing* nations, in which *Third World* peoples are expected to conform to Euro-Western values in order to escape conditions of poverty that often resulted from colonial legacies and global inequities (Bigelow & Peterson, 2002; Cannella & Viruru, 2004; Escobar, 1995; Marable & Agard-Jones, 2008; Spariosu, 2004; Willinsky, 1998). In schools, this translates into curricula, teaching methods, assessment tools, and behavior expectations that privilege and speak to middle-class, Euro-Western ways of living in and understanding the world. As such, teachers are directed to police, colonize, and coerce children into conforming to a worldview that relegates their cultures, identities, and origins as inferior, deficient, and even deviant (Denzin, 2003; McLaren, 1995; Tejeda et al., 2003).

Methodological-Epistemological Orientation for Representation

Denzin (2003) wrote that performance ethnography can be a teaching tool that "makes sites of oppression visible" (p. 14). This performance contrasts one-dimensional stories that portray students as exotic and damaged with stories of complexity, multiplicity (Kincheloe & Berry, 2004), agency, and humanity. I hope to expose the stereotypes and deficiency labels often imposed in educational settings, while negating them with the real-life experiences and interactions of children and teachers. Contrary to standard academic writing, I invoke shared emotionality as a powerful way to bridge gaps in understanding about human experiences in diverse locations and times (Denzin, 2003).

Denzin (2003) characterized critical performance as a form of intervention that foregrounds "the intersection of politics, institutional sites, and embodied experience" (p. 9). The Act Two performance provides actors with a form of "embodied aesthetic practice" (Alexander, 2005) in which they enact the experiences and voices of young children living with troubling circumstances. Like Alexander's (2005) narratives featuring migrant street vendors in Los Angeles, the children in this ethnography are engaged in everyday "acts of survival and sustenance grounded in their current predicament and their relation to space, place, and time" (p. 413). Drawing on Alexander's approach, my intent is to instigate a shift in the way performers and audience members perceive themselves in relation to children who have been othered, to break down the false barriers of *us* and *them*, and to "disrupt the perpetual stasis" (p. 412) that is common among educators who have been indoctrinated to accept and perpetuate the status quo.

My goal is to avoid the *bad teacher* versus *victim student* dichotomy that is very common in popular and political discourses about education, while nevertheless acknowledging some ugly realities that plague our educational relationships. Teachers, including myself, frequently have been trained to prioritize *behavior management* as our primary job description, and indeed, rigidly regulating students' behaviors is necessary for efficiency schooling to function. The overflowing classrooms of business-model schooling require obedience and conformity to predetermined requirements and schedules (Tyack, 1974; Gatto, 2005). Yet this model, which has been standard in most public schools for over half a century (Spring, 2008; Tyack, 1974), is dehumanizing for both students and teachers. In a profession that historically has been dominated by white women (Altenbaugh, 2003), teachers too often take up roles as gendered police who unthinkingly accept and enforce orders from their administrative authorities. My intention is to compassionately portray and speak to present and future teachers who both participate in and rebel against these roles, and who must navigate through the daily power relations of educational bureaucracies.

The performance that follows is part autoethnography (Ellis, 2004) and part ethnodrama (Ackroyd & O'Toole, 2010), and is based on interviews, participant observations, and literature research. Act One is drawn from interviews with four district and school staff members collected by two other researchers (Anders & Bates, 2008–2009), and is presented nearly verbatim. Some sentences have been condensed or rearranged for better comprehension, but the language and context remain true to the speaker. Character lines serve to describe staff attitudes and perceptions of the Burundian students and their transition, as well as contextual details that tell the story of the students and their new school from the point of view of district staff.

In addition, Act One includes an autoethnographic monologue presented in poetic form by the character Researcher/Academic, and incorporates theory with personal reflections on the data, educational policies, and research processes and relationships.

Like Spry's (2006) autoethnographic performance text *Being There/Being Here*, this aspect of the performance conducts an "emotional texturing of theory" (p. 187), using "poetic structure to suggest a live participative embodied researcher" (p. 187). This character blatantly inserts the researcher into the text to demonstrate the researcher's epistemological orientation (i.e., attitude and beliefs about the research) and the voice of the researcher as "teller" (Kincheloe & Berry, 2004; Noblit, Flores, & Murillo, 2004); hence, the character's location in the *Talking About* section of the script. My intent is to demonstrate that no matter how well-meaning or positioned as advocate, the researcher's voice is still partial and positional, and can be both valuable and limited.

Act Two is based on my participant observations with the Burundian children both at their school and during afterschool tutoring sessions, and it consists of a montage of poetic vignettes that describe observed events and verbatim quotes, as well as some of my interpretations. Each vignette, though performed by only one actor, consists of multiple characters, and highlights interactions, lived moments, relationships, and emotions. The Burundian children's verbatim quotes serve as the central and organizing element of each vignette.

Although my intention is to present a critical performance that privileges marginalized voices, I cautiously approach an endeavor in which I, a Euro-Western academic and educator, take poetic license, so to speak, with the perspectives and experiences of children struggling within a neocolonial context. Having wrestled with whether to write about their perspectives at the risk of objectifying them, I have decided it would be worse to exclude them. Instead, I have chosen to take ownership of my interpretations by describing, in third person, what I observed and perceived to be the phenomenon. In this way, I insert myself into the Act Two text to highlight my role as researcher and writer in representing others (Kincheloe & Berry, 2004; Noblit, Flores, & Murillo, 2004). I believe the vignettes offer an important counternarrative to the reductionist and totalizing discourses—ELL, LD, ESL, ED³—imposed by mainstream educational frameworks. I hope that as a performance text, the piece conveys critical messages that inform teachers' future practices and attitudes toward students who are systematically labeled as problems because they are different—and because they refuse to conform. I also strive, as Ackroyd and O'Toole (2010) advocate, to re-present the Burundian children's stories with dignity.

Research Description

Research context. The Burundian children who participated in this research had been resettled in a midsize city in the southeastern U.S. in 2007. Prior to that resettlement, they had lived in a refugee camp in Tanzania that was created for "the 1972 Burundians," who had escaped genocidal massacres between the Hutu and Tutsi ethnic groups in 1972. The United Nations determined that it would never be safe or logical for them to return to Burundi, yet the Tanzanian government made clear it could not accept the Burundians on a permanent basis, and restricted their movement, property, and employment rights. Therefore, the U.N. began a process of resettling the Burundians as permanent residents in various other countries (Ranard, 2007; United Nations High Commissioner for Refugees, 2007).

Many of the 1972 survivors had suffered or witnessed atrocities, and post-traumatic stress symptoms were not uncommon. The camps were rural, and residents lived in small huts, relying on U.N. rations, small gardens and animals, and natural fuels and technologies such as firewood for subsistence. Hunger was common, as was violence due to intermittent attacks by militia groups. The majority of Burundians did not read or write, and their spoken languages were Kirundi and sometimes French (Ranard, 2007; UNHCR, 2007). Upon resettlement, nontransferrable job skills, language barriers, and insufficient resettlement supports kept the Burundian families impoverished.

The elementary school in the study was composed of primarily white staff and students, and a majority of the student body was from low-income families. The district was located in a politically conservative, "English Only" state. At the time of my research, the school had matriculated 10 Burundian students, most of whom were boys. There was one ESL teacher, who floated among classes and conducted pull-out sessions with selected students.

Data Collection and Analysis

This performance is based on data collected by an interdisciplinary research team. The team's principal investigators interviewed four staff members—an ESL teacher, principal, district administrator, and teacher assistant—in fall 2008, with one follow-up interview in fall 2009 (Anders & Bates, 2008–2009). I conducted participant observations in the school in fall 2008, visiting the school four times for 2 hours each over a 2-month period. I also conducted participant observations as an afterschool tutor/mentor with the Burundian children, attending twice a week for 1½ hours from October 2008 to December 2008 and February 2009 to May 2009. I originally applied open codes (Hardy & Bryman, 2004) to the five interviews and the original report based on my school observations, using Atlas.ti to support the analysis process. For the construction of the performance, I reread the interviews and my original participant observation notes to retrieve additional details and verbatim quotes.

Positionality

As a white, economically secure, U.S.-born citizen whose first language is English, I approached my interactions with and representations of the Burundian children with many privileges and great caution. I have consistently reassessed my process to see if I am falling into the trap of objectifying or "otherizing" research participants, and to examine the ways in which I am inserting my worldviews into the research (Noblit, Flores, & Murillo, 2004). Most of all, I am cognizant of my position as a highly educated *researcher* associated with a university, and the power this confers on me to represent and even possibly define other people for anonymous audiences. I feel it is necessary for me to work with a heightened awareness regarding the interpretive possibilities of my reader-audiences, because we always bring our assumptions and worldviews to our interpretations of any text (Barker, 2003). As a product of my culture-society, I am well aware of the racial, global, and national biases that imbue our everyday perceptions. Given the above, I strive to predict and overcome such embedded attitudes, but I know it is impossible to do so for every reader.

As a former teacher, I conducted this research in order to critically analyze a situation and try to imagine approaches that might better support the Burundian students during their transition. I had been trained in California and earned CLAD (Crosscultural, Language, and Academic Development) certification emphasizing cultural and linguistic diversity. My experiences working in California schools showed me what schools *could be*, and in my opinion, *should be* for multicultural student bodies. Teachers were prepared to employ inclusive methods such as pluralistic and anti-bias curricula, culturally responsive instruction, and adaptations for learners of English as a second language. Yet, California was far from perfect, particularly in its support systems for students who endure severe stress or trauma.

As a survivor of chronic childhood trauma, I could identify with children who sometimes struggled to get through the day. I remember the lack of support from the adults in my life and their angry directives and threats in response to my intense emotions and (mis)behaviors. Nevertheless, I know I cannot impose my own experiences and perspectives onto the Burundian children, as each of them has had a unique journey quite different than my own. My focus has been on transforming schools and teachers. In my academic journey, I have been trying to address the following notion: How do we (i.e., teachers) become better informed and equipped to fully and holistically support all of our students through the tumultuous cycles of life? More specifically, how can we improve our understandings of human beings from all walks of life, and recognize and reject the harmful attitudes and discourses in which we have been socialized?

A Note to Readers, Performers, and Audience Members

Though the script is written for the stage, it may be read in various locales, such as classrooms, coffee shops, and community centers. Although the target audiences are pre-service and practicing educational professionals, the script also may be helpful for community organizations and groups interested in the intersections of schooling and children who have experienced forced immigration. I only ask that this performance be read or enacted responsibly; that is, that all performers and audiences participate in conscientious discussions about the performance. I worry that it may be too easy for some audiences to get "sucked in" to the negative discourse in Act One and to find themselves believing and agreeing with some of the more egregious statements and terms. The preceding Theoretical Orientation section may provide some background for students unfamiliar with concepts in multicultural and critical global education. The questions for dialogue that follow both acts provide students an opportunity to critically examine the discourse used in Act One, and to compare their experiences of the different forms of representation in both acts. This performance is, above all, a learning tool rather than a form of entertainment.

However you participate in this performance, please keep in mind that this representation is necessarily partial and positional. It is *my* interpretation and representation of people and events (Noblit, Flores, & Murillo, 2004). There are many other stories and perspectives to which you have not been exposed, both within and beyond this particular research context. Perhaps this experience may inspire you to explore or share some of them.

Finally, a note about character descriptions: As you will see, the List of Characters provides only titles and names, with no additional description. I made the decision to exclude character descriptions for a number of reasons. First, I want to take extra care not to reveal the identities of research participants through deductive disclosure by sharing too much contextual information. Second, Act One is deliberately one-dimensional. My intent is to demonstrate the power of words and descriptors—especially when they are divorced from the context of everyday life, the way most research results are presented—to portray children who have been othered in limited and negative ways. Third, I don't want to describe the Burundian students yet because I want readers, performers, and audiences to be exposed to the discourses in Act One first. My goal is for my audiences to examine and contrast their initial conclusions and assumptions about the Burundian students with those they formulate after experiencing Act Two. Fourth, I don't want to describe who the Burundian children *are*. Rather, I want to demonstrate who I perceived them to be in flashing, temporary moments of interaction and coexistence, and in their own words. That is, I want their *beingness*—and that of other characters in Act Two—to come forward in the performance to demonstrate the reflexive and relational nature of our interpretations of other people.

"I Am Proud to Be African"

Act One: Talking About

Characters
District Administrator
Principal
ESL Teacher
Teacher Assistant
Researcher/Academic

Setting
The stage is dark. The actors sit in chairs dotted haphazardly around the stage. The spotlight directs to one actor at a time, leaving the other actors in the dark. Upon being illuminated, each actor stands and recites their lines, holding a white picket sign with their character title printed in large, black, capital letters. When they have finished, the light goes out before they sit back down. The stage stays dark for a few seconds before illuminating another actor.

A loudspeaker announces the setting: Somewhere in the southeastern United States, there is a school district that has encountered DIFFERENCE.

[*The first spotlight illuminates District Administrator*]

District Administrator: You know, a year ago, I had never heard of Burundi. And this year we have Burundian refugees in our schools. In the beginning it was absolute chaos. We got descriptions of behavior problems that we had not seen from anybody. Things like kicking and biting and hitting and having to be forcefully picked up by the principal and placed on the school bus kicking and screaming and biting every step of the way. I could be wrong—you'll have to ask him—but I think he had to go get a tetanus shot for human bites. Of course, these are children who have been traumatized. They've seen a lot of violence.

Principal: I actually had people quit work here or threaten to leave because they just could not handle the children. So we quickly put together a transition classroom. This was the little meeting place for our refugees. I had assistants, an ESL teacher, and they were always with the children, and they would go into the mainstream classrooms with them for literacy lessons, then bring them back to their transition room and teach them there. And it made a huge difference, just being together and having someone they knew there all the time. The biggest surprise—outside of the initial shock of them coming and us not knowing what to do with them or how to educate them—came when we realized what was working.

ESL Teacher: The ESL teacher is usually treated like some kind of "foreign language student whisperer." I mean, they think we've got some kind of magic. We can speak any language that they speak. We can just get control over students. The ESL teacher is always called to help in any kind of foreign language student issue. Sometimes they would call while I was at another school and ask me to come immediately, like I had some idea of what to do. I don't! I'm just there to teach them English.

Teacher Assistant: I graduated five days before I started working as an assistant in the transition classroom. I went to a college where you can get your teaching license while earning your bachelor's degree. I'm really glad I went there, because they drill behavior management. It is taught in every aspect. I had one whole class that that's everything we did, the entire class. At first I hated it, but I am so thankful now after getting this job because that's all I do is behavior management, and it's come in so handy, all that training.

District Administrator: Now we went to our congressman and said, "You know, if you're going to say that you're letting in large numbers of families from other countries that are so vastly different, you can't just do that and dump them on school systems. It's not that we mind to have them. That's not it. Taking care of kids and meeting their needs is what we do. But if you're going to, as a government, say that this is the way it will be, then you also need to give us the resources to do it." You know, what we did at that school ended up costing about $75,000. For that one year, for those few children. I think at the maximum the classroom had 12 students. That's a lot of money for 12 kids.

Principal: We rented a room and transformed it into a really neat ESL classroom. It is now my pre–K classroom because the ESL children have transitioned into the mainstream classroom and no new ones came. So the monies that were spent to put this room together as an official county school classroom were not only for this Burundian group of refugees, but now it's serving the 4-year-olds of this community.

Teacher Assistant: It's not that they have a behavior problem. These children are often misdiagnosed as behavior problems or mentally unstable or damaged, or whatever, and while they might have some behavior problems, it needs to be understood as a difference. They can't be expected to behave as Johnny, who is in third grade because he's gone to pre–K, K, 1, and 2. He knows how to sit and write, and, yeah, he has his wiggle worms, but he's been taught this. Until a child has been taught this, they cannot be expected to do it. So these children need to have an environment where they can, over an extended period of time, be shown how to walk in a line. Practice it. Not just, "This is a line, let's go." No. Let's practice. Let's have a specific order we line up in every day.

Principal: Public education is not prepared to take on a group of people with such different cultures and language barriers and ideas. But, you know, the skills needed are probably those that come with any successful classroom teacher, and that's patience and understanding and commitment and love and forgiveness. I don't think you can sit in a classroom and learn the skills from a university to take on refugee children and be successful. You can learn about their culture, you can learn about the habitat and what's needed for this transition, but you're not gonna be successful by reading a book.

ESL Teacher: I think the reason they call me is because the relationship with the ESL teacher is very different, because you don't have the whole classroom. It's a really intimate relationship. It's usually just one-on-one. And you form a bond just so much faster than you do in a classroom of 20 or 30 students. And because you have that bond, you have more trust and you can de-escalate or help a situation so much easier.

District Administrator: There were some serious problems that I knew to expect, but that I would expect with any refugees. Physical needs. Parenting failures, but that is from our perspective. We're accustomed to that in ESL.

Principal: The greatest satisfaction for me has been their success.

District Administrator: Many classroom teachers have an attitude that the ESL teacher is supposed to fix whatever is wrong with the student. And we frequently get phrases like "your kids." Well, they're our kids. And the ESL teacher can't fix them any more than the classroom teacher can.

ESL Teacher: Physical Education is our biggest problem area because to participate in gym, her rules are that if you're not wearing tennis shoes, you don't get to participate. Well, this population, along with half the school, can't always afford tennis shoes. You have the shoes that somebody handed down or donated to you. Your parents can't just go out and buy you brand new shoes. So the P.E. teacher was making them sit on the wall during her class.

Principal: Some of them were very angry. One did not speak the entire 6 weeks. Did not speak and did not pick up a pencil for 6 weeks. One of the most successful stories in the building, now, but at the time, it was not. That's just one of the many things that I think we dealt with. I think that one of the successes of this endeavor that we took on last year was getting them back together. I guess probably if you want to think about their behaviors and their differences, they were very sad children, initially. Very sad.

Teacher Assistant: Every once in a while, one of them would just be "whoooo," nonsensical crying. Just crying to be crying. Well, you're not allowed to cry at school, 'cause that's a big problem. And it needs to be defined that, when you're hurt or you don't feel good, then it's okay. But if your feelings are hurt or you're just unhappy, then it's not okay. We made it a class rule and posted it on the board.

District Administrator: And so we had a summer program, kind of in the middle of the summer. We would have liked to bring in some of the ones from other places in the county, but it was just too costly. 'Cause, you know, they don't have transportation. I think the bill for one bus is 7½ thousand. Don't quote me on that. I would have to make sure and check that number. But buses are very expensive.

ESL Teacher: Last year it was stupid for them to transition. It was the superintendent's decision. For him to fund it, he said he wanted them to be done and fully transitioned by the end of the year. Well that's just not how children's developmental stages work. They're not little puppets that we can say, "I know you're not used to this but you need to be done by this date." Well, they're not done. They're not okay right now. I see the need for them to still be with me in a transition classroom. I've got a few of them that still don't know the alphabet! And they're in the third grade. When, exactly, are they going to learn the alphabet? In their hour with me? And there's a few behavior issues. Half of the guys are still having problems.

District Administrator: The fact that our superintendent was willing to put our resources, and that includes money, into working with those children was a wonderful move on his part. He was willing to say, "Okay. You can have a teacher. You can have a bus. You can have a classroom." We also sent the teachers to a discipline training program. All those things cost money. So I have all the support and resources I need now. We even decided not to use all the funds.

Teacher Assistant: They realize that these behaviors that worked and got them attention before, it doesn't work anymore, and we've seen huge strides with these kids. They are helpful now, they are walking in a line, they line up in order every day. Cynthia even put her book bag and coat on her number without any direction.

Principal: I don't know if anyone out there would have a better success story as far as social, emotional, cultural, language, and academics than we've had here. It's amazing. I can now speak to these Burundian children in English and in their broken English, we can now communicate. And when you think of now, October 2008, and you go back to last year, when we were having to pull them out of trees and get them off fences and put their clothes back on them, these children have come a long way. Very successful over the last year.

[*Lights out*]

[*Suddenly and simultaneously, a dim spotlight illuminates the seated characters and another spotlight illuminates a new character, Researcher/Academic. The seated characters are frozen and unmoving. Researcher/Academic stands at far stage right and walks to downstage center, carrying a picket sign in the same design as the other characters. The first line of the sign reads "Researcher," the second line reads "Academic," and the third line reads "Poet?" Researcher/Academic balances the picket sign on the floor in front of her and addresses the audience to begin the monologue.]*

Researcher/Academic:
There are many reasons to cry.
Remembering loved ones killed
or left behind.
Remembering hunger
and sorrow
in a country they said
was not yours,
and a camp
where futures sank into
endless days of internment.
There are many reasons to cry.
Losing a place of ancient beauty
that echoed with the heartbeats of
magnificent creatures—
lions, elephants, antelopes.
Losing culture and language
and knowing the ice-water shock
of a brave new world
rife with endless machines
and hostile faces.
Leaving one kind of poverty
for another.
Becoming a stranger
who is *Black*
in a sea of *white*,
who is seen as *Third World*
and *primitive*
among the so-called *civilized*.
Becoming a *struggling reader*
and an *ESL*
in their eyes,
a number

in their bureaucracy.
Becoming a target
for hate and ignorance
or the violence of family traumas relived.
There are many reasons to cry,
but do not think this means
they are not strong.
They are small,
but they have survived.

[*Throughout the rest of the monologue, Researcher/Academic gesticulates, paces about, and holds the sign in a variety of positions, e.g., by the top, dragging on the floor, etc., as if it is an afterthought.*]

[*sighs*]
So what happens when
bigotries and money
make the big decisions?
When behavior regulations
and capitalist efficiencies
trump emotional healing and supports?
When learning means
walking in a straight line
and teachers are expected to behave
like prison guards on the beat?
What happens when
multiculturalism is a dirty word
and whiteness is assumed to be rightness?
When children are reduced
to caricatures of good and bad
and their experiences and cultures deemed
alien,
irrelevant,
obstacles to be overcome?

We are not paper dolls,
we human beings.
We do not fall from the sky unbroken.

"I Am Proud to Be African" 23

Sometimes we need time
to mend
to sit and breathe
with a friend
who looks in our eyes
and sees the richness of our humanity
even if they don't fully understand
our journey.

Our stories are never simple.
They do not conform
to standards and efficiencies.
Do they?

[*Researcher/Academic walks to downstage left and exits the stage. Lights out and curtain down.*]

Act Two: Talking With

Characters
Vignette 1 Actor (Emile[4], classmate, Researcher/Academic)
Vignette 2 Actor (Mrs. Pollard, Eric)
Vignette 3 Actor (Freddy, Researcher/Academic)
Vignette 4 Actor (Cynthia, Mrs. Pollard, recess duty teachers)
Vignette 5 Actor (Jojo, Emile, Shabani, Thierry, Miss Hailey, Miss Rukundo)
Vignette 6 Actor (Eric, classmate, Researcher/Academic)
Vignette 7 Actor (Jojo, three classmates, teachers)

Setting
The stage is lit, and the actors, one for each vignette, mill about the stage, looking around them, at each other, at the audience in great curiosity, interacting without speaking. They may murmur, gesture, reach out and touch each other in greeting. After 20 seconds, all actors freeze but the one giving their monologue. Each of these pieces should be acted out expressively and physically, with the actor taking on all the roles in the monologue and acting out the behaviors described. When each actor finishes

their[5] vignette, all actors return to milling about for 10 seconds, then freeze again while the next actor performs their monologue.

Vignette 1:

"You African!" the boy spits out at him
like being African is a bad thing.
Emile puffs out his chest,
stares down his harasser
until he looks away.
Emile is Burundian
but has never been to Burundi
because he was born in a refugee camp in Tanzania.
Now, he has been "resettled" by the United Nations
and lives in the southeastern United States.
He did not choose any of these things.
I ask him, "How do you see yourself?"
He answers with conviction:
"I am African. I am proud to be African."

Vignette 2:

Mrs. Pollard does not have
a No Crying rule.
Eric weeps into her sweater,
moaning slightly,
as she stands in front of the class.
Swaying gently, she holds him
with one arm
and a book in the other
and reads to her students.
She tells me
later
this is a daily rite of passage.
Each day she holds his grief,
just for a little while,
and he seems to greet the afternoons
with a lighter heart.

Vignette 3:

"OH MY GOODNESS GRACIOUS!"
Freddy takes a liking to my silly phrase,
rolls it around his 5-year-old tongue
and launches it into the blue spring sky
over and over
while he rides his bicycle
back and forth
laughing with singular glee
at the funny new words
he has just learned.
"OH MY GOODNESS GRACIOUS!"
We laugh and laugh
and the floating clouds,
and the green-gold hillsides,
and the warm sun
all seem to laugh with us.

Vignette 4:

"I am baby!"
Cynthia snuggles deeper into her teacher's lap
during recess as the teachers on duty giggle and
insist that she is 7 years old.
"No!" she smiles, "I am baby!"
and Mrs. Pollard hugs her, bouncing her up and down
to play along.
Months later, I learn
that the woman who lives with Cynthia
is not her mother.
Cynthia tells me, softly,
"My grandmother is in Africa.
I talk to her on the phone
every week."
She has never spoken
of a mother.

Vignette 5:

Jojo, Emile, Shabani, and Thierry
play Word Bingo
with Miss Hailey, their ESL teacher,
and Miss Rukundo, their interpreter.
Emile says quietly,
"Kenny tells the teacher that I say
I am going to kill everyone.
He is lying."
Miss Hailey stops the game.
She tells him he has to tell his teacher
he did not say this.
Miss Hailey tells me
that the whole class has ganged up
on the Burundian students,
but the teacher and the principal
don't see it as a problem.
Miss Rukundo adds, "They tell them
they are bad, bad, bad."
Miss Hailey nearly leaps out of her seat.
"They're not bad! They're not!"
The children wait for Miss Hailey to calm down.
Then they go back to playing Word Bingo.

Vignette 6:

"This my teacher!"
Eric announces proudly to his second-grade classmate
as he throws his body across my lap.
"What you doing here? Go away!" he grins jokingly.
We have worked together for a month now
in the afterschool program
and he has begun to trust me.
Later, I return after 2 months of extended winter break,
ready for reunion.
"No one here remembers you!"
he asserts angrily,
then rushes past me,

slams into the bathroom,
and shouts through the door,
"YOU FORGOT!"
I learn stupidly
and painfully.
One does not enter a child's life carelessly. [6]

Vignette 7:

In the cafeteria,
Jojo sits by three girls
who talk and laugh
with each other, but
say nothing to her.
She does not meet their eyes.
but looks out into the distance
or down at her food,
eating in silence.
Everyone thinks
Jojo may be 11 years old
even though she is in fourth grade.
When she first came,
the teachers changed her name to Jojo
because they said Joel was "a boy's name."
For a year, Jojo tells everyone to call her by her new name.
Then she changes her mind.
She says,
"Call me by my real name.
I am taking it back."

[*The actors freeze and turn to face the audience. Vignette Actor 1 is at stage center. Each actor says their line one at a time. After all have taken their turns, all actors repeat the lines as they see fit, changing tones and overlapping and interspersing lines in a cacophony of voices. The voices crescendo, then fall silent.*]

Vignette 4 Actor: My grandmother is in Africa.

Vignette 6 Actor: YOU FORGOT!

Vignette 7 Actor: Call me by my real name.

Vignette 3 Actor: OH MY GOODNESS GRACIOUS!

Vignette 1 Actor: I am African. I am proud to be African.

[*Vignette 1 Actor steps forward and stares pointedly at the audience before repeating his line, first in English, then in Kirundi.*]

I am African. I am proud to be African.

Ndi umu ny' afrika. Ndashima kuba ndi umu ny' afrika.[7]
[*Lights out*]

Questions for Dialogue

1. After careful examination of the discourse used by the participants in Act One, identify and discuss words and phrases that serve to exoticize and otherize the Burundian children, children categorized as ESL, and their families. Which deficit-oriented and assimilationist attitudes can you identify?
2. As you reflect on your own experiences and background, what might be some alternative approaches to educating students who come from different experiences and backgrounds or speak a different language than your own?
3. Who are the various stakeholders in Act One and what are their perceptions of the students? In what ways might their professional roles shape the way they see and talk about their new students?
4. What have you learned about the characters in Act Two? After reviewing the act, what types of interactions and emotions are evident? What emotions do you experience in response to the vignettes? In what ways might these emotions as well as newly acquired understandings affect your future teaching?
5. What view of the Burundian children do you have after participating in and reenacting Act One? How have your views changed after hearing students' voices in Act Two? What does this tell us about research and the power of representational methods to convey information and shape our views about people?

Notes

1. I wish to thank Allison Anders and Denise Bates for allowing me to use their interview data for this article. The research reported does not necessarily reflect the views of Allison Anders, Denise Bates, or any member of the Healing Transitions research team at the University of Tennessee.
2. I ask readers to be aware of the power of words to define individuals in our minds. People who have had to live with conditions of forced migration are, first and foremost, people.
3. English language learner, learning disabled, English as a second language, emotionally disturbed.
4. Pseudonyms are used for all proper names.
5. I purposefully use the pronoun *their* to avoid (a) privileging masculine pronouns and (b) using language that only acknowledges two genders.
6. This data is described in an earlier publication by Mariner, Lester, Sprecher, and Anders (2011).
7. Pronunciation (using phonetic sounds, not symbols): "N'dee oomoo n'yahfreeka. N'dahsheemah koobah n'dee oomoo n'yahfreekah." English to Kirundi translation and Kirundi pronunciation provided by Fleurette Sambira.

References

Ackroyd, J., & O'Toole, J. (2010). *Performing research: Tensions, triumphs and trade-offs of ethnodrama*. Stoke-on-Trent, UK: Trentham Books.

Alexander, B. K. (2005). Performance ethnography: The reenacting and inciting of culture. In N. K. Denzin & Y. S. Lincoln (Eds.), *The Sage handbook of qualitative research* (3rd ed., pp. 411–441). Thousand Oaks, CA: Sage.

Altenbaugh, R. J. (2003). *The American people and their education: A social history*. Columbus, OH: Merrill Prentice Hall.

American Psychological Association. (2010). *Resilience and recovery after war: Refugee children and families in the United States*. Washington, DC: APA Taskforce on the Psychosocial Effects of War on Children and Families Who Are Refugees From Armed Conflict Residing in the United States. Retrieved from http://www.apa.org/pubs/info/reports/refugees.aspx

Anders, A., & Bates, D. (2008–2009). Healing Transitions. University of Tennessee: Center for the Study of Youth and Political Violence.

Anyon, J. (1980). Social class and the hidden curriculum of work. *Journal of Education, 162*(1), 67–92.

Apple, M. W. (2001). Comparing neo-liberal projects and inequality in education. *Comparative Education, 37*(4), 409–423.

Barker, C. (2003). *Cultural studies: Theory and practice*. London: Sage.

Bigelow, B., & Peterson, B. (Eds.). (2002). *Rethinking globalization: Teaching for justice in an unjust world*. Milwaukee, WI: Rethinking Schools.

Bowles, S., & Gintis, H. (2002). Schooling in capitalist America revisited. *Sociology of Education, 75*(1), 1–18.

Cannella, G. S., & Viruru, R. (2004). *Childhood and postcolonization: Power, education, and contemporary practice*. New York: Routledge Falmer.

De Lissovoy, N. (2009). Toward a critical pedagogy of the global. In S. L. Macrine (Ed.), *Critical pedagogy in uncertain times: Hope and possibilities* (pp. 189–205). New York: Palgrave Macmillan.

De Lissovoy, N. (2010). Decolonial pedagogy and the ethics of the global. *Discourse: Studies in the Cultural Politics of Education, 31*(3), 279–293. doi:10.1080/01596301003786886

Denzin, N. K. (2003). *Performance ethnography: Critical pedagogy and the politics of culture.* Thousand Oaks, CA: Sage.

Doka, K. J. (1995). *Children mourning, mourning children.* Bristol, PA: Hospice Foundation of America.

Ellis, C. (2004). *The ethnographic I: A methodological novel about autoethnography.* Walnut Creek, CA: AltaMira Press.

Escobar, A. (1995). *Encountering development: The making and unmaking of the third world.* Princeton, NJ: Princeton University Press.

Frater-Mathieson, K. (2004). Refugee trauma, loss and grief: Implications for intervention. In R. J. Hamilton & D. Moore (Eds.), *Educational interventions for refugee children: Theoretical perspectives and implementing best practice* (pp. 12–34). New York: Routledge.

Gatto, J. T. (2005). *Dumbing us down: The hidden curriculum of compulsory schooling.* Gabriola Island, BC, Canada: New Society.

Haasl, B., & Marnocha, J. (2000). *Bereavement support group program for children: Leader manual.* Philadelphia: Accelerated Development.

Hamilton, R. J., & Moore, D. (Eds.). (2004). *Educational interventions for refugee children: Theoretical perspectives and implementing best practice.* New York: Routledge.

Hardy, M., & Bryman, A. (Eds.). (2004). *Handbook of data analysis.* Thousand Oaks, CA: Sage.

Keddie, A. (2011). Pursuing justice for refugee students: Addressing issues of cultural (mis)recognition. *International Journal of Inclusive Education, 16*(12), 1–16.

Kincheloe, J. L., & Berry, K. S. (2004). *Rigour and complexity in educational research (Conducting educational research).* Philadelphia: Open University Press.

Kincheloe, J. L., & Steinberg, S. R. (1997). *Changing multiculturalism.* Philadelphia: Open University Press.

Lustig, S. L., Kia-Keating, M., Grant-Knight, W., Geltman, P., Ellis, H., Birman, D., Kinzie, D., Keane, T., & Saxe, G. (2003). Review of child and adolescent refugee mental health: White paper from the National Child Traumatic Stress Network Refugee Trauma Task Force. Substance Abuse and Mental Health Services Administration, U.S. Department of Health and Human Services. Retrieved from http://immigrantchildren.org/Reports%20and%20Studies/refugeereview.pdf

Marable, M., & Agard-Jones, V. (Eds.). (2008). *Transnational blackness: Navigating the global color line.* New York: Palgrave Macmillan.

Mariner, N., Lester, J., Sprecher, K., & Anders, A. (2011). Relational knowledge production and the dynamics of difference: Exploring cross-cultural tensions in service learning through narrative. In N. Webster & T. Stewart (Eds.), *Exploring cultural dynamics and tensions within service-learning* (pp. 63–80). Charlotte, NC: Information Age Publishing.

McLaren, P. (1995). White terror and oppositional agency: Towards a critical multiculturalism. In C. E. Sleeter & P. L. McLaren (Eds.), *Multicultural education, critical pedagogy, and the politics of difference* (pp. 33–70). Albany: State University of New York Press.

Nieto, S. (1996). *Affirming diversity: The sociopolitical context of multicultural education.* White Plains, NY: Longman.

Noblit, G. W., Flores, S. Y., & Murillo, Jr., E. G. (Eds.). (2004). *Postcritical ethnography: Reinscribing critique.* Cresskill, NJ: Hampton Press.

Office of Refugee Resettlement. (2012). About the Office of Refugee Resettlement. U.S. Department of Health and Human Services: Administration for Children and Families. Retrieved from http://www.acf.hhs.gov/programs/orr/

Ranard, D. A. (Ed.). (2007, March). COR Center refugee backgrounder no. 2: The 1972 Burundians. Retrieved from http://www.cal.org/co/pdffiles/backgrounder_burundians.pdf

Roey, A., Fergus, E., & Noguera, P. (2011). Addressing racial/ethnic disproportionality in special education: Case studies of suburban school districts. *Teachers College Record, 113*(10), 2233–2266.

Sarroub, L. K. (2008). Living "glocally" with literacy success in the midwest. *Theory into Practice, 47*(1), 59–66.

Sleeter, C. E., & Grant, C. A. (2003). *Making choices for multicultural education: Five approaches to race, class, and gender* (4th ed.). New York: John Wiley & Sons.

Spariosu, M. I. (2004). *Global intelligence and human development: Toward an ecology of human learning.* Cambridge, MA: MIT Press.

Sprecher, K. (2011). *Decolonial multiculturalism and local-global contexts: A postcritical feminist bricolage for developing new praxes in education.* (Unpublished doctoral dissertation). University of Tennessee, Knoxville.

Spring, J. (2008). *American education* (13th ed.). Boston: McGraw Hill.

Spry, T. (2006). Performing autoethnography: An embodied methodological praxis. In S. N. Hesse-Biber & P. Leavy (Eds.), *Emergent methods in social research* (pp. 183–211). Thousand Oaks, CA: Sage.

Tejeda, C., Espinoza, M., & Gutierrez, K. (2003). Toward a decolonizing pedagogy: Social justice reconsidered. In P. P. Trifonas (Ed.), *Pedagogies of difference: Rethinking education for social change* (pp. 10–40). New York: Routledge Falmer.

Titone, C. (1998). Educating the white teacher as ally. In J. L. Kincheloe (Ed.), *White reign: Deploying whiteness in America* (pp. 159–176). New York: St. Martin's Press.

Tyack, D. B. (1974). *The one best system: A history of American urban education.* Boston: Harvard University Press.

Tyack, D. B. (2003). *Seeking common ground: Public schools in a diverse society.* Cambridge, MA: Harvard University Press.

United Nations High Commissioner for Refugees, (2007, January). Group resettlement of "1972 Burundians" from Tanzania. Retrieved from http://www.unrefugees.org/atf/cf/%7BD2F991C5-A4FB-4767-921F-A9452B12D742%7D/Burundifactsheet.pdf

United Nations High Commissioner for Refugees. (2012). Refugees: Flowing across borders. Retrieved from http://www.unhcr.org/pages/49c3646c125.html

U.S. Department of Education Mentoring Resource Center. (2009, January). Helping a grieving mentee: A mentor's ultimate expression of caring and support. *Mentoring Resource Center Fact Sheet, 26.*

Willinsky, J. (1998). *Learning to divide the world: Education at empire's end.* Minneapolis: University of Minnesota Press.

Wolfelt, A. (1983). *Helping children cope with grief.* Muncie, IN: Accelerated Development.

Worden, J. (1996). *Children and grief: When a parent dies.* New York: Guilford Press.

Chapter 2

I Live in a Curled World...: Stories from Immigrant Students and Their Teacher

Irina S. Okhremtchouk and Rosa M. Jimenez

> I love the world I live in.
> At school,
> I live in a curled world.
> I love the world I live in.
> At home,
> I live in a curled world.
> I love the world I live in.
> I eat, I drink, I think,
> I live in a curled world.
> I love the world I live in.
> I split into a hundred ways,
> I live in a curled world!
> —*Zorya*

Introduction

A staggering one in five students in America is a child of immigrants, and speaks a language other than English in the home (Capps, Fix, Murray, Ost, Passel, & Hernandez, 2005). Many view this student population as homogeneous, neglecting to notice its vast diversity. The differences are plenty, including cultural and ethnic backgrounds, academic preparation, age and entry into U.S. schools, and socioeconomic status, to name just a few (Suárez-Orózco, Suárez-Orózco, & Todorova, 2008). In addition to these monolithic views, English language learners (ELLs) are also viewed in deficit terms, which we aim to challenge in this chapter. In defining the term, ELLs may be immigrants themselves or U.S.-born children of immigrants. It is important to note that the term *Englishlanguagelearner* is problematic due to its focus on students' weaknesses—that is, the language they are acquiring—rather than their strengths. While we are cognizant of its limitations, we use this term for consistency with the body of literature in the field to which we aim to contribute. We invite our audiences to interrogate the ways these students' stories deconstruct, counter, and rupture deficit orientations.

The overarching purpose of this study is to present a twofold approach for disseminating research findings through students' narratives and a teacher's story. To that end, in this empirical work we aim to counter the monolithic understanding of who immigrant ELLs are, where they come from, and how they experience school as well as home environments in their new worlds: the United States and U.S. public schools. We selected performance ethnography as a method due to its innovative approach, which allows audiences to relive the lives and schooling experiences of the populations studied.

This work invites all audiences interested in issues of immigrant ELLs to participate. More specifically, this performance ethnography is designed to benefit pre-service teachers, practicing teachers, school administrators, and those who create policies. In this work, we aim to confront preconceived notions about immigrant and ELL students, and prescriptive curricula. We aim to widen and deepen audiences' perceptions of this significant and vastly expanding student population. This approach leads to multiple implications for teaching practices and a better understanding of immigrant students and their classrooms. The stories told in this study invite participants to tell, retell, and re-embody the empirical data (Alexander, 2005; Denzin, 2003b; Denzin & Lincoln, 2000). Thus, these stories, described in three acts, provide an avenue to introduce, discuss, question, and transform understandings of immigrant students and their educational contexts.

After engaging the audiences in three acts, we invite the readers to further partake in the analysis of data, and to engage in questions for dialogue. To initiate this engagement we provide a brief narrative of the findings, focusing on several pertinent subthemes, including negotiating identity, negotiating environments, and participants' journeys from their own points of view.

These themes were derived from the extensive review and data analysis using content analysis coding methods. In its design, this performance ethnography addresses the social context of ELLs and their teacher through their own voices and expressions.

On the Course toward Fruition

This study is situated in a semi-urban Title I[1] middle school English Language Development (ELD) classroom with 21 ELL students of diverse backgrounds. The classroom teacher, an immigrant herself, repeatedly defies mandated scripted curricula imposed by the school and district administration by using unconventional teaching approaches for ELLs—including expressive writing centered on students' own lived experiences. To that end, the teacher challenges students to draw upon their everyday skills, knowledge, and lives to write essays, poetry, and journals. While trying to create a meaningful and rich academic environment for her students, the teacher is under siege by curricular restrictions and demands imposed by the Program Improvement[2] status of the school. She is successful, but finds herself in a constant struggle, having to navigate the torturous waters of scripted education, which led us to name the site of our study "Script/Ed Middle School."

In writing this work, the multitude of obstacles, struggles, and uncertainty of the road behind and ahead inspired the title of this chapter. The poem by one of the student authors, which serves as an epigraph for this work, describes the circumstances of all participants: Their worlds are "split into a hundred ways," yet these fractured pieces of history, culture, language, and memory curl together to create new, multifaceted, and unique lives—a "curled world."

With that, we began our journey. Our questions were many, but perhaps the one that was most apparent was, how does this classroom, given the circumstances, challenge the odds? Shortly after meeting the students and their teacher, it became apparent that in spite of the environment and isolation, the classroom is full of hope, dreams, and purpose—a place that a child never forgets because this is where she was inspired.

Representation of Findings and Methodological Discourse

In this section we will explain how the findings and methods used are represented. Additionally, we will engage the readers in a discussion of the layers of findings and how the methods support the analysis.

We chose performance ethnography to foster audiences' awakening to multiple dimensions of the human experience that may have been "inaccessible or gone unnoticed" (Barone, 2002). Through this approach, as audiences become active participants, they are challenged beyond traditional formats such as lecture, discussion, and small group dialogues (Barone & Eisner, 2006; Conrad-Cozart, Gordon, Guzenhausser, McKinney, & Patterson, 2003; Gibson, 1985). Additionally, we employ performance ethnography's methodological and theoretical principles of social justice as we leverage its political tools to expose and counter deficit constructions of ELL students' lives, knowledge, and experiences (Alexander, 2005; Denzin, 2003a; Denzin & Lincoln, 2000). While little is known in the field about the

ELL student population from a heterogeneous perspective, this study seeks to add unique and complex layers to the extant literature. It is our hope that our readers will participate in rich interactions, robust engagement, and critical analysis through participants' voices.

Data Sources and Analysis

Our work is drawn from qualitative data gathered by Irina Okhremtchouk (chapter co-author) about a middle school ELD classroom, the teacher, and her ELL students over the course of one year in a northern California school. The participants in this study include one teacher and her 21 ELL students. In total, eight countries and nine languages are represented in this classroom. Because this study is situated in an ELD classroom, the students vary in grade levels (sixth through eighth) and ages (10 through 14).

Multimethod qualitative data collection strategies were utilized in the course of the study, including audio recordings of classroom instruction, participant observations, interviews, and document collection. The primary data in this performance ethnography is the collected student work, including narrative and expository essays, student stories, and reflective journals, as well as teacher interviews. We conducted semiformal interviews with the teacher about her own background, upbringing, educational philosophies, pedagogical practices, and views of the school, her students, their parents, and the community.

Together, we—the co-authors—analyzed the data and collaboratively designed and wrote this performative ethnography. All transcripts underwent three coding passes in which codes were created, recalibrated, and refined (Erickson, 1986). Initially, we used open coding in order to look for emergent patterns. Broad analytic categories were drawn based on students' immigrant lives and schooling experiences. We then conducted a rereading and second coding based on how students' negotiated their identities and home and school environments, and their reflections of their immigrant journeys. Lastly, we developed micro-codes to analyze data with more specificity for each of the findings/performative texts that were unfolding, including:

- My Journey: This theme deals with the factors relating to how students arrived in the U.S. and came to their current school; who and what they left behind; and how they felt about their journey.

- My Life: This theme deals with the current lives students lead as youth in the U.S. including their everyday interactions, behaviors, and experiences across multiple contexts within and beyond home and school.
- My Family and Community: This theme examines students' family—their background, cultural practices, and social roles. In addition, this theme includes student experiences across multiple social communities.

We examined the data separately and individually by student (reading through each student portfolio, one at a time) and by themes (reading through data excerpts from different students about common themes), as well as intermittently among all data sources (using field notes alongside transcriptions and student work documents).

Writing of Performative Texts

In order to preserve the integrity of each student's experience, we sought to keep each character and their script as close as possible to the "actual words" of the individual students, rather than create composite characters. We corrected more serious grammatical errors and misspellings for the sake of clarity, but left minor errors and some slang intact for a sense of how English language learners and middle school students talk (e.g., "like, for reals"). In other scenes, it may seem that the student dialogue is a bit academic rather than social, with phrases such as "I, on the other hand" and "I developed the English skills of a regular American student." In fact, these were the actual words students used in their student work, and in almost all cases they reflect the teachers' instruction and influence. We purposefully chose to create acts around the overarching themes we found in the data. While we used creative liberties to craft scenes with the students in dialogue with each other, these are composite scenes derived from the data (Ellis, 2004). That is, during the course of the project, students indeed worked in small groups discussing their projects, and gathered around the ELD classroom during lunch to socialize, but the scripts we wrote are not actual accounts of those interactions.

Our Positionalities

We, the co-authors, are researchers, teacher-educators, and education advocates. In our former schoolteacher roles we taught ELD classes and worked with immigrant students as well as students who are ELL. In our current professional roles we conduct research and teach classes that focus on issues pertinent to English language learners, immigrant youth, and language minority students. As a result, we came to this project with a considerable depth of knowledge that includes language minority and immigrant student issues along with their educational contexts.

One shared reason—and perhaps the primary reason—why we chose to work with and study language minority students is our backgrounds. We are both bilingual and daughters of immigrants. I (Irina) am a first-generation immigrant. I immigrated to the United States at the age of 15. My initial school experiences were at a small Alaskan high school in a town of 2,100 people. Although I was very much influenced by my high school experiences, my experiences as a lone immigrant student in a small high school greatly differ from what immigrant students currently experience in urban, suburban, and rural areas across the nation. I was privileged to have been taught by educators who recognized my academic potential and encouraged me to attend college. In addition, I come from a professional household, with both parents having high-skilled professional careers.

I (Rosa) am a daughter of Mexican immigrants. I was born and raised in a midsize city (150,000) in central California. My parents were employed primarily as factory workers and as agricultural fieldworkers. Both of my parents instilled in me a love for learning and nurtured my childhood dreams. I grew up in a working-class neighborhood and attended low-income, Title I schools throughout my K–12 education. At times, I felt some of my teachers had a general understanding of my life; other times, especially during middle school, I fell through the cracks and was shuffled through classes where student discipline dominated class time. It was not until my sophomore year in high school that a counselor saw my potential, reviewed my cumulative record, and helped me access college preparatory and advanced placement classes. I went to college, and later became a middle school social studies teacher in Los Angeles. Most of my students had immigrant and Latino backgrounds, and many were learning English. As a researcher, I examine many facets of education for diverse learners, including curriculum and instruction with language minority students.

Together, we (co-authors) bring diverse perspectives both personally and professionally. In this work we positioned ourselves as researchers and not active participants.

An Invitation to Engage

This section is written as an open invitation for the readers to engage and make their own assumptions about the text, as opposed to reporting conclusions of the study. Although we present a summary of findings at the end of this chapter, these are offered as our thoughts for your consideration, debate, and further dialogue. Such an approach provides a starting point for thinking about the monolithic issues often associated with English language learners, and at the same time affords readers an opportunity to expand the discussion. Furthermore, this section will be closely aligned with the methods section—to which we will circle back throughout this chapter.

We present our performative text with the understanding that it is one interpretation—our interpretation—for you to engage, consider, challenge, question, re-interpret, re-envision, and extend. We invite your active "interjection" into the dialogue and lived experiences of students and their teacher (Barone, 1995). We ask you to step into the conversations of these students and critically examine the label *English language learners*, which connotes a monolithic student narrative loaded with assumptions and misconceptions about who they are and what they can do, and which reduces the complexity of their lives to one single component—learning English. Although these students indeed are learning English, this label does not represent that they also are becoming bilingual/multilingual, and that they have dynamic lives, rich experiences, complex thoughts, and vibrant dreams (Cummins, 2000; Gonzalez, Moll, & Amanti, 2005; Gutiérrez, Baquedano-López, & Asato, 2000; Valdés, 1996, 2002). We ask our readers to engage each character as multifaceted, conflicting, and overlapping, for they are complex human beings moving through adolescence. Furthermore, in our representation of findings, we draw audiences' attention to the fact that ELLs' experiences, in both their school and home lives, are more similar to the experiences of the monolingual English-speaking students than one would typically perceive. Their stories and your interpretations may also push back or amplify these notions. We aim for this forum to challenge our readers in "moral truths about the self and other" to question your own positionality as you unpack your examination of an ELL student "other" (Christians, 2000, p. 147).

In this work, we aim to represent students' own words, while recognizing that these are snippets of their lives, "partial" stories (Noblit, Flores, & Murillo, 2004) written for their classwork. Nevertheless, with these stories we seek to create a unique opportunity for our readers to step into the lived experiences of ELL students and discover "multiple truths" and "pockets of critical consciousness" (Christians, 1996). With our readers' uptake and engagement in this performative text, we hope you will share "untold" stories (Krog, 1998), illuminate blind spots, and dialogue about its fruitfulness, what was lacking, and what remains to be done. Furthermore, we hope educators and those interested in various facets of education move through the spectrum of performance to discussion of these acts and their potential implications for pedagogical practice and educational policy about ELLs. Rather than linear, we view this spectrum of engagement in a dialogic, circular, and holistic manner.

The next section describes the list of characters based on individual students and their teacher. We invite you to select a character and participate in a live reading. We close with a series of questions inthe hope that you will view them as malleable tools. Please enter into the lives of immigrant youth who are learning English and much more.

Welcome to the English Language Development Classroom Where "Better Than Your Best..." Is Expected

The Setting

Script/Ed Middle School is only 6 years old, but it has steadily increased in population since it was built, and by year 3 was over capacity. From the main school entrance and the adjacent street, campus buildings appear new and well kept. Yet, a short walk from the apparent newness of the structure, one will find relatively old, second hand portable buildings stacked next to each other. English Language Development (ELD), special education, and vocational education classes were amongst a few other classrooms scattered here and there in the section of the campus relegated to portable classrooms, far removed from the well-marked and distinguished main school buildings that housed science, social studies, language arts, and math programs.

The ELD classroom is situated in the "portable classroom" farthest from the main campus. A distinct image overpowers one's first-glance impression of the classroom—that of a large, rusty, dark-yellow water stain on the ceiling, which extends all the way along the wall to the floor. The rest of the walls are poorly painted and suggest someone other than a professional attempted to make the dark room look more cheery and welcoming. Classroom desks are arranged in a U-shape with much space in the center of the room intended for reading activity circles.

Well-stacked bookshelves hold dictionaries, encyclopedias, and textbooks. The teacher's desk is organized but incredibly busy with various forms, student assignments, and artwork. Countless sticky-notes, with an array of reminders tacked along the wall above the teacher's desk, depict an author who never rests. Student work and certificates of accomplishments cover the classroom walls. The physical environment of this room is different from other classrooms: Besides lacking a welcoming feeling, this is the only classroom in the entire school that lacks the various disciplinary wall posters that enumerate consequences for student misbehavior and endless lists of the state standards.

In all, the portable building section of the campus does not exemplify hope to anyone, let alone students. The obvious structural decay, remote from the newness of the main campus, reflects the low expectations for students and the deficit perspectives that permeate the portable climate—a far remove from what education is meant to be and could be. In this environment, the only hope is —the human capital, that is, teacher and her students. Somehow, if the human capital is there, then everything else—poor learning conditions, old buildings, stains on the walls, and so on—becomes diminished. This alone makes a difference between education and learning versus painful day-in and day-out tolerance. In a global sense, the significance of the human capital is important for any classroom and any school, but it is especially critical in this case—the portable climate—due to the simple fact that the human capital is the only element that provides hope.

Ms. Liebermann, or "Ms. L," is the talk of the school. Students describe her as "super nice" and "hecka strict." The colleagues respect her, administration fears her, and parents go to her for advice on a range of topics from how to make their students do homework to what classes are needed to ensure college opportunities after high school. She is assertive, fearless, and confident in both her knowledge of the subject matter and pedagogy. Ms. L is an immigrant (like her students), young (in her late twenties), but a veteran teacher due to her 8 years in the profession. She describes her students as "the best" and "leaders," and does not let others say otherwise. As a coordinator of the ELD program (an extra duty without real monetary compensation), she has control of the categorical site budget, a portion of which was received through grants she had obtained. Ms. L's allies are parents, her colleagues, and the principal of the school, who had been asked multiple times by the district superintendent to find a reason to remove Ms. L.

In her classroom, one might hear Ms. L say, "I don't want your best work, I want better than your best work," and "I am not in the business of educating followers, I am in the business of educating leaders." Ms. L uses her strict and no-nonsense demeanor to achieve the goals of her program. She is rigid and gentle at the same time, and the master of both. Ms. L sets high expectations for her students as well as herself, and demands that these expectations are met. She leaves no room for negotiations with her students or school administration. Provided the above, no one would ever sense that Ms. L is exceptionally sensitive. She spends countless hours examining her students' work. In that, she is more than just empathetic in her awareness, she relives her students' lives. At the same time, Ms. L does not feel sorry for her students, and her instruction strategies reflect this. Instead, she is certain that the best way she can help her students is by going beyond the standards and giving them the gift of knowledge, so they are better equipped to navigate through their multifaceted, "curled" lives (Darling-Hammond, 2010; Ladson-Billings, 1995; Nieto, 1992).

Ms. L's students are just as she describes them: "the best." Once they enter her classroom, they transform and mimic their teacher by engaging in a proactive discussion with assertive views and confidence. The students are from various parts of the world, with disparate backgrounds, cultures, home languages, and academic preparation. However, it is apparent to anyone who cares to know that every student is unique in her own way.

Act One: My Journey

Characters
Narrator

Sakshum immigrated from India with his family 2 years ago. Script/Ed Middle School is his first school in the United States. At the time of enrollment, Sakshum was 11 years old, and was placed in the sixth grade. He and his family temporarily reside with their relatives (in a multifamily household) as they try and establish themselves in the United States. Although confident in his English abilities due to attending a school in Punjab where English was taught, Sakshum's oral, reading, and writing skills in the English language were minimal at the time of enrollment. In other words, Sakshum has had prior exposure to the English language, but his demonstration of English language skills was minimal, possibly due to the quality of the instruction he received. Sakshum is savvy and has an easy going, good-natured personality, which inspired our choice of the pseudonym "Sakshum," meaning "skillful. Presently, Sakshum attends eighth grade.

Rafey and his family immigrated from India when he was 9 years old. Rafey is 11 years old now and in the sixth grade. He and his family have moved several times since they immigrated to the United States. Script/Ed Middle School is his second U.S. school. Rafey is very resourceful and resilient. His first 2 years in the United States were filled with hardships and heartaches due to his mother's death and the family's financial struggles. In spite of all the hardships, Rafey is very studious, imaginative, and social. He has learned how to cope with different situations in various contexts. We selected "Rafey," which means "pioneer," as his pseudonym. Indeed, Rafey is a pioneer in the sense that at a young age he has traversed novel and multiple terrains, both social (e.g., constant mobility and financial struggles) and emotional (e.g., the loss of his mother).

Oyunbileg is 11 years old. She is enrolled in the seventh grade at Script/Ed Middle School. Oyunbileg and her family immigrated from Mongolia when she was 8 years old. Since then, the family has moved three times, and Script/Ed Middle School is Oyunbileg's third U.S. school in 3 years. Although Oyunbileg's family is experiencing multiple difficulties associated with immigration, the home environment and family dynamic is very stable and nurturing. Oyunbileg likes learning and being in school, and is very driven in her educational pursuits. She is also wise beyond her years and often interjects in arguments amongst counterparts by sharing her opinions or instructing those involved on "how it should done." We chose "Oyunbileg" as her pseudonym because its meaning is "gift of wisdom."

Ye is 14 years old. He moved from China to live with his father and stepmother. Script/Ed Middle School is Ye's first school in the U.S., and he is now in the eighth grade. He has made incredible strides in learning English considering that he had no knowledge of the language when he first arrived a year ago. Ye has a very cheerful and happy personality and is always eager to entertain his audience. He is also very studious, invests much time on school assignments, and is enthusiastic about learning. In selecting pseudonyms we chose "Ye," which means "bright," an accurate depiction of both his personality and mind.

Act One: Scene 1

Narrator: A typical lesson in the ELD classroom, which started with an opener, followed by direct instruction and now the lesson, slowly progresses to a group activity. The teacher, Ms. L, stands in front of the class stating directions for the next assignment, "My Journey." A word bank with various adjectives and nouns (which were called out by the students, recorded by the teacher, and later reviewed by all) is on the whiteboard to help students with the activity. Ms. L reminds her students that they are to use the word bank, class notes, dictionaries, and atlases as resources. She continues by stating that students are not allowed to waste time, and (for the third time) reminds them to keep their discussions on the topic at hand. After the "expectations" talk, the students are instructed to get into groups and discuss their journeys

I Live in a Curled World...

to the United States and brainstorm key elements for their next task—an essay. She allows 20 minutes for the in-class discussion and 10 minutes for expressing their thoughts on paper. The students are clearly happy about the group work, because they get to visit with each other, but are reluctant about writing.

Sakshum: Ms. L wants us to talk about our "journey" experiences ... who's gonna start?

Rafey: I am not sure what that means? Journey? She wants us to talk about...travel?

Oyunbileg: No. Ms. L wants us to talk about how we got here, you know, like how we got to America.

Sakshum: Hmmm, we got here by plane. Oh, and car!

Oyunbileg: Me too, but that's not what she wants us to talk about. [*raises her hand and shouts out*] Ms. L, what are we supposed to do?
Ms. L walks over to the group of student.

Ms. L: I need you to talk about and brainstorm your journeys to the United States. What have you left behind? What do you miss most? How did you get here? And, I had also asked you to discuss your first memories of America.

Rafey: You want us to write this down too?

Ms. L: Yes, after you share, I need you to write your individual stories down and draw an image of your journey.

Rafey: [*reluctantly*] Oh man, we have to write too?!

Ms. L: Yes, but you need to share and discuss first, and then write down your experiences. Do you understand the task at hand and are you ready to proceed?

Sakshum: Yes, I guess...

Oyunbileg: I will start.... As you already know I am from Mongolia and that makes me Mongolian. When I was 8 we moved to the United States. My country means a lot to me because my family was all born there.
[*Ms. L walks away*]

Sakshum: Oyunbileg, do you want to go back?

Oyunbileg: Yes, maybe for a visit, but I can't live there anymore because we are here now and I belong with my family...

Sakshum: Yeah, me too. When we moved, I left behind my family, my uncles, cousins, and many friends. Leaving India was very sad though. My family was crying when I was on my way to the airport. I wish I could go back to Punjab because I miss my friends and family.

Ye: Me too... I would do anything to see my old friends... friends are everything! I moved here last year. I was so lonely at first because I had no friends. But, my friends in China called me and told me to be strong and to make new friends.

Sakshum: Oh, you get to talk to your friends on the phone? Your parents let you do that?!

Ye: Yes. I was sad at first and my parents let me call them and then they called me. I was so happy to talk to them—they are so nice... I miss them still. I want to go back to China very much. I cry less now, but was crying hard a lot when I first got here.

Sakshum: You really cried, like for reals? [*chuckles*]

Ye: Yes...

Sakshum: Maybe that's why your parents let you call your friends. My parents tell me it's too expensive...

Rafey: Yeah... my dad says the same thing.... After a while you start missing your family and friends less ... why did your parents move?

Sakshum: We moved to America because my parents said they wanted us to have a good life.

Rafey: That's what my dad said too. We came here because our cousins wanted us to get better education.

Oyunbileg: Yeah, same thing. My parents tell us to study hard because we moved here for better life and they tell us that we have to do good in school…

Ye: [*sighs*] I moved to America to live with my dad and my stepmom.

Oyunbileg: Your mom is still in China?

Ye: Yes. On the day I moved to the United States my mom cried. My mom, cousins, and my friends took me to the airport. I took the airplane by myself and flew to America. When I was on the airplane, I looked outside the window and saw the blue sky. I was so sad …. When I got off the plane, I saw my dad and uncles. They drove me to my dad's home…

Oyunbileg: Do you miss your mom?

Ye: Yes. My mom and I were just like friends. I always told my secrets to my mom.

Rafey: I miss having a mom. I don't have a mom anymore. My mom died of cancer after we moved to the United States…

Oyunbileg: I am so sorry. [*hugs Rafey*]. I wouldn't know what to do without my mom…

Rafey: That's ok, I just miss her and miss being with her. We were so happy when we were in India…

Sakshum: You know, at first, I was happy when I found out that I am going to the United States, but I was also sad because I didn't want to leave my friends and wasn't sure what the school is going to be like here. I really didn't like going to school because of the teachers there.

Ye: Not me, I loved going to school. I still remember when I first started pre-school in China. I was 3. Then I went to first grade and started elementary school. I was a very active boy; I liked running, playing basketball, and soccer. I studied all the time and was at the top of my class!

Rafey: Do you miss your old school? [*looks at Ye*]

Ye: Yeah, kinda. When I was in China, I lived at my school. My school was far away from my house, so I couldn't go home very often, only like once a month. Most of the time I stayed with my classmates. We studied and played together just like a big family. I miss my big family very much.

Sakshum: I never liked my school in India because teachers used to hit me with a big stick when I talked to someone or got bad grades.

Oyunbileg: The teachers were a lot stricter in Mongolia, but they didn't hit us! Did they hit you a lot?

Sakshum: Yeah.... I like school here though because teachers don't hit you with a stick and they're always kind to you. The schools are free in the United States and my dad doesn't have to pay money for me to attend school.

Rafey: Do your parents like it here? [*looks at Sakshum*]

Sakshum: Ummm... I am not sure. My parents worry a lot now, more so than before. My dad used to be happy in Punjab because he had his own business and he had a lot of people working under him. He misses his business because his business was real good. It was a farming business and he liked it.

Rafey: That's cool... my dad was an engineer in India, now he works at a motel that my cousins own. In America, it got really hard. We were losing a lot of our money really bad. Our cousins let us stay in their motel. At first, I really did not like living here and neither did my dad. It's really hard. But, my family and I are staying here for a better education and to become citizens.

Oyunbileg: You live in a motel?

Rafey: Yes, I have a cool life there. I do a lot of fun things at the motel. I go swimming and play basketball. I always play with my little brother. We have a lot of fun. In the night I go to the gym to workout. That is why I am really strong!

Oyunbileg: We live in an apartment. I think my parents are happy, but they are always tired, especially my dad. My dad is a truck driver, which is very hard, because he doesn't get enough sleep. My mom always worries about him, because he goes everywhere in the U.S.A. Sometimes he goes on icy roads, which is slippery. My dad has been in a lot of states now. He has to make the delivery on time or he doesn't get much money. That's why he doesn't sleep or eat much. My mom work at Granite's Subs Wings and Things. On Tuesday she works the full day. When she gets home she is always tired.

Ye: My dad told me that we are gonna move to San Francisco next year because that's where his work is going to be. When I told my friends I will have to move, they all don't want me to go. I don't wanna move, too. But there is nothing I can do; I will just have to listen to my dad…

Oyunbileg: You know, if I were to move again or if I could go back to the past, I would go back to Mongolia, the only thing I would change is my grandma's life. I remember her being sad… I would do everything for her to make her happy. I love her so much.

Sakshum: Me too… I want nothing more than to go back and spend some time talking to my friends and cousins about what has happened. The friends and family whom I left behind are part of my life and that part is missing…

Ms. L: Okay, people, I need your attention please… one, two, three…thank you. I hope you enjoyed your group discussions. Now, I need you to start writing your stories on a piece of paper. Remember, this is just a draft. We will be in a computer lab tomorrow typing and developing your stories further. If you want to be creative, you can write a poem, which will serve as a preface to your "My Journey" essay. You have exactly 10 minutes to write down the information and ideas you just brainstormed with your peers. Happy writing ladies and gentlemen! Start, please!

Narrator: Everyone knew the pattern for the task ahead, since it has been rehearsed many times before. The students quickly move back to their assigned seats, get pieces of paper and writing utensils out, and start writing. All are on task and the classroom is silent, one could hear only an occasional shuffling of paper and strokes of the pens… After sitting at her desk motionless with a notebook and pencil in front of her for about 10 seconds, Oyunbileg starts writing…

Title: Who I am, Where I am From, and Who I Adore
I am Mongolian.
I am American.
I am a girl.
I am eleven.
I am a tween and,
I live in between
Two worlds.
My culture is in my heart,
And in my mind.
My culture is my birthplace,
And it is seeded where I was born.
If I could go to the past, the only thing
I will change is my grandma's life.
I will make her happy, but not sad.
I will make her feel better but not bad,
That is why I love her.

Act Two: Family and Community

Characters
Student A, Student B, and Student C are students in the ELD classroom; their contributions in these scenes are minimal.

I Live in a Curled World... 51

Sachi is 14 years old and in the eighth grade. Her father and mother met 15 years ago when Sachi's dad, an African American, was stationed in Japan for his military service. Sachi's parents divorced when she was 3 years old. Sachi was born and raised in Japan with her mother and grandmother. When she was 13, Sachi moved to the United States to live with her dad, stepmother (a Japanese American), and two stepsiblings. Initially, the move was a significant cultural shock for Sachi. However, with family support and her new friends in school, she was able to overcome these struggles fairly quickly. Sachi has a very strong personality and high ambitions. She often challenges cultural norms and preconceived notions about gender roles. Sachi is blessed with a strong character, hence her pseudonym "Sachi," meaning "blessed."

Balbir is of Indian descent. He and his family immigrated from Fiji when he was 6 years old. The family has moved many times since then. Balbir attended five different schools in 7 years and thus had no consistency or continuity in academic instruction. As a result, Balbir scored low on all standardized tests and has been placed in ELD repeatedly since first grade. Balbir is now in the eighth grade. Between the household responsibilities imposed by parents and his lack of faith in school, his goals centered on the one thing that was consistent in his life—his interest in and ability to work on cars. In spite of the obstacles he has experienced in life, Balbir is firm and sets clear goals for himself. As a result, we selected the pseudonym "Balbir," which means "strong."

Act Two: Scene 1

Narrator: Another typical lesson in the ELD classroom, which started with an opener, followed by direct instruction, and now the lesson slowly progresses to a group activity. The teacher, Ms. L, stands in front of the class stating directions for the next assignment. Today, the students are more eager than usual to participate and see each other because they just returned from a 3-day weekend.

Ms. L: Ladies and gentlemen, I hope you had a good weekend and are now ready to produce quality work today. We are one third through with the new unit, which focuses on your families and your communities. What I would like you to do first is turn to the person next to you and interview them about their lives and their communities. The possible questions that you might want to ask your peers have been brainstormed last week and are written on the whiteboard. I need you to record the interviews in your notebooks, meaning write the answers down. Then, I want you to exchange the interviews—that means give each person who has been interviewed their own interviews. In the end, everyone in this class will have a record of their own answers that have been recorded by their partner. Once you complete this task, I ask that you create a concept-map depicting your communities, which will include all possible communities we had brainstormed last week and anything else you might want to add. As previously discussed, you will be at the center of your own diagram, since you are the center of your world and your communities. Without you, your communities would not exist and vice versa, that means without your communities your lives would be dramatically different. Are there any questions?

Student A: Can we draw our maps first and then do the interview?

Ms. L: No. I would like you to first focus on your interviews because you might have something to share with your partner that you haven't thought of before. In other words, I need you to express your thoughts and engage in a discussion first, then record your partner's answers to help your partner conceptualize his or her ideas as well as think of how you might want to conceptualize your own work, which might be different due to the interview/discussion with your partner. Do you have any more questions?

Student B: What is "conceptualize"?

Ms. L: Does anyone want to answer this question?

Student C: [*raises her hand*] That means think of an idea?

Ms. L: Great answer, correct. Conceptualize means to form a concept, such as your community maps or form/create an idea.... I will be walking around and helping each group, so please ask questions. Are we ready to start?

Students: Yes...

I Live in a Curled World...

Ms. L: I can't hear you, are we ready to start?!?

Students: Yes!

[*Students turn to their partners and open their notebooks.*]

Balbir: You wanna start?

Sachi: Ok, I guess... tell me about yourself.

Balbir: Ok, well... is this an interview, like for reals?

Sachi: Yeah... I'll be writing your answers down. So start already!

Balbir: Ok, ok, jeee! Here it goes... hmmm...today I will be talking about my life. [*laughs*] I am 14 years old. I like to play football a lot. I also like to play video games, watch TV, and do a lot of stuff outside. I like to be outside a lot. I like to play a lot of sports, oh did I say that already?

Sachi: Yes you did! [*chuckles*] What else?

Balbir: Hmmm... I also like to play with my baby brother. I am the main person in my house to take care of my brother. His name is Nicky and he is 6 years old right now.... Oh, yeah... my brother always gets in trouble and I always get blamed for it. I plan to raise him and teach him all the stuff I learned.

Sachi: I have a little brother too! Well my little stepbrother. And, I take care of him all the time too; he is my responsibility...

Balbir: Oh, yeah...cool. I also like working on cars. I told my dad that I would like to work on cars when I grow up. I have an older brother, too. My older brother really takes good care of me. My brother is teaching me how to work on car engines now because I already know how to work the body kits and other things. My brother promised to get me a car when I go to high school so he won't have to drive me to school and pick me up every day. [*laughs*] Good for me!

Sachi: Where were you born?

Balbir: I was born on Fiji and my family is from there. We still have a lot of family there. They moved to the Bay Area when I was little. I was raised in Oakland, though, until I was 6 years old, then my family and I moved to south San Francisco when I was still 6. In San Francisco, we had an old house but we turned it into a big mansion that cost a lot of money from all the stuff we bought for the house. I had always wanted to live in San Francisco and I like all the stuff that happens there.

Sachi: So how did you end up here?

Balbir: Well, then, one day things had changed for my family and me. I remember going to the store with my dad because he had to sign a paper that said we won a lottery! After that, we went home and the next day we put the house up for rent and moved to Sacramento. I really got tired of moving. I really don't like it here [Sacramento] as compared to living in San Francisco because I can't do a lot of stuff here that I can do over there.

Sachi: So what's your favorite place to live?

Balbir: Hmmm... as I said, I like living in San Francisco... I wish we could have our old life back, but my dad says we have to stay here and can't go back. One place I don't want to go back to is Oakland!

Sachi: Oh, really, why?

Balbir: When I lived in Oakland I really did not like it there because every time I stepped out of my house, I would see someone getting jumped or getting shot. We lived in a very bad area to save money. Every Friday there was a drive-by shooting down the street from my house. There were always cops outside everyday. I almost got shot when I was in my garage sitting in my dad's car playing with the speakers in the back trunk, and all I could hear is my mom yelling, "Balbir, Balbir! Get inside! Hurry!" .... I hate the way my mom yells at me.

Sachi: Wow, is that true?!

I Live in a Curled World…

Balbir: Yeah, we didn't live there for long though. So, how about you? Do you like it here?

Sachi: Well I do and I don't. I am half Japanese. I have two cultures, Japanese and American. Mostly I love my Japanese culture. I was living in Japan for 13 years, so I know everything about Japan.

Balbir: That's cool, how many sisters and brother do you have?

Sachi: I have one brother and one sister and they are little. I live with my dad and I have a stepmom. My mom is in Japan with my grandmother. I really miss them so much.

Balbir: Is Japan a cool place?

Sachi: Oh, Yes! Japan is very fun place. Everyone thinks that Japan is small place, but I think it's big. When you see the Japanese map they have 47 cities. I was living in Yokohama.

Balbir: Do you have the same stuff like holidays and stuff as we do here?

Sachi: Sometimes we celebrate some holidays with America. Like we always celebrate the New Year's. And, Christmas, but some people don't celebrate Christmas in Japan. We also have a "Kids Day." We celebrate a lot of things in one year.

Balbir: How are the people there? Are they different?

Sachi: Some of the Japanese people are very smart people. They study really hard for tests. Japanese and Chinese worlds are very hard. That's why we have to make good grades and study hard.

Balbir: So what do you do for fun here? You like it here?

Sachi: Yeah, I guess. It's nice to be with my dad, but I miss my mom a lot…. I go to church all the time. I look after little kids in my church. I study with church members. My church has a big community and we always talk to each other. My church is a Japanese church, so that means that everyone is

Japanese there. We also bring Japanese food and socialize with everyone. During the morning service we sing for God and we read Bible with others. We always help each other and lean on each other.

Balbir: We go to Temple on weekends too! It's mostly boring, but I like the food! So what else do you like to do?

Sachi: Hmmm ... oh, I like shopping a lot! But, I am mainly at church or at school... the school is my learning community where we learn together. When I first got here, a year ago, I just knew two people, now I know many and I love my friends! I talk to my friends all the time and they are always helping me with the new things. One of my best friends is from Mexico. At first, it was hard to communicate with her. But now I am with her every day and we talk every day. I'll miss them a lot when we move...

Balbir: Are you moving? Where?

Sachi: Yes, we are moving next year to another state because of my dad's work. I don't want to go since I moved so much already! But there is nothing I can do about it... I will miss this place.

Balbir: I wish we could move back to San Francisco! I so wanna go back! Do you do anything outside, like around your house?

Sachi: Oh, yes. I live in an apartment though; in my neighborhood we have three parks. I love the skate park the best...

Balbir: [*interrupting*] Why is that?

Sachi: I love to skate and I love my skateboard!

Balbir: You have a skateboard?! That's so cool! I thought only boys do that.

Sachi: I do that and I am not a boy!

Balbir: Yeah, I know, that's cool...

I Live in a Curled World...

Ms. L: Alright everyone, good work and good discussions! Now all eyes on me, please. I need you to give your written records of the interview you just recorded to your partners whom you just interviewed. The next task is for you to start working on your conceptual maps involving your communities and activities. Remember, you are the centerpiece of all your communities and everything around you, so you are the most important element, and therefore your name must be in the middle of your conceptual maps. Also, if your discussion/interviews triggered some thoughts that you might want to include as part of your essay project, please write these thoughts down before you forget. So, now you should be working on one of two things, your community conceptual maps or brainstorming some ideas that have developed as a result of your discussions/interviews. Any questions?

[*Students take their notebooks and pencils out and several asked for colored markers. Ms. L walks to her desk and hands over boxes of colored pencils to students.*]

Ms. L: Are there any questions? And, do you need anything else to help you with this project?

[*Students are focused on their assignments and on making sure they get the colored pencils they like for their drawings.*]

Ms. L: I guess we're ready to start. Please let me know if you have any questions. Start everyone!

Narrator: Sachi selected the colored pencils she wanted for her community concept map and quickly walked over to the teacher's desk to get a white piece of paper to draw on. She then returned to her desk and organized her things in all the appropriate places to ensure that she has easy access to everything she needs in drawing her map. Sachi wanted to draw her map, but then after a moment of thinking, she took her notebook out and turned it to a blank page. She then started writing.... Sachi writes silently...

Sachi: [*reads to herself the poem she wrote*]

Title: I Am a Skater

My hobby is to ride my cool skateboard
I am a skater, and I am a girl.
They say, "Skateboards are for boys!"
But I am not cool with that…
I want to be a great skater-girl on the skateboard,
I am a skater, and I am a girl
I don't care about how I look
Sometimes they look at me and say,
"She is a skater and she is a girl?"
Yes, I am a skater and I am a girl!
I want to have skater friends
I want to be better than anyone
I am a skater!

Act Three: My Life

Characters

Jian was born in the United States. He is 11 years old and in the seventh grade. His family has strong ties to their country of origin, China, and often go back to visit for extended periods of time. Jian has had a fairly stable life without many struggles. Jian's parents own a restaurant in the community. Although Jian was born in the United States, he repeatedly scored low on standardized tests, hence his placement in the ELD classroom. He is easy-going and adapts well to new environments; however, he struggles with outside perceptions. Jian is an only child and relies on his many friends as well as online computer games and community to keep him company. We selected the pseudonym "Jian," which means "prosperous."

Terbish is Oyunbileg's (Act One) older brother. He is now 12 and in the seventh grade. Like his sister, Terbish values education and likes going to school. He is very friendly and gets along well with his classmates and other students at school. Because Terbish is an older sibling, his parents often ask him to perform many household tasks, including translating and filling out forms, making phone calls, and writing letters. As a result, Terbish often misses out on his afterschool time with friends. We chose pseudonym "Terbish," which means "helper."

I Live in a Curled World...

Abelardo and his family are from Mexico, and immigrated to the United States 3 years ago. Although the move itself was a culture shock to Abelardo, his parents are very supportive and frequently tell him that life in America will ensure better opportunities for Abelardo's future. The parents worked in the fields picking grapes and moved several times before settling in northern California. Abelardo is now 14 years old and in the eighth grade. He is shy and has few friends. Abelardo is fairly new to Script/Ed Middle School and still adjusting to the new environment. He is very kind, respectful, and generous in his interactions with his peers and teachers. We chose the pseudonym "Abelardo" because of its meaning—"generous."

Sancho is very ambitious and imaginative. He is also very mature for his age (13), perhaps because of his life experiences. For a time, Sancho lived with his grandmother in Mexico while his mother immigrated to the United States to find work. Sancho moved to the U.S. and joined his mother and new stepdad 4 years ago. In addition to adapting to life in a new country, Sancho was adapting to a new family construct—a new stepdad, an African American who did not speak Spanish. Sancho is very truthful, humble, polite, and always eager to help, hence the pseudonym "Sancho," which means "sincere."

Zorya and her family immigrated to the United States from Ukraine 3 years ago. Zorya's family has multiple relatives living in the area, which made the transition and acclimation to a new life much easier. Zorya is 13 years old and in the eighth grade. She is very artistically talented and has high aspirations for her future, hence the pseudonym "Zorya," or "rising star." Her family environment has been very stable since immigrating; the family has moved only once, to a nicer place within the same area.

Kamil is 11 years old and in the seventh grade. He and his family immigrated to the United States from Jerusalem when Kamil was 7 years old. Kamil and his family are very happy about their lives in the United States and Kamil's essays and journal entries reflect his favorable opinions of their new life. He is very studious and a perfectionist, hence the pseudonym "Kamil," which means "perfection."

Act Three: Scene 1

Narrator: Several ELL students are sitting on the ground outside the ELD classroom during lunch. Some are reading, others are trying to get caught up on math homework for their afternoon class, but for the most part, students are enjoying their free time because they get a chance to socialize.

Jian: Hey Terbish, what did you do after school yesterday? Me and Ye were at the KFC waiting for you! You never came online to play either. We played online for hours yesterday!

Terbish: I had to go straight home after school. My mom had a day off and she needed help.

Jian: Aww, cool. So what did you do?

Terbish: We have to fill out these forms for, you know, stuff... like to get help and stuff. So I helped my mom translate her Mongolian language to English for forms and letters. I had little time to myself.

Abelardo: Me too! I have to do that all the time too.... The first thing my mom said when we got here is that I would have to go to school because I have to know how to speak English and help out. I, on the other hand, told her that I don't want to go because I don't have any friends here, but my dad told me that I shouldn't worry because I am going to make new friends. Now, I have you guys to hang out with!

Sancho: Yeah, it was hard for me too, but my mom said the same thing...the first school I ever went to here was an elementary school and it was my favorite school. I was in third grade for the first time and my teacher spoke English and Spanish so he helped me out a lot. By the time I was in fifth grade, I developed the English skills of a regular American student.

Terbish: When I first came here, I was only good at math. Language Arts class was very hard since I only knew Mongolian language. There were only a few Mongolian kids at my school so it was fun learning with them how to speak English. I like the schools here though because we have less homework. But the classwork is so hard.

I Live in a Curled World...

Jian: Yeah, less homework is always good, it gives us more time to hang out! I don't even remember my first time in school ... it is all a blur now... I just remember that everyone looked at me weird and probably thought that I was dumb.... Now I speak English just fine but people still look at me weird. They always ask where I am from and whether I am a Filipino. I tell them I am Chinese! So annoying!

Terbish: [*laughs*] People think I am Chinese all the time, too! I have to correct them and tell them I am Mongolian... argh so embarrassing!
[*Zorya overheard the conversation and walks over to the group of boys sitting outside of the ELD classroom door.*]

Zorya: At least people take a guess with you two! No one takes a guess with me until they hear my accent and then ask... I hate being asked, since I am from here now.

Jian: I don't care anymore... I have many friends now.

Zorya: Yeah, me too. I like living here. I love my beautiful apartment and the school is close to my house, so it is a very good thing for me. When I first started this school I was very nervous, though. I went to the sixth grade and I did fit in with all the people, so it's cool.

Sancho: Who do you hang out with?

Zorya: At home, mostly with my sister, we also go to church a lot so I know all kinds of people there. Here I hang out with Maria, Thao, and your sister, Terbish!

Terbish: Yeah, I know! You talk on the phone a lot!

Abelardo: I miss my old school, my teacher, and friends a lot! I didn't want to move this year, but we had to.... Ms. Carla was my favorite teacher at my old school. She was the best teacher ever! Ms. Carla was from Mexico. The first day of school, I had asked her several times if I could be with her all the periods, but she told me that I cannot because of the school rules. I felt so scared....

Jian: Why were you scared? Was your school in a bad neighborhood or something?

Abelardo: No, because I didn't speak English. After Ms. Carla's class, I went to another class. I looked around and the teacher started to ask me things like my name and some other stuff, but when I told him that I don't know how to speak English, he told me that I just have to take a seat in the back of a room. I was bored because I was sitting for like 2 hours in the back of the room.

Sancho: I hate when teachers do that! I was sitting in the back of my class a lot when I first got here.

Terbish: How do you like it here now?

Abelardo: It's ok, it got better after a while. Now I have you guys to hangout with! I still miss my old friends though....When we had to move again last year, my friends told me that they are going to miss me a lot. Instead, I realized that I missed them more because I was all alone at the new place.

Zorya: I was very sad when we moved here from Ukraine 3 years ago. But I was happy to see all the people I missed when we got to America. That night was the best night ever. We went to my cousins' house where we had a big party with many new dishes that I had never seen before. The food was very delicious, weird, and interesting at the same time! Then my family and I went to live with my grandmother and now we have our own apartment.

Terbish: We stayed with my cousins when we first got here! And boy did I hate my stepcousin! He always acts like he knows everything in the world. Well, he knew more about America just because he came here first. But after a while I made new friends and my English started to improve. I owed it all to one and only television, especially Toon Disney, Disney Channel, Cartoon Network, and Nickelodeon. Now we have our own apartment too.

Jian: Why did you move Sancho? What's your story?

Sancho: Well... after my mom divorced my dad, she decided to leave Mexico and move here. Me and my sister went to live with my grandma, so my mom could gather enough money to get us here without having to cross the desert. My mom came to the United States with my aunt and my uncle and stayed with relatives that lived here. She worked in a restaurant and saved money every month so she can get us here. After sometime working in that restaurant she met my stepdad. My stepdad didn't speak Spanish and also didn't understand it…. They got married and then they brought us over here.

Abelardo: How did you get here?

Sancho: My grandparents helped us get to the border and after that they went back and someone else helped us get here …I really don't remember how now….

Zorya: Was your mom happy to see you? I wouldn't know what to do without my mom!

Sancho: Yeah… the first time she saw me and my sister here, I was 8 years old, she was so happy that she started crying. The day after that she introduced us to our stepfather and I was surprised because I never knew that she got married. My sister and I got to know our stepdad and we also learned to accept him as our stepfather, which was not difficult at all. He was nice and understanding, even though he was strict sometimes.

Narrator: Ten minutes left before the tardy bell. The traffic on campus has increased and students are walking to their assigned classrooms. Kamil's next class is ELD. He walks up to the group of students sitting on the ground and standing against the wall of the portable classroom talking and eating Hot Cheetos.

Kamil: Hey, Terbish, can I have some?

Terbish: Sure.

Kamil: Thanks … so what are you all talking about here?

Terbish: Oh just life….

Kamil: What about it?

Zorya: You know, how we got here, what we do now... family... you know, life.

Kamil: Ok. Cool.

Sancho: Where are you from, Kamil?

Kamil: [*chewing*] Me? I am from Jerusalem.

Sancho: Where's that?

Kamil: [*chewing*] Palestine, Israel….

Sancho: Hmmm... Ok. When did you move here?

Kamil: I am not sure, can't remember, long time ago…. Can I get more Cheetos? [*looks at Terbish and extends his hand. Terbish hands his bag of Hot Cheetos, or what is left of it, over to Kamil*]… My family wanted to have a fresh new start, so we moved. Everyone in my family came here to have a better life. My dad always says that he wanted to get paid well and treated well too! America is a free state. You can do whatever you want. We are happy here. Ever since my family moved to America, we had a great life.

Jian: Yeah, I like it here, too man! I love my big house and all the stuff I have. When I was visiting China last year, my mom and I went to dinner with my mother's friends. The food was good but the restroom looked nasty. There are no toilets, just holes in the ground... Yeeak! [*shrugs his shoulders*]

[*Ms. L walks briskly towards the classroom. As she reaches the door, the students quickly stand up and line up alongside the portable building.*]

Ms. L: Hello everyone! Let's go inside… please get your notebooks out; we will start with a journal entry.

I Live in a Curled World… 65

Narrator: Students enter the classroom while chatting quietly and get in their assigned seats. Ms. L leaves her unfinished lunch on the teacher's desk and walks over to the whiteboard in the center of classroom. She picks up the marker and starts writing under the agenda, "Journal Entry: My Life." The bell rings, students take their notebooks and writing utensils out and start writing. The classroom is silent. The only noise in the room is a slow clicking of Ms. L's shoes as she walks around the classroom and checks student work. Ms. L approaches Jian's desk and over his shoulder, reads to herself what he has written.

Ms. L: [*reads Jian's poem to herself*]

Title: Jian's Poem
My life has no ending
If I want to leave I can't
I can walk the walk
And talk the talk
But I am Chinese and
I am also American
If I want to go
Then I would go
With the wind
I can fly to China on a cloud
China is poor
But we should help the poor way more
I think, I play, I eat, I sleep,
But my life is so boring
It is so ANNOYING
I am INVINCIBLE
But people treat me like
I am invisible.
When I walk to school
They say, "Are you Filipino?"
Because of my skin.
But I say, "I am Chinese."
Because that's what I am!

Ms. L: [*whispering*] Good work, Jian! So you decided to write a poem instead?

[*Jian nods his head. Ms. L pats Jian's shoulder and walks towards Zorya's desk and reads her journal entry.*]

Ms. L: [*reads Zorya's poem to herself*]

Title: Me
Who am I?
I ask myself that question.
Am I Ukrainian?
Or am I American?
I might be Russian or American…
How should I know?
I can ask my mother …
I can ask my father…
I can ask my uncle…
Or I can ask my aunt…

Who can tell me who I am?
Maybe my grandmother…
Maybe my grandfather…
Maybe someone I don't know…
Can tell me who I am.

Maybe it will be a secret?
Maybe it will come one day to me?
But for now I will wait…

Fruition in Due Time

As we analyzed the multiple layers of data collected in the course of this study, some consistent threads came to light, leading us to construct the overarching themes illustrated in the three acts above and subthemes discussed below.

In moving through their curled and at times unpredictable lives, the mobility itself (literal and otherwise) is part of life for our participants. The adjustments are many, inherent, and unavoidable—and they relate not only to their new lives in the United States, but also to schools, neighborhoods, and life situations. The students are well aware that they are perceived differently by the mainstream culture, which requires them to negotiate their own identities in multiple environments; nevertheless, they are told, and are convinced, that America equals a "better life." In their out-of-school contexts, family and family networks (i.e., relatives) play a significant role. They find solace with members of the same cultural and language groups, which also contribute significantly to socializing newcomers into the new world. In that, the English language serves as a gateway and is perceived as a key to success. For those students who were born in the United States or who have been in the country for sometime, the challenges take a slightly different shape as the students struggle to find themselves and their place in the United States, which is the only home they know.

In our journey toward fruition, we recognize that fruition will be achieved in due time, and that it will mean different things for this work, the study's participants, and our readers. The small segment of our participants' lives described in this chapter is just that, a small segment. Their lives, struggles, and challenges are ongoing. That said, this study depicts a small fragment of U.S. school realities and obstacles that stretch from the work of a teacher whose goal it is to reshape scripted curricula to the life experiences of students who are immigrant and learning English. As our readers engage in their own journeys toward fruition in analyzing this work and making their own assumptions, we have listed starting points for engagement, while leaving room to form opinions and new understandings that challenge monolithic notions associated with the students who are learning English and their learning environments. It is our hope that this study will stimulate discussions, debates, and further dialogues.

Questions for Dialogue

1. Think of the premise of the U.S. public educational system ("the great equalizer" in our society). Does the learning environment described in this chapter fulfill its goals? If so, how? If not, why not?
2. Discuss how the *English language learner* label constructs the identity of immigrant students who are learning English. What does the label focus on, and what does it conceal? How do you think these students' stories deconstruct the monolithic perceptions the ELL label may conjure?

3. In what ways are these students' stories and experiences similar to or different from your previous understandings of ELLs?
4. To what degree did the life challenges and circumstances experienced by the participants (both the teacher and students) relate to your own?
5. How do these characters resonate with or disrupt your knowledge of immigrant students in the United States?

Notes

1. *Title I* is a label assigned to schools that are more than 40% composed of students living in low-income households, and therefore qualify for additional school services facilitated through federal programs.
2. Schools in Program Improvement (a California-specific term) are Title I schools that do not make Adequate Yearly Progress (AYP) under the No Child Left Behind (NCLB) Act, and are therefore subject to sanctions.

References

Alexander, B. K. (2005). Performance ethnography: The reenacting and inciting of culture. In N. K. Denzin & Y. S. Lincoln (Eds.), *The Sage handbook of qualitative research* (3rd ed., pp. 411–441). Thousand Oaks, CA: Sage.

Barone, T. (1995). Persuasive writings, vigilant readings, and reconstructed characters: The paradox of trust in educational story sharing. In J. A. Hatch & R. Wisniewski (Eds.), *Life history and narrative* (pp. 63–74). Washington, DC: Falmer Press.

Barone, T. (2002). Who cares? A play about passion in teaching and in the researching of teaching. In E. Mirochnik & D. Y. Sherman (Eds.), *Passion and pedagogy: Relation, creation, and transformation in teaching* (pp. 75–94). New York: Peter Lang.

Barone, T., & Eisner, E. (2006). Arts-based educational research. In J. Green, G. Camilli, & P. Elmore (Eds.), *Handbook of complementary methods in education research* (pp. 93–107). Mahwah, NJ: Lawrence Erlbaum Associates.

Capps, R., Fix, M., Murray, J., Ost, J., Passel, J. S., & Hernandez, S. (2005). *The new demography of America's schools: Immigration and the No Child Left Behind Act*. Washington, DC: Urban Institute. Retrieved from http://www.urban.org/publications/311230.html

Christians, C. (1996). Social ethics and mass media practice. In J. Makau & R. Arnett (Eds.), *Communication ethics in an age of diversity* (pp.187–205). Urbana: University of Illinois Press.

Christians, C. (2000). Ethics and politics in qualitative research. In N. K. Denzin & Y. S. Lincoln (Eds.), *Handbook of qualitative research* (pp. 133–155). Thousand Oaks, CA: Sage.

Conrad-Cozart, S., Gordon, J., Guzenhausser, M. G., McKinney, M. B., & Patterson, J. A. (2003, spring). Disrupting dialogue: Envisioning performance ethnography for research and evaluation. *Educational Foundations*, 53–69.

Cummins, S. (2000). *Language, power, and pedagogy: Bilingual children in the crossfire*. Tonawanda, NY: Multilingual Matters.

Darling-Hammond, L. (2010). Recruiting and retaining teachers: Turning around the race to the bottom in high-need schools. *Journal of Curriculum and Instruction, 4*(1), 16–32.

Denzin, N. K. (2003a). *Performing ethnography: The politics of culture*. London: Sage.

Denzin, N. K. (2003b). Reading and writing performance. *Qualitative Research,3*(2), 243–268.
Denzin, N. K.,& Lincoln, Y. S. (2000). Introduction: The discipline and practice of qualitative research. In N. K. Denzin & Y. S. Lincoln (Eds.), *Handbook of qualitative research* (pp. 1–29). Thousand Oaks, CA: Sage.
Ellis, C. (2004). *The ethnographic I: A methodological novel about autoethnography*. Walnut Creek, CA: AltaMira Press.
Erickson, F. (1986). Qualitative methods in research on teaching. In M. Witrock (Ed.), *Handbook of research on teaching* (3rd ed., pp. 3–36). New York: Macmillan.
Gibson, M. A. (1985). Collaborative educational ethnography: Problems and profits. *Anthropology & Education Quarterly, 16,* 124–148.
Gonzalez, N., Moll, L. C., & Amanti, C. (Eds.). (2005). *Funds of knowledge: Theorizing practices in households, communities, and classrooms*. Mahwah, NJ: Lawrence Erlbaum Associates.
Gutiérrez, K., Baquedano-López, P., & Asato, J. (2000). "English for the children": The new literacy of the old world order, language policy and educational reform. *Bilingual Research Journal, 24*(1&2), 87–112.
Krog, A. (1998). *Country of my skull: Guilt, sorrow, and the limits of forgiveness in the new South Africa*. New York: Three Rivers Press.
Ladson-Billings, G. (1995). Toward a theory of culturally relevant pedagogy. *American Educational Research Journal, 32*(3), 465–491.
Lincoln, Y., & Guba, E. (1985). *Naturalistic inquiry*. Beverly Hills, CA: Sage.
Nieto, S. (1992). *Affirming diversity: The sociopolitical context of multicultural education*. New York: Longman.
Noblit, G. W., Flores, S. Y., & Murillo, E. G. (Eds.). (2004). *Postcritical ethnography: Reinscribing critique*. Cresskill, NJ: Hampton Press.
Suárez-Orózco, C., Suárez-Orózco, M. M., & Todorova, I. (2008). *Learning a new land: Immigrant students in American society*. Cambridge, MA: Harvard University Press.
Valdés, G. (1996). *Con respeto! Bridging the distances between culturally diverse families schools: An ethnographic portrait*. New York: Teachers College Press.
Valdés, G. (2002). *Expanding definitions of giftedness: The case of young interpreters from immigrant families*. Mahwah, NJ: Lawrence Erlbaum Associates.

Chapter 3

The Naming of the Dis/abled within U.S. Special Education

Jessica Nina Lester and Rachael Gabriel

There is a place,
a meeting
where many experts gather,
entering the space of naming the "other."
"To help,"
is the storyline they tout.
"No other way to help,"
apparently.
The place of naming
the "other"
dis/abled.
Welcome to the *Theatre of the Absurd*.

Beginnings

We came to this work as former classroom teachers and current teacher-educators with the aim of making sense of the ways in which various stakeholders experience special education meetings (i.e., IEP meetings, as they are called in the U.S.). Scholars in disability studies in education (e.g., Corker & French, 1999; Corker & Shakespeare, 2002; Sleeter, 1987) have placed increasing emphasis upon the socially constructed and contingent nature of dis/abilities. Learning disabilities (LDs) are relatively new constructions, and some scholars disagree on appropriate diagnostic criteria. Some scholars in disability studies argue that the "disability" is constructed between a person and his or her environment; it is not a fact of that person's biology. In saying this, scholars do not minimize the learning challenges, but question the idea that someone is inherently DIS-abled. Rather, they suggest that the notion of disability is socially constructed and historically specific. Other scholars maintain that there is a biological basis for learning difficulties that is a static and observable reality inherent to the individual.

Little research has attended to the ways in which the "official," privileged, and culturally familiar ways of talking about LDs play out in the context of special education meetings. The performative script we share here was constructed using data from a larger project exploring the "landscape" of the special education process in the southeast region of the United States. Within this script we focus on a particular aspect of this project: the meetings in which a person, often a child, is officially designated LD. From the outset, we oriented to the practices in such meetings as performances, and situated our analysis within and against the discourses and practices of the technical and routine doings of special education meetings. Taking up a critical performance methodology (Madison, 2008), we explore here, through a performative text, the everyday lived moments (de Certeau, 1984) of those who participate in special education meetings, working to complicate ideas surrounding educational "help," "dis/ability," and "expertise" within such settings.

Methodological Orientation and Representation of Findings

When deciding which layers of our findings to share and how to do so, we were particularly drawn to the idea of constructing our findings in a way that created a space with the potential of "art-making for transgressive and transformative experiences" (Garoian & Gaudelius, 2008, p. 1). We thus grounded this work in a performance studies framework (Conquergood, 1998), and aimed to craft our findings as a staged retelling (Alexander, 2005). As we engaged in the data analysis and writing process, we used the performative text as a means to question taken-for-granted practices and to interrogate unjust systems and processes (Madison, 2008). Since its initial construction we have shared and invited others to re-enact the stories in a variety of spaces, including community centers and teacher-education courses (Gabriel & Lester, in press).

Date Sources and Analysis

As part of a larger research study, we conducted 15 in-depth interviews with individuals who had participated in special education meetings. Our participants included seven special education professors, two psychologists, one special educator, four parents, and one student. We identified each "group" of participants in different ways. For those participants who identified primarily as teacher-educators, we contacted department chairs and departmental secretaries at universities that housed the 15 largest teacher-education programs in the selected region of the U.S., and requested the contact information of those individuals responsible for teaching courses in the area of special education. For those individuals who identified primarily as teachers, we used snowball sampling, beginning with graduates of a local teacher-education program. For parents, we used both snowball sampling and a contact list of local parent groups, including special education support groups and homeschool support groups. For the student participant, we used word-of-mouth, contacting students who were 18 years or older through our network of colleagues and participants. Most interviews were conducted via phone because participants were often hours away. Those that were local had the option of a phone or in-person interview. One participant, the student, preferred a face-to-face interview.

All interviews were transcribed and uploaded into Atlas.ti, a software program we used as an organizational tool while reading and rereading the interview transcripts and engaging in the analysis of the individual transcripts. Over the course of 6 months, we met together and analyzed the data iteratively, attending first to broad patterns within individual interviews and across the data set. We then explicitly attended to moments of variability and contradiction within and between our participants' stories. We used in vivo coding and sociologically constructed codes (Coffey & Atkinson, 1996) to analyze our interviews, and eventually developed broad themes around which we organized the findings/performative text.

Additionally, we approached our analysis with an understanding that "talk creates the social world in a continuous, ongoing way," with each participant's discourse standing as only one production among many possibilities (Wood & Kroger, 2000, p. 4). So, in the construction of this text, we attended to the varied discourses that act to position, manage, and at times contest labeled identities often framed by normative and deficit models of human development. We worked to problematize the very practice of labeling one's way of being dis/abled. Further, in order to capture what we came to understand as "absurdities," that is, those technical practices presented by "experts" as rational and normalized "truths" and "necessities," we named this work a "theatre of the absurd."

In an effort to provide a structure for the representation of our participants' words, we looked to examples of dramatic texts within the tradition of the theatre of the absurd. Pirandello's 1924 play *Six Characters in Search of an Author*—a controversial work in which the six characters invade the stage and demand to be included—served as a mentor text. As such, it provided an example of staging and organization for a play in which several characters enter a set with minimal props or scenery and negotiate their roles and purposes among each other. We leaned into this example as inspiration, borrowing the beginning stage directions as well as the image of a starkly decorated set. This allowed us to stage performances in a wide variety of locations, as we did not depend on props, artifacts, or furniture to create the world of the play (Lester & Gabriel, 2012). Like Pirandello, we also constructed this text in a polemical spirit, working to present the characters as shifting and complex beings, regardless of how the script casts them. For the majority of the characters[1] we created composites (Ellis, 2004), drawing upon the data we collected. We attempted to represent the commonalities that we noted across each group we interviewed. In doing so, we recognized that we may undermine our desire to attend to the particular, yet we remained willing to work with and against such tensions.

Though students are not always present at their own special education meetings, our student participant, who was 22 years old at the time of the interview, shared her story of being labeled at age 7 and attending her own meetings in high school. We were struck by the absence of the student in many descriptions of special education meetings, and by the ways in which the student we interviewed sought a venue to interrogate those who had made decisions for her. As she said, "It's what they thought, not what I thought. It's what they thought was best and that's how it was gunna be." So, we asked her what she would have asked her teachers, administrators, and parents on the very first day they met, when she was only 7 years old. We asked, "What would you tell them to do differently? What questions do you wish you could have asked? What questions do you hope/wish to ask now?" As we listened and learned from the student participant, we were compelled to share our findings in a way that privileged her perspective. In doing so, we acknowledged, both literally and figuratively, her felt absence from special education meetings. Thus, we worked to retell the stories of special education meetings from her perspective, allowing her to direct the action both within the play and with us as we constructed it. She worked through the text at the side of one of the researchers, reminding us of the stories we often failed to represent and of our previous work as educators.

Our Positionalities

As we collected and analyzed the data and constructed the text, we worked to practice recursive reflexivity (Pillow, 2003), recognizing that our biases and presuppositions shaped how we chose to represent the findings. As such, we position ourselves "as no longer transparent," but as "classed, gendered, raced, and sexual" beings who engage in constructing and negotiating our social locations (Fine, 1994, p. 76). In that our positionalities (Noblit, Flores, & Murillo, 2004) on the process of labeling another's identity affected the ways we constructed the performative text, we chose to make our positionalities explicit in order to be maintain transparency and inform the reader.

As practicing K–12 teachers and teacher-educators, we both have witnessed and participated in the nominating and/or labeling of children as dis/abled in academic and therapeutic settings. We also have witnessed the consequences and affordances of the moment of labeling in a child's life and academic career. I (Jessica), as a white, privileged special educator, have tested, labeled, delabeled, taught, learned from, hurt, constructed, and/or deconstructed many children. Over time, the stories of the students with whom I have worked have become a part of my story. When I began academic work, I made an explicit commitment to find ways to complicate the stories that are told and retold about educational labeling, tracking, and placements. Indeed, their stories, losses, smiles, and tears carry me in many ways to this work. Though saturated with privileges, I choose to speak back, to retell in partial, and biased ways. I (Rachael), as a white, privileged former middle-school teacher, have both nominated students for and shielded them from placement in special education. When I first began teaching, I thought the best way to help students who struggled in my classes was to get them out of my room and into the hands of "experts" who could teach them better than I could. I learned that removal from mainstream classes was, at times, more punishment and avoidance, both socially and academically, than "help." I also learned that preparation to teach students who struggle in mainstream classes is not a matter of titles, degrees in special education, or specialist licenses. It involves a belief in every human's ability and desire to learn, and a relentless pursuit of ways to ensure that they do. As teachers and researchers, we find that such "ways" are too often thwarted by the very structures put in place to support them.

An Invitation to the Reader/Performer

We offer this rendering, constructed as a performative text, as only one among many possible interpretations of our findings, and resist the notion of a single definitive meaning of experiences in special education meetings. Across the performative text, we ask you to consider: Who benefits? Who is heard? What else might be imagined? Like Barone (1995), we suggest that:

> [W]e do not always need, within the same textual breath, to deconstruct in another style and format, the epiphanies they foster. Sometimes the conversation between writer, reader, and characters should be allowed to wane before additional voices interject themselves into the dialogue. (p. 72)

As such, in our representation of the participants' words, we opted not to incorporate theorized interpretations or a final, concluding paragraph. Instead, we leave space for you to fill in the gaps, note what we have failed to share, and "interject [your]selves into the dialogue" (Barone, 1995, p. 72). We ask you to imagine each character as complex, contradictory, and layered. Although we stayed close to the "actual" words of the participants, we believe that getting the story "right" is impossible. We did not seek to do so. Instead, we retell a partial version, recognizing that for every story told, there is a story untold (Krog, 1998). So, we invite you to tell us what we cannot yet see, noting what we have learned and have yet to learn.

The following section details the list of characters. In groups of two or more, we encourage you to assign yourself a character and to engage in a live reading. We have provided initial discussion questions to follow the reading. They are meant as a guide, not an assignment, as we hope your reading will provoke discussion far beyond them. Welcome to the theatre of the absurd.

The Naming of the Dis/abled

Characters
Professor Used-to-Teach: a special education teacher at a higher education institution in the southeast region of the U.S. that graduates well over 100 Ms. Care N. Paperworks each year.

Ms. Care N. Paperwork: a special educator working particularly with children identified as learning disabled (LD) and emotionally-behaviorally disordered (EBD). She regularly participates in special education meetings.

Mom: attends special education meetings due to a child needing and/or desiring "extra services."

Ms. Diagnosis: a psychologist who represents the school and clinical psychologists involved in the diagnosis process. She has extensive experience, having worked in both clinical and educational settings.

Katrina[2]**:** a 22-year-old who was labeled LD at the age of 7. She began participating in her own special education meetings at the age of 14. She graduated from high school and now works in a daycare center.

Interpreters: One or two interpreters are often present at special education meetings to translate for students, parents, and/or school personnel. In the performative text they do not have any lines because they rarely have the opportunity to provide input during meetings, though they are often the only people with total access to the communication of everyone in the room.

Directors 1 (Rachael) and 2 (Jessica): The two directors take up this work with particular assumptions, biases, and commitments. They ask questions, and at times ask and/or tell the actresses and actors to STOP, REPEAT, and SHH.

Act One

Setting
The spectators find the curtain raised and the stage as it usually is during the daytime. It is half dark and empty, so that from the very beginning of this

rehearsal, the public has the impression of an impromptu performance. The actors and actresses of the company enter from the back of the stage: first one, then another, then two together, with the final actress, a blond haired 20-something-year-old, slowly walking onto the stage. Five altogether wait—some sit, others chat, one smokes, and the 20-something-year-old eventually sits down off in the corner. Finally, the two directors enter and go to the table prepared for them to watch and listen. They bring a recorder and a notebook with them.

Director 1: [*throwing a notebook down on the table and looking at the other director*] I can't see. Let's have a little light, please!

Director 2: LIGHTS! [*all turn toward the audience, attach their nametags, and take their seats, looking to the Directors' table for clarification as if the lights had just gone on to signal the start of rehearsal*]

Director 1: Now Katrina, remember you're the one who's learning disabled.

Katrina: Excuse me?

Director 1: So I need you to actually be learning disabled.

Katrina: Be learning disabled?

Director 2: But what does that mean?

Director1: We'll get to that. Katrina?

Katrina: Yes?

Director 1: You're here as the one who is learning disabled so that you can go back to the day you weren't, and ask the people who named you all the questions you'd like to ask them.

Katrina: When I was 7? The things I would have asked them when I was 7?

The Naming of the Dis/abled within U.S. Special Education

Director 2: Maybe partly, but in the script, it's more what you would have wanted to ask them now.

Ms. Diagnosis: Okay, is this a run-through or are we doing this for real now?

Director 1: Real now?? What do you mean by "real now"?

Ms. Diagnosis: I mean are we starting? Do I get to begin?

Director 2: We're starting, but in this play Katrina begins.

Ms. Diagnosis: But that's not how it goes. I mean that's just not how these things go.

Director 1: Then tell us, Ms. Diagnosis. Tell us what happens at a special education meeting. Is it you all and the child?

Ms. Diagnosis: Not often, but if the child is over 14 they are more likely to be involved.

Director 2: STOP. We want to do this differently. We've invited a student to be here. She starts; she ends; she asks questions; she is present.

Ms. Diagnosis: Well, how old is she? Does she have a disability?

Director 1: She is 22. And her name is Katrina.

Ms. Diagnosis: Well, she shouldn't be sitting at the table unless she's of age and has the capacity to understand. The law supports me on this.

Director 2: This meeting's *about* her. Why can't she be here?

Director 1: It's about what they're going to do for her.

Director 2: [*aside*] To her.

Ms. Diagnosis: Well, technically she can come now. She's 22.

Director 2: Today, we aren't playing by your rules, Ms. Diagnosis. Katrina is our leading character. [*The other characters look around at each other in surprise, some audibly gasping, others rolling their eyes, some nodding in agreement.*] Katrina, where do we begin?

Katrina: Well, I want to know what other people's experiences were like. Aren't there other students coming? I wanted to know what their experiences were like.

Director 2: No other students spoke to us, but we did speak to parents. Can you [*looking at Mom*] share about your experiences?

Mom: Well, my first experience was not in this state, so I don't know if that makes a difference, but our first experience was in another southern state. My son had the normal, typical "preemie" issues. And so he had been in the special education system through early intervention, since he was a baby. And he went to kindergarten, first, and second—so he had an Individualized Education Plan, an IEP, from that point on. When we took him out of school to homeschool him is when things got a little iffy, because he still qualified for services, but they were not willing to give him any.

Director 1: You are supposed to say "who." Who wasn't willing?

Katrina: [*whispers*] The messed-up system.

Mom: [*looks at Katrina and nods her head in agreement*] We have not had that problem here in this state though. They've been much more cooperative. And helpful. They sit down and they go through the whole process. They even discussed with us that if they had the funding, that they would have liked to have given our son 2 days a week of specialized reading help. They just didn't have the funding for it.

Katrina: How is that helpful?

Mom: Listen, where I used to live, the special education meetings were not so easy and I would go in with a tape recorder and record everything that was said by everyone because we had had problems where they would say they were going to do something and then not provide it. So we had to really fight. We fought and fought and fought with them. And we ended up taking him to the clinic at a university. They agreed to work with him 4 days a week. It was wonderful. It was probably the most life-changing thing for him. They actually taught him to read before he could talk. He's 14 now and you could never tell he didn't start to speak until he was 6.

Katrina: [*mumbles*] No one ever taught me to read.

Mom: And the other thing that we always say about our kids is our kids are cubes, and society, well, we're trying to put them in a round hole.

Director 1: What did you say, Katrina? Can you REPEAT that?

Katrina: No one ever taught me to read.

Mom: They didn't?

Katrina: Two years after high school, I went to a clinic and these two ladies taught me what I wanted to get better at, what I wanted. Not what they thought I needed. What I wanted, which is great because I worked on my writing, spelling, and we worked on reading, and that's really what I wanted, you know. They taught me.

Mom: See, when you try to put a cube into a round hole, you chisel off some of their best parts. And so when we're trying to make these children fit into a one-size-fits-all educational system, we're losing some of their best abilities and their best parts. You know because that's, that's how our son is—just the most wonderful child—but he does not fit the typical, sit-for-8-hours-a-day school system. They can't handle him and he can't handle them.

Katrina: Couldn't handle him? They couldn't handle me either. They said I was too stubborn.

Director 1: Is stubbornness a common symptom of LD, Ms. Diagnosis?

Ms. Diagnosis: What I think we all have to keep in mind here is that school psychologists and private educational consultants test and diagnose for different reasons, but we all have to work together.

Director 2: Let's get back to the actual meeting, Katrina. Can we talk about what's important at a special education meeting?

Mom: Mom input. It's important for the Mom to be there, or at least to send her notes if for some reason she couldn't attend. It's nice to know the faces of the people who are with him all day and that they want what's best for him. You know sometimes I just want to be mom and love on my kid and not be teaching or managing all the time.

Professor Used-to-Teach: Well, in my class, I hand out a psychological report on the various specific disabilities and the students have to complete an IEP for that specific child. So, if it's health impaired or if it's learning disabled or if there's a dual diagnosis or mental retardation with a language impairment, then they have to complete the IEP on that child. So they, to some extent, they have to assume some things so when they're writing the present levels of performance page, obviously they have the scores, you know standard or scaled or whatever they have. They then have to assume certain things that a second-grade student should know. So when they come to write the narratives, of course, they can get some of this from the psychological report, but you know, I'd say, well, you know, if you assume that by the first grade they're learning multiplication facts, obviously if the child has a learning disability in math, then probably he doesn't know those.

Director 2: You can assume that?

Mom: I don't think that's fair to say. My kids didn't each know all the same things by second grade, but they all learned it all eventually.

Professor Used-to-Teach: Well, I have the students build up a picture of the child from the psychological report.

Director 1: A picture of the child from the psychological report? Wouldn't they need to be working with the child?

Ms. Care N. Paperwork: Not always.

Professor Used-to-Teach: So most of the information they have, but some they have to assume and some they have to research. Like, what would a child look like, uh, who had a learning disability in math and what might or might not they have been able to do according to a certain grade level? Does that make sense?

Director 1: Yeah, that makes lots of sense if you think that grade levels are a natural thing, instead of something we invented to help organize classrooms of approximately equal size with approximately equally sized children. Are you saying if you don't fit into the grade level expectations, you're disabled?

Ms. Diagnosis: We know statistically that students who don't know certain things by certain grades don't do as well later.

Professor Used-to-Teach: Well, in my class, they have to actually write the IEP, um, and then we do a simulation of an IEP team meeting. And it's probably the most stressful thing they do in special education here. I actually have had a guy hyperventilate.

Director1: Why?

Professor Used-to-Teach: They have to do the whole meeting as if they were the special education teacher. One person has to review the rights and responsibilities and explain what the disability means to the eligibility decision, um, and then the other person has to take the notes and has to go through the IEP and explain, um, the modifications, and so they explain the whole IEP to the other members of the class, who assume the role of a parent or surrogate parent and special education teacher, general education teacher. So we do actually go through an entire IEP team meeting.

Director 1: So that's what happens?

Katrina: Without the student.

Director 2: About a fake student based on a fake psychological report.

Director 1: So you teach them that you write an IEP based on what a report tells you. And so what do you hope they learn?

Professor Used-to-Teach: Well, I also teach them that it is important for the parent to be there and for the teacher to work to put the parents at ease in the process. It's also important for the general education teacher to be there and be part of the team. Not just sign that they will do these accommodations, but—

Director 1: Wait a second! Are professors in these IEP meetings?

Professor Used-to-Teach: Yes, I sometimes go as an advocate.

Director 1: Right, there are sometimes parent advocates.

Professor Used-to-Teach: There are, but I go as a student advocate.

Ms. Diagnosis: Well the data doesn't lie. It's all right in here. [*pats overstuffed manila folder*] It says everything here on these tests.

Director 1: That's why they pay you the big bucks.

Professor Used-to-Teach: You have to put data into parent-friendly language. The IEP meeting should not be the first communication about the child's progress with parents.

Ms. Care N. Paperwork: You know, I think there are some meetings that are positive and some that are negative. I've been involved in all kinds of special education meetings. I mean, the best meetings I've been in are the ones where I can actually get kids out of comprehensive special education, you know, out into a regular education situation with support. Those are the most gratifying to me.

Katrina: The best year of my life was the year I didn't have to go to the "special" room. No one knew about my problem that year. I was normal.

The Naming of the Dis/abled within U.S. Special Education   85

Ms. Care N. Paperwork: Well, "resource" is considered special education. It is not for extremely special special-education students. They are not really high needs, mostly learning disabled, other health impairments, autistic sometimes. But we have others. Resource is the higher up.

Director 1: Higher up on what? What does "extremely special *special*" mean? Should I be writing this down?

Katrina: I don't believe in that room at all. I don't believe in what they do there. I don't believe in some of the teachers that are in there.

Professor Used-to-Teach: Well, we have to first ensure that it's the least restrictive environment. The law requires assessment of students, and where they are, also what kind of needs that they will have, what kind of goals and objectives that need to be written. I definitely stress the parent participation as much as possible. And I also stress the fact that they need to make sure that the parents actually do understand their rights.

Mom: That's what I learned to look for. But I went down to the county office and I took every pamphlet and packet they had on special education and I put it in a huge 3-inch binder and I sat with all that information every night with my highlighter until I got through it and knew my rights. And now I go to those meetings with other parents and help them make sure they understand.

Director 1: Like a parent advocate. Though everyone else seems to think they're acting as parent advocates too. So special education meetings are about the parents?

Professor Used-to-Teach: It's the team approach that's important.

Ms. Care N. Paperwork: Well, ideally, we assess the kids and try to meet them where they are and try to help them make progress. I didn't expect them to make straight A's once they got back into regular education, but I did think it was possible with the right accommodations for kids to do well. So, the very first time it happened, one of my colleagues took me aside and asked why I did that because this kid is never going to thrive. But he ended up thriving. And now, as a matter of fact, he is a senior in high school this year, and he told me that he is doing really well and he never looked back.

Director 1: Because he got out?

Katrina: I totally feel that way, that they'll—you know, what if they wouldn't have done this and what if they would have worked harder with me on stuff? You know, maybe I would be different. Maybe I'd still have trouble, but I mean, maybe I could have got better. It could have, you know, [*breathing out hard*] I don't know.

Ms. Care N. Paperwork: A lot of the teachers came to think that if the student isn't out of special education and not in a resource class or something like that by the time they hit middle school, they'll never get out of it. I came to think that it was my job to help my students get to the point where they could actually survive in a regular education class. Because, you know, that is just what I thought I was supposed to do, so that is what I did.

Director 1: You mentioned there are sometimes bad meetings. Can you say more about what makes one bad?

Ms. Care N. Paperwork: I can understand the need for the IEP process and I think it's a good thing, but at least the ones that I had dealt with, the staff that had came in to work with us seemed to be very gung-ho, very fresh out of school, full of ideas that they were anxious to put into practice. That was great, but I felt a real lack of teamwork, a real lack of willingness on their part to listen to what the teachers had to say. Sometimes what looks good on paper just looks good on paper and does not work.

Katrina: I really would like to know why do I have a learning disability? Why? What is it that I can't, that I don't know? I would like to know why I have a learning disability. What, is my brain different?

Professor Used-to-Teach: [*turns body away from Directors and gazes at Ms. Diagnosis*] A learning disability has, uh, can be manifested in accordance with the IDEA '04 regulations, actually.

Director 1: There's a law that defines disability? So, like, can you sue someone and say they break the ability law? Or the disability law? Can I sue for a misdiagnosis?

Professor Used-to-Teach: You've got to take the state definition. For every disability that you talk about, you have to know what is the definition and how do you assess it. Really, this is complicated and we don't have time for it.

Katrina: You know, sometimes I don't think a learning disability is really something, because like, sometimes I think that they put it in your head that that is what's wrong with you, and you can't fix it.

Professor Used-to-Teach: I answer that question by saying that a learning disability is a valid construct supported with research and consensus of the learning disability roundtable that is characterized by intra-individual cognitive and academic variability. But this is sort of a debate really.

Ms. Care N. Paperwork: Well, I tell parents that if their child is learning disabled, they've been learning disabled since like whenever they were first diagnosed.

Director 1: I'm confused. You are disabled once you are diagnosed, named disabled?

Ms. Care N. Paperwork: My professor said "it prohibits them from performing in their academic classrooms. It hinders their learning." That's why it's a learning disability instead of a physical disability.

Director 1: Is that right, Katrina? Did it hinder your learning?

Katrina: I feel like I can't get fixed because of what everyone's said. Like, they put this in my head and that's how I'm going to be the rest of their life.

Ms. Diagnosis: Now Katrina, I understand that you're angry, but statistics show us that many children who have learning disabilities…

Professor Used-to-Teach: See, well, now you're making me think back to my textbook. It's, I would say, it's not that these children can't learn. I think the word *disability* gives a false impression. They may have to work around situations. And they may have to develop new skills in order to master the content.

Katrina: I didn't have the skills to do anything, because no one gave me the skills or helped me, you know—show me some skills to do it, you know. No one helped me.

Mom: Oh, gosh. Do you want my thoughts?

Katrina: Yeah.

Mom: My child, my oldest son, was in the fifth grade and began having discipline problems because he refused to stand up in front of the class and recite his multiplication tables. His teacher was upset and my son was shy, so I understood where he was coming from. She was very upset and I said, "Well, look, he's doing long division, so he obviously knows how to multiply because you can't do one without the other." But she insisted that he stand up and she goes, "Well, I think he has a learning disability." I thought, "Huh, okay. Well let's have him tested."

Director 1: And then what happened?

Mom: We did and the test results came back and they laid the paper in my face and said, "see, we told you he had a learning disability." You know what it was?

Ms. Diagnosis: Oppositional defiant disorder? Dyslexia? Dyslexia is extremely common, you know, and it manifests itself in many areas. It could also be ADHD. There's some oppositional behavior and anxiety with that often.

Director 1: And stubbornness?

Mom: As a fifth grader, he tested at tenth-grade level. They labeled him as learning disabled. He did not fit the square little peg.

Director 2: Wow. What happened next? Was—did you end up—

Mom: He eventually dropped out, got his GED, and moved on with his life.

Ms. Care N. Paperwork: Now where is he?

Mom: He's out in Washington. He has grown kids of his own.

Director 1: [*holding up copies of the special education law*] It says here: "implementation [of the law]...has been **impeded by low expectations**" under 20 U.S.C. 1400(c)(4), whatever that means.

Katrina: They just started taking things away from me, not making me do it, you know. But at that time, I didn't really realize that, but now I do. I realize that they just didn't even say anything to me about it. [*pushes away from the table and gazes at her feet*] The start of taking things away and pushing me through.

Director 2: Oh, and here it says "... having **high expectations** for such children and ensuring their access to the general education curriculum in regular classrooms, to the maximum extent possible ... to meet the challenging expectations that have been established for all children; and be prepared to lead productive and independent lives to the maximum extent possible" 20 U.S.C. 1400(c)(5).

Katrina: They didn't do that for me. No expectations. They took it all away.

Ms. Care N. Paperwork: Are you talking about us?

Katrina: Yeah. Maybe. Sort of. I want you to help children. Just, like, help them learn how to do it, you know. Make them more confident in themselves. Put effort into it, you know. Don't do it *for* them. Don't do it *for* them. Show them ways to do it.

Ms. Care N. Paperwork: I always try to get the students into the mainstream classroom. Like I said earlier, that's my goal.

Mom: Everybody seems to—I don't know if it's putting kids in their little pegs in their little, you know, this child's autistic, this child's learning disabled, this one, whatever. They just—it's like they need those labels to place them.

Director 2: That's really, really interesting. Do you imagine an alternative?

Mom: An alternative to labeling. Gosh, I don't know. You know, they did it forever before, putting kids through schools and without the labels and you just work with each child on their level. It—

Director 2: Ironically, the most logical alternative—working with each child on their level. They didn't do it forever before. Kids got sent away to institutions or stopped going to school. There were no "good old days" for kids with LDs.

Ms. Diagnosis: Aha! So you DO believe in it, in LDs!

Director 1: Well, honestly, we had a lot of trouble figuring out how to talk about all this.

Katrina: So why can't we get rid of labels? Why can't we do something different? Why can't we figure it out? Do different things that would build skills?

Ms. Diagnosis: Well, we HAVE it figured out; it's just that…

Directors 1 and 2: [*say in unison*] SHHH! Everyone quiet. [*look toward Katrina*] Do you want to say something, Katrina?

Katrina: Stop labeling. It hurts. It puts you down. How come this is all about what they, the people in charge, think should be done? It's what *they* think. *They* choose the program. *They* pull you out of class. *They* test you on *their* time. Never asking *you* what you think about all this. It's not what the student thinks; it's not what the student wants. It isn't. It's not, which is ridiculous. That's crazy that they don't even ask that. I've never been to a meeting where they've asked what I thought about all this. It's what they think is best and that's how it's gunna be.

Director 1: That's amazing! [*laughs*] It's supposed to be about the student, right?

Director 2: So if you had to name your educational story, what would you name it?

Katrina: [*laughs and looks directly at Ms. Care N. Paperwork*] The Start of Taking Things Away and PUSHING Them Through!

Director 1: Cut! Repeat that, Katrina. Say it again. The start of what?

Katrina: The Start of Taking Things Away and PUSHING Them THROUGH! That hurts. That hurts.

Mom: What hurts dear?

Katrina: The whole thing. I don't really have that much confidence. My confidence, my self-esteem is very low. Yeah, it still is. I hope no one has to go through what I've gone through. [*pushes her chair away from the table, stands up, picks up her purse, and begins walking away from the stage. As she walks away, she looks back at the table*] One more thing, you need to quit pushing these kids through the system, because you're not helping them out in their future. That's a big thing I would say right away. You need to work with them. You need to figure out how they learn and how you can help them, and how to get their confidence up, you know. Get these kids [*breathing out hard*], get them help. Help them, don't push them through.

Director 2: Ok, um, we end when she ends.

Ms. Care N. Paperwork: But what did we accomplish today? We can't be done.

Director 2: LIGHTS OUT! [*everyone looks toward the Directors*] We said we would end as Katrina ended. She got up and walked away. Get up and walk away. It's over now without her. CUT.

Questions for Dialogue

1. From your perspective, what is the purpose of an LD label?
2. Are the stories told here similar or dissimilar to what you know about special education meetings?
3. How do the characters fit or not fit with what you believe about learning disabilities?
4. What do you believe would be an ideal educational system?

Notes

1. The Directors and Katrina (see "Characters") were the only characters who were not constructed as composites.
2. Pseudonyms were used throughout.

References

Alexander, B. K. (2005). *Performance ethnography: The reenacting and inciting of culture*. In N. K. Denzin & Y. S. Lincoln (Eds.), *The Sage handbook of qualitative research* (3rd ed., pp. 411–441). Thousand Oaks, CA: Sage.

Barone, T. (1995). Persuasive writings, vigilant readings, and reconstructed characters: The paradox of trust in educational story sharing. In J. A. Hatch & R. Wisniewski (Eds.), *Life history and narrative* (pp. 63–74). Washington, DC: Falmer Press.

Coffey, A., & Atkinson, P. (1996). *Making sense of qualitative data: Complementary research strategies*. Thousand Oaks, CA: Sage.

Conquergood, D. (1998). Beyond the text: Toward a performative cultural politics. In S. J. Dailey (Ed.), *The future of performance studies: Visions and revisions* (pp. 25–36). Washington, DC: National Communication Association.

Corker, M., & French, S. (1999). Reclaiming discourse in disability studies. In M. Corker & S. French (Eds.), *Disability discourse* (pp. 1–20). Buckingham, UK: Open University Press.

Corker, M., & Shakespeare, T. (2002). *Disability/postmodernity*. London: Continuum.

de Certeau, M. (1984). *The practice of everyday life*. London: University of California Press.

Denzin, N. (2003). *Performance ethnography: Critical pedagogy and the politics of culture*. Thousand Oaks, CA: Sage.

Ellis, C. (2004). *The ethnographic I: A methodological novel about autoethnography*. Walnut Creek, CA: AltaMira Press.

Foucault, M. (1980). *Power/knowledge: Selected interviews & other writings 1972–1977* (A. Fontana & P. Pasquino, trans. 1977). New York: Pantheon Press.

Fine, M. (1994). Working the hyphens: Reinventing self and other in qualitative research. In N.

Denzin & Y. Lincoln (Eds.), *Sage handbook of qualitative research* (pp. 70–82). London: Sage.

Gabriel, R., & Lester, J. N. (2013, in press). Community performances and performative texts as tools for critical exploration. *Power and Education.*

Garoian, C. R., & Gaudelius, Y.M. (2008). *Spectacle pedagogy: Art, politics, and visual culture.* Albany: State University of New York.

Habermas, J. (1988). *Theory and practice.* (J. Viertel, trans.) Boston: Beacon Press.

Krog, A. (1998). *Country of my skull: Guilt, sorrow, and the limits of forgiveness in the new South Africa.* New York: Three Rivers Press.

Lester, J., & Gabriel, R. (2012). Performance ethnography of IEP meetings: A theatre of the absurd. In P. Vannini (Ed.), *Popularizing research* (pp. 173–178). New York: Peter Lang.

Madison, D. S. (2008). Narrative poetics and performative interventions. In N. K. Denzin, Y. S. Lincoln, & L. T. Smith (Eds.), *Handbook of critical and indigenous methodologies* (pp. 391–405). Los Angeles: Sage.

Noblit, G. W., Flores, S. Y., & Murillo, E. G. (Eds.). (2004). *Postcritical ethnography: Reinscribing critique.* Cresskill, NJ: Hampton Press.

Pillow, W. S. (2003). Confession, catharsis, or cure? Rethinking the uses of reflexivity as methodological power in qualitative research. *Qualitative Studies in Education, 16*(2), 175–196.

Sleeter, C. E. (1987). Why is there learning disabilities? A critical analysis of the birth of the field with its social context. In T. S. Popkewitz (Ed.), *The formation of school subjects: The struggle for creating an American institution* (pp. 210–237). London: Palmer Press.

Wood, L. A., & Kroger, R. O. (2000). *Doing discourse analysis: Methods for studying action in talk and text.* Thousand Oaks, CA: Sage.

Chapter 4

Needing Intensive Remediation: How a Reading Identity is Negotiated, Interpreted, and Lived

Anne McGill-Franzen and Renee Moran

Inequality—whether in income distribution, access to higher education, or career opportunities, to name but a few of its manifestations—has long vexed social scientists. Those vested in educational institutions, as we are, may be complicit in perpetuating inequality insofar as schooling contributes to social outcomes beyond the school itself. Instead of viewing the school as simply transmitting knowledge, ethnomethodologists such as Mehan (Mehan, 1978, 1979, 1992; Mehan & Wood, 1975) see schooling as an "interactional device that shapes students' careers on the basis of an interplay between students' background characteristics and the institutional practices of the school" (Mehan, 1992, p. 16). Regardless of the routinized nature of the work of educators within schools—teaching, testing, attending meetings—Mehan holds that students' IQ scores, access to coursework, academic self-concepts, and ultimate achievement and careers are "assembled" from these everyday, mundane school practices. As we illustrate with our performance, testing interactions are powerful examples of the structuring that takes place in schools that contributes mightily to the unequal outcomes of education.

Negotiating a Score

Constitutive analysts such as Mehan (1978) have made explicit evaluators' assumptions about testing. Those who administer tests take as a given that correct answers signal the presence of the underlying ability, whereas incorrect answers signal the absence of that ability. Testers also assume that the language of the test means the same thing to the testers and to the student; in other words, that they share the meanings of the questions, instructions, or words. Testers also assume that the context of the assessment, that is, the setting and other factors, are either controlled for or standardized, and therefore, not implicated in the behavior of the student. Last, the tester is assumed to simply record the responses of the person being assessed, exerting no influence whatsoever on the student's behavior. The results of the tests that rest on these assumptions are treated as facts: Scores are reported and acted upon. The constitutive process through which an individual student and individual tester jointly produced the test score is hidden from view. Access to the student's actual reasoning processes is hidden as well, even though, as Mehan (1978) stated, "the student's reasoning ability is the very thing most educational tests were set up to measure" (p. 50).

Contrary to the tester's assumptions, Mehan (1978) demonstrated that videotaped testing interactions complicate this simple view. Student and tester do not necessarily share the same meaning for the items, and incorrect answers may arise from a different interpretation of the questions or items, rather than from an inability to perform the cognitive task at hand. During the testing situation, the tester may emphasize one aspect over another in determining whether the student's responses are correct. The tester may also repeat a question or prompt, as in "Can you think of something else you might do?" (Mehan, 1978, p. 52), rather than immediately asking the next question. Such interactions deviate from the format of a testing encounter, which should be Question-Answer/Question-Answer. In his videotapes of intelligence testing, Mehan found that more than one third of the questions diverged from testing protocols. In his videotaped study of the assessment of children's understanding of basic language concepts, testers managed to increase correct scores by 44% by providing cues such as "Is that the only one?" and "Good" (p. 54), and by stressing key words in the questions. Mehan maintained that these occurrences are not evidence of "sloppy test administration, but are the inevitable aspects of the social interaction that comprises testing encounters" (p. 55). Thus, Mehan identified three different constituent processes that are typically obscured in educational testing: the reasoning through which students arrive at answers, the inadvertent cueing and interpretation by testers of what counts as an answer, and the ensuing interaction between student and tester that jointly produces scores.

Similarly, students typically engage in a "searching" strategy (Mehan, 1979, p. 291) wherein they float various "trial" (p. 291) answers as they try to please the teacher, determine the parameters of the task, and guess the right response. Individually administered tests represent an extreme variation of "known answer questions" (Mehan, 1979, p. 285), a query that takes place only in schools. To illustrate, consider a question posed by Mehan: "What time is it, Denise?" Typically, if asked that question, the listener would say, for example, "2:30." And the questioner would probably say, "Thank you!" But what if the questioner instead said, "Very good"? Outside of school, a "very good" response would raise more than eyebrows. In school, *known answer questions* are typical of everyday discourse wherein the teacher asks a question, the student answers, and the teacher evaluates the answer as right or wrong (Question-Response-Evaluate, or QRE). Individual testing interactions, such as the ones we represent in the performative text below, are extreme examples of the QRE interaction: a discourse, if you will, of uninterrupted single known-answer questions relentlessly lobbed at a student who may be clueless about the dimensions of knowledge under scrutiny, but gamely searches for the right answer to please the teacher.

Performance as Language and Identity

"Language performs a reality" (Madison, 2012, p. 179), and it does so within particular contexts—in this case, educational testing. It also does so in a way that is "recognizable in [its] repetition" (p. 179) across time. As former teachers, we have participated in countless hours of classroom lessons, marked by QRE interactions, and in countless individual testing situations as well. In our present roles as teacher-educators and researchers, we have been socialized into the epistemology of constructivism; we have developed deeper insight into literacy and the display of literate behavior; and we are learning to reflect upon our own language as language-in-use, its performative nature, and a potential object of study.

Thus, it behooves us, in service of equity, to examine interactions within educational institutions and the role of participants, including ourselves, in contributing to inequity within this context. To accomplish this work, we turn to the concept of analytic bracketing or, in the words of Gubrium and Holstein (2000), "oscillating indifference to the realities of everyday life" (p. 499). Similar to ethnomethodologists (and phenomenologists), we must set aside, or bracket, our belief in what is "real" in order to observe and document the everyday practices through which and by which social structure—reality—is constructed. Wittgenstein (cited in Gubrium & Holstein, 2000, p. 499), a philosopher of "language games," noted that in this instance, language has taken a holiday to make visible the ways that language itself constructs the reality it is usually thought of as simply describing. Put another way, a careful stepping back to examine what is said during familiar interactions—in this case, testing interactions—may enable us to see not only how we as assessors co-construct the "score" along with the student (by inadvertent cueing), but also how the student perceives the assessment tasks. By identifying patterns in the talk between assessor and student, we may be less likely to take for granted the meanings that members of a school community typically assign to students' scores. Rather than assuming that test scores are indicators of true ability or development, we may be more likely to view scores as artifacts constructed within the negotiated space of language interaction.

In the scenarios that follow, a number of participants perform language-in-use (specifically, assessment) using a common psychometric instrument (DIBELS) and the interpretation by school personnel of the score that is negotiated between assessor and assessed. The words that participants perform, or read aloud, are the naturally occurring talk between tester and student that was recorded during individual testing interactions and later transcribed. By stepping aside or bracketing the social "facts" of test answers and test scores, which we as educators have been accustomed to treating as indices of individual cognitive abilities, we hope to lay bare the process by which an identity as a reader is accomplished and named: *needing intensive remediation, performing strategically*, or *achieving benchmarked status*.

Performance studies, of which this chapter and performance are part, inject academic analysis with "artistic ways of knowing" (Conquergood, 2002, p. 151). Called a "hybridity" (p. 151), performance provides a deeper experience for all participants—the audience as well as performers; it provides a lens that "illuminates the constructed creative, contingent, collaborative dimensions of human communication" (p. 152); and further, it may provide the impetus for intervention in service of equity and social justice. By re-enacting DIBELS assessments—an everyday constitutive activity in schools—and teachers' interpretations of the identities that students accomplish—*benchmark, strategic*, and *intensive*—we hope that the audience can re-imagine these practices in a way that might enable the transformative potential of education.

Dynamic Indicators of Basic Early Literacy Skills

But first, we provide some background on the testing instrument itself. Dynamic Indicators of Basic Early Literacy Skills (DIBELS; Good & Kaminski, 2002) is a measure of early reading skills used by virtually all school districts in the United States. DIBELS includes subtests that its developers claim measure the areas of phonemic awareness, phonics, fluency, vocabulary, and comprehension. As an aside, political pressure during the Bush era of No Child Left Behind (NCLB) coerced most districts into using DIBELS as the standardized testing measure in order to obtain funding through the provisions of Reading First, a reading improvement grant subsumed under NCLB (Goodman, 2006). Although widespread, its use remains controversial because on the face of it (face validity), reasonable educators do not believe that there is a valid connection between the rapid pronunciation of nonsense words and authentic, meaningful reading and writing.

Some of the tasks—for example, segmenting individual phonemes within words—may be difficult and abstract for a child who can already read and spell the words, just as it would be for an adult. On the oral reading fluency task, students are timed for 1 minute and scored on the basis of the number of words read correctly. A 1-minute retelling follows the timed oral reading. The number of words generated during the retelling constitutes the comprehension score. Again, there is scant empirical evidence that what the DIBELS developers refer to as "benchmark" performance on isolated tasks models authentic reading and writing proficiency. In fact, research into the utility of short-term curriculum-based assessments has called into question the assumption that "short-term accomplishments accumulate into broad-based competence" (Fuchs, 2004, p. 188). Even though an oral reading fluency measure can predict oral reading fluency later in the year (on the same assessment), "single-skill measures cannot model global learning over time [and] may correspond poorly with overall learning of the broad academic domain" (p. 191). The tenability of any measure, but particularly curriculum-based assessments such as DIBELS, should be based not only on psychometric sophistication of the instrument but also, most importantly, on the usefulness of the information for teachers in providing appropriate instruction to individuals.

Pressley and his colleagues (Pressley, Hilden, & Shankland, 2005) found that DIBELS did not provide information to classroom teachers beyond what they already collected through informal assessments. Likewise, McGill-Franzen, Solic, Payne, and Mathson (2006) examined correlations between DIBELS, informal classroom spelling and word recognition tasks, and global measures of reading level and writing at two points in the kindergarten year. The highest correlations of any tasks with authentic (or global) reading was that of the informal classroom sight word recognition ($r=.73$; .80) and spelling ($r=.61$; 60).

Identity as *Intensive, Strategic,* or *Benchmark*

Yet, the DIBELS assessment yields a score that the developers transform into categories of probability; that is, the probability that children so labeled will or will not achieve the goal of being able to read. Children who score at *benchmark* are likely to meet the goal; at *strategic*, the test developers cannot make a prediction about the likelihood that these children will learn to read. Children who score within the *intensive* category are unlikely to learn to read without intensive remediation in the skill tapped by the subtest on DIBELS (for example, rapid pronunciation of nonsense words). In the kindergarten study cited above, 20% of the sample was categorized as intensive (35 students), although 20 of these students were already reading on a Guided Reading Level A and five were reading on Level C or above!

How did this happen, and what does the score mean for children who are so identified? We turn now to our performance of four acts to examine the ways in which such identities were made "real."

Performance

In this performance, we adhere to the following stage directives (after McCall, 2000, p. 424): We use no costumes; we play multiple characters, including ourselves; and we sit in chairs around a table and address each other directly when in character. When we make analytic statements as researchers, we stand up and address the audience directly. These statements represent our interpretation of the meaning of the children's responses to the assessment probes; that is, what we, as researchers, can infer about the children's reading development. Our inferences are informed by scholarship to which the teaching assistant is not privy. Similarly, we directly address the audience when thinking out loud in character, as the teaching assistant and children sometimes do, in order to give voice to what our experience suggests they may be thinking.

Act One: Negotiating a Score

Characters
Girl 1: a kindergarten student

Boy 1: a kindergarten student

TA 1: Ms. Smith, a teaching assistant at the school who has been given the assignment of administering the DIBELS assessment

Timer: Set by the teaching assistant for one minute for each task; goes off loudly at the end of each task

Setting
Hallway outside the classrooms in the kindergarten wing. There is a table and chairs, and a timer which the TA in each act sets for 1 minute for each task; it goes off loudly at the end of each task.

Girl 1: [*walks down the hall, notices the table and chairs that line the hallway, and stops*] We practice for the test. Sometimes we do it at rest time. We go into a hall and we sit in chairs and we wait for our turn. But it's not always a test. Sometimes we're practicing. We do it every year and we sit on these chairs that are different colors and we gotta be really quiet. I just hate it when they're talking. It's so loud in the hall [*her voice is rising*] and I'm trying to do my test but it's too loud. What I really hate about it is when people get in time out. In the hall people are talking…and my friend, he's a bully, and he was talking so loud I couldn't even do the test and she had to put him in time out! [*Girl 1 walks away*]

Boy 1 and TA 1 are seated across from each other at a small table with two chairs. There is a timer on the table. TA 1 holds a DIBELS manual, reads the script in a business-like manner, sets the timer, records the student's answers in the record booklet, and so on. Boy 1 smiles nervously, looks at the student's booklet, and responds to the TA 1's probes.

TA 1: This is mouse, flowers, pillow, letters. Mouse begins with the sound /m/. Listen, /m/, mouse. Which one begins with the sounds /fl/?

[*Boy 1 is silent*]

TA 1: Flowers begins with the sounds /fl/. Listen, /fl/, flowers. Let's try it again. Which one begins with the sounds /fl/?

[*Boy 1 is silent*]

TA 1: Flowers begins with the sounds /fl/.

TA 1: Pillow begins with the sound /p/. Listen, /p/, pillow. What sound does letters begin with?

Boy 1: L

TA 1: Good. What sound does *L* make?

Boy 1: /l/

TA 1: Very nice. Letters begins with the sound /l/. Here are some more pictures. Listen carefully to the words. This is yard, giraffe, present, bridge. Which picture begins with /y/?

Boy 1: yard

Needing Intensive Remediation

TA 1: Which picture begins with /j/?

Boy 1: giraffe

TA 1: Which picture begins with /pr/?

Boy 1: present

TA 1: What sound does bridge begin with?

Boy 1: B

TA 1: Ok. This is crutches, feather, toothpaste, city. Which picture begins with /s/?

[*Boy 1 silently points to each picture*]

TA 1: Which picture begins with /f/?

TA 1: Which picture begins with /t/?

TA 1: What sound does crutches begin with?

Boy 1: K

TA 1: This is dime, sofa, peanuts, horse. Which picture begins with /h/?

Boy 1: horse

TA 1: Which picture begins with /s/?

[*Boy 1 silently points to picture*]

TA 1: Which picture begins with /d/?

Boy 1: dime

TA 1: What sound does peanuts begin with?

Boy 1: P

TA 1: This is mop, footprints, dishes, goat. Which picture begins with /m/?

Boy 1: mop

TA 1: Which picture begins with /f/?

[*Boy 1 silently points to picture*]

TA 1: Which picture begins with /g/?

[*Boy 1 silently points to picture*]

TA 1: What sound does dishes begin with?

Boy 1: D

TA 1: Nice work.

[*Timer goes off*]

Researcher: [*aside*] Every time he provides the teaching assistant with a letter instead of a sound, she marks it wrong. It's a shame. He not only knows the beginning sound represented by those pictures, but he can map that sound onto a letter—he knows the letter that represents the sound! He has mastered the alphabetic principle, so his skill is already beyond the task being measured here. It's a shame! He may be identified as needing intensive remediation in recognizing beginning sounds.

Boy 1: Would you like me to flip it over?

TA 1: I would like you to flip it over. Thank you. Here are some letters. Tell me the names of as many letters as you can. When I say begin, start here, and go across the page.

Needing Intensive Remediation

Boy 1: [*interrupting before TA 1 finishes directions*] How should I know what this line is? Look! [*makes a straight line in the air*]

Boy 1: [*aside*] Now you tell me…is that a 1 [one] or an I [uppercase I] or an l [lowercase l]? It can be any of those!

TA 1: [*nods and continues the directions*] Point to each letter and tell me the name of that letter. If you come to a letter you don't know, I'll tell it to you. Put your finger on the first letter. Ready, begin.

Boy 1: S L U N S X K U X I L

Boy 1: [*aside*] I called the first one an L, I'll call the next one an I, and the last one an 1, and just to be sure, I'll call one of these lines an explanation point!

Boy 1: D H H T C R B G

Boy 1: [*aside*] Where are we?

Boy 1: T U N M R U W C N M J! I M P Q R M T X O R B

[*Timer goes off*]

TA 1: Wonderful job. You must be practicing your letters.

TA 1: [*aside*] It's already spring and I can't believe he still doesn't know his letters.

Researcher: [*aside*] The assessment of constrained skills, such as letter recognition, which must be mastered by all students, can be manipulated by using unfamiliar or timed tasks, or by using fonts that are difficult to interpret. These manipulations have nothing to do with the student's actual knowledge of the letters of the alphabet.

TA 1: I am going to say a word. After I say it, you tell me all the sounds in the word. So, if I say, sam, you would say /s/ /a/ /m/. Let's try one. Tell me the sounds in mop.

Boy 1: mop M

TA 1: the sounds

Boy 1: M

TA 1: The sounds in mop are /m/ /o/ /p/. Your turn. Tell me the sounds in mop.

Boy 1: /m/ /o/ /p/

TA 1: Very nice. OK. Here is your first word. Hat.

Boy 1: H A uhhh T

TA 1: Remember, we are looking for the sounds of those letters. What sounds do you hear in hat?

Boy 1: H O T

TA 1: hear

Boy 1: H E R

TA 1: Very good. You're spelling these words. Can you tell me the sounds in hear?

Boy 1: /h/—

[*Timer goes off*]

Researcher: [*aside*] This student scored a zero on this task, putting him at risk, identifying him as *intensive*, meaning he needs remediation in segmenting phonemes. It's ridiculous! He is actually spelling the words, a much more sophisticated task than simply segmenting sounds. He segments the sounds automatically because he—you—I—all of us who know how to spell segment the sounds first and then match those sounds with appropriate letters to spell words.

TA 1: Look at this word. It's a make-believe word. Watch me read the word: /s/ /i/ /m/, sim. I can say the sounds of the letters, /s/ /i/ /m/, or I can read the whole word, sim.

Boy 1: sim

TA 1: Your turn to read a make-believe word. Read this word the best you can. Make sure you say any sounds you know.

Boy 1: /t/ /l/ /t/

TA 1: Remember, you can say the sounds or you can say the whole word. Watch me. The sounds are /l/ /u/ /t/ or lut.

Boy 1: lut

TA 1: Let's try again. Read this word the best you can.

Boy 1: lut

TA 1: Very nice. Here are some more make-believe words. Start here and go across the page. When I say "begin," read the words the best you can. Point to each letter and tell me the sound or read the whole word. Read the words the best you can. Put your finger on the first word. Ready, begin.

Boy 1: /z/ /w/ /a/ /z/ /o/ /s/ /l/ /t/ /z/ /v/ /m/ /t/ /p/ /d/ /p/ /j/ /t/ /s/

[*Timer goes off*]

TA 1: Wonderful work. I like the way you pointed to each letter.

TA 1: [*aside*] Did he really think he was reading words?

Researcher: [*aside*] Most students try to make sense of the words they are given to read. For example, if given the nonsense word mik, most students will say Mike or milk. They think the teacher made a mistake and spelled the word wrong.

TA 1: Ok, our last activity is looking at words. Listen to me use this word: green. The grass is green. Here is another word: jump. I like to jump rope. Your turn to use a word. Rabbit.

Boy 1: I like to hop. I like to flip.

TA 1: Very good. Listen to me use rabbit. The rabbit is eating a carrot. Your turn. Rabbit.

Boy 1: A rabbit is eating a carrot.

TA 1: A rabbit is eating a carrot. Very good.

Boy 1: Let me try another one. I like to play in the snow.

TA 1: Make sure that you use rabbit.

Boy 1: A rabbit likes to play in the snow.

TA 1: I bet that rabbit likes to play in the snow. Ready for your first word? Fence.

Boy 1: F

TA 1: Can you use fence just like you used rabbit?

Boy 1: A rabbit did jumped over the fence.

TA 1: coach

Needing Intensive Remediation

Boy 1: A coach is eating a rabbit.

TA 1: front

Boy 1: A front is eating a rabbit. [*laughs*]

TA 1: which

Boy 1: A witch is changing a rabbit into a ladybug.

TA 1: nobody

Boy 1: A witch can.

TA 1: nobody

[*Boy 1 is silent*]

TA 1: That's your next word. Can you use nobody?

Boy 1: Nobody can eat a rabbit.

TA 1: meant

Boy 1: A meant can eat a rabbit.

TA 1: felt

Boy 1: A felt is eating a rabbit and spits him out.

[*Timer goes off*]

TA 1: Those are some good sentences. Thank you so much for working with me today.

TA 1: [*aside*] Whew. Another zero. I wonder if his teacher knows how bad his language development is.

Act Two: More Negotiating

Characters
Boy 2: a kindergarten student

TA 2: Ms. Jones, a teaching assistant

Researcher

Setting
Hallway outside the classrooms in the kindergarten wing. The participants are seated across from each other as in the previous act, holding the same booklets, timer, and so on.

Boy 2: Please don't tell me I have to spell because I don't like spelling. I can't read or I can't get math. I don't like this math. What's 2 + 2? It's 4. I only know 2 numbers. 2+2 is 4, 1+1 is 2.

TA 2: Well, you just do the very best you can, because you know what? This is not for a grade and I am not your teacher.

Boy 2: Are you one of the, one of the kindergarten teachers?

TA 2: No, I'm not a teacher at all right now.

Researcher: [*aside*] Teachers usually do not give DIBELS. Typically, the assessment is administered by someone that the student does not know. Teachers cannot see how their students perceive the tasks or how they respond to the probes. Teachers are simply given a number (score) and an identification of the student as "benchmark," "strategic," or "intensive."

TA 2: So we are just going to do some tests and you can help me. I want to know what you think.

Boy 2: I only think about, I only think about jumping on a trampoline.

Needing Intensive Remediation 111

TA 2: Oh, okay, let's see if we can think about this for just a minute. Alright, this is my stopwatch right here on my phone.

Boy 2: Ohhh, are those games?

TA 2: You're already done with the first test. You are super speedy. Ready to do another one?

Boy 2: I thought I lost a test. I thought this was a timer test. I thought if I won again I would lose.

TA 2: No, you didn't lose. After 1 minute we stop. So you take some other tests where they use a timer?

Boy 2: Yeaaah. You get horrible things like you get in time out you go to the principal's office, you walk the fence, your teacher calls a message to your mom and dad—that is bad!

TA 2: What? If you get in time out? Or if you don't do good on the test?

Boy 2: No, if you get your clothespin moved. Like there's this thing called "excellent." There's this thing called "friendly reminder." There's a thing called "time out." There's a thing called "walk the fence." There's a thing called "note to home." And the worstest thing is "principal's office."

TA 2: Oh, I see. I see. If you get in trouble. Got it.

Boy 2: All I got on. The only worse thing I got on is the first thing "warning: friendly reminder," but it's not bad it's just people telling you...

TA 2: Just a friendly reminder, just a warning.

Boy 2: [*aside*] I didn't think I'd still have to take the test after I told her all of that...

TA 2: OK we're going to try one. I want you to listen to this word. And I'm going to use it. The grass is green. Here's another one.

Boy 2: Green

TA 2: Jump I like to jump rope. See how I'm using it in a sentence? Your turn to use a word. Rabbit.

Boy 2: I like to see a rabbit.

TA 2: Good job. Let's try some more. Happy.

Boy 2: I like to be happy.

TA 2: Rained.

Boy 2: I don't like the rain.

TA 2: Ago.

Boy 2: I love to go.

TA 2: Ones.

Boy 2: I like ones.

TA 2: Anything.

Boy 2: I want to do anything.

TA 2: Rags.

Boy 2: I like to rag.

TA 2: Opened.

Boy 2: I want to open a jar.

TA 2: Makes.

Needing Intensive Remediation

Boy 2: I want to mix cream with carrots.

TA 2: Cried.

Boy 2: I like to cried soup.

TA 2: Alone.

Boy 2: I like to be alone.

TA 2: Afraid.

Boy 2: I am afraid of ghosts. Actually, I'm afraid of zombies. That's all I'm afraid of.

[*Timer goes off*]

TA 2: But, not really ghosts?

Boy 2: No, ghosts aren't real. They can't, they can't hurt you. They can only haunt you and turn you into ghosts.

TA 2: But zombies are real or zombies are not real?

Boy 2: No, if you actually see a zombie, it's not going to hurt you. It's like a guy dressed up for Halloween.

TA 2: [*aside*] I've never met such a talkative student. Because he scored "at-risk" on this assessment, he will definitely need a program to practice using words in sentences.

Researcher: [*aside*] Because the task provides no context within which to use the targeted words, children, who aim to please the examiner, often resort to patterned sentences—such as "I like to see a rabbit; I like to be happy; I don't like the rain; I like the ones"—so that they can give an answer to each probe.

Act Three: Understanding Equals the Number of Remembered Words

Characters
TA 3: Mrs. Smith, a teaching assistant

Boy 3: a third-grade student

Setting
Hallway in the intermediate grade wing. The participants are seated at a table across from each other as in the previous act, holding similar booklets and a timer. They have completed several tests and are about to begin the DIBELS comprehension test, an assessment that requires students to retell what they remember after orally reading a passage for 1 minute. The comprehension score is based only on the number of words that the student recalls during a 1-minute probe. There are no follow-up questions.

TA 3: We are going to do the next test. And in this one you are just going to read a passage out loud. If you get stuck, I'll tell you the word so you can keep reading. When I say stop, I may ask you to tell me about what you read, so do your very best reading.

Boy 3: Okay.

TA 3: Okay. This is the first one, called "My Friend."

Boy 3: My Friend.

TA 3: And this is where you are going to start. Go ahead and begin.

Boy 3: I have a new friend at school. She can't walk so she uses a wheelchair to get around sss so she comes to sc-school in a special van that can transport four people who use wheelchairs. The van brings my friend and another boy to school. My friend is in third grade with me and the boy is in fourth grade. I like to watch my friend get in and out of the van. The driver pushes a button and part of the van floor lowers to the driveway to form a ramp. My friend just wheels up to the ramp and goes inside. After she is inside, the driver pushes a button and the ramp puts itself away.

Needing Intensive Remediation

[Timer goes off]

TA 3: Stop. I want you to tell me about what you just read. Try to tell me everything.

Boy 3: About someone's friend that can't walk so she uses a wheelchair.

TA 3: [*aside*] He only used 11 words in his retelling. He definitely did not understand the story. He will need to be placed in the computer lab with me for comprehension during his classroom reading block.

Act Four: Struggling to Make Sense of DIBELS Labels

Characters
Kindergarten Teachers: Mrs. Lindsey, Mrs. Worth, Mrs. Wishart, Mr. Coleman, Mrs. Carr, Mrs. Anderson, Miss McComas, Mrs. Whitman, and Miss Sheffield

Mrs. James: instructional leader

Researcher

Setting
Teacher's lounge. Teachers have received their DIBELS scores and student classifications and they are grouping their students for instruction and remediation. It is district policy that all students be screened on DIBELS, and those students labeled as needing intensive remediation placed in an intervention program. Some schools require teachers to use DIBELS scores to group students for all reading instruction. The teachers are seated around a table with printouts of students' scores in front of them. Their talk overlaps one another.

Mrs. Lindsey: The thing that bothers me about mine is...well, we have to group them by their scores. Like, who's benchmark, who's strategic, who's at risk? I have a kid who scored at-risk, but he's fine. He just did poorly on nonsense word fluency and so I have to put him in the lowest group, but he doesn't need it.

Mrs. Worth: Umm…I've got a student—I think he's doing fine. I had him in my middle group for reading and everything and then I got DIBELS scores back and he was at-risk because he also did poorly on nonsense word fluency …you know, segmenting those nonsense words. That was the one thing he did really, really bad on so I had to put him down in my lower group. He does that for reading and then we also have, like, kind of during the day, intervention—30 minutes of nonsense word decoding—and he gets so bored.

Mrs. Wishart: [*to Mrs. Lindsey*] Do you have to do DIBELS or does someone do it for you?

Mrs. Worth: We have an assistant.

Mrs. Wishart: Does your assistant know them, because I think too when the child is tested by someone they don't know, they're more concerned about …you know…what's your name and what are you doing?

Mr. Coleman: I do think that is a factor because I know there is one child in her class and he was working with me the other day. You were there. [*gestures to Mrs. Worth*] He will not talk in front of people he doesn't know. I mean, he will just sit there and I'm sure he did not do well on this test. Whether he could actually do it or not, I don't know, but he's not going to do well regardless.

Mrs. Worth: Because someone…

Mr. Coleman: Because he doesn't know the person…

Mrs. Worth: Because he doesn't respond well to strangers

Mrs. Carr: When Ms. Smith came out to test him, he just broke down in tears because he wants to be right and he wants to know what he's doing is right but he just kind of loses it, falls apart, with someone new and strange and if the test is out of his routine.

Needing Intensive Remediation

Mrs. Anderson: Did you notice that the letter-naming fluency test that we gave them had a lot of letters and sounds in the first two or three lines that, if you're on the one-letter-a-week program in the core reading program, you haven't introduced yet. And so, if you're just an average kid and you're learning everything you've been taught, you haven't had much exposure to many of those letters. Yet they came across those letters in the very first two or three rows. It was not based on what we taught!

Mr. Coleman: Um... two of mine that are at-risk for initial sound fluency are speech students, so you know, that's understandable, but...one of mine was at-risk in one area and in need of intensive remediation in another, but he is already reading Level B books.

Miss Sheffield: And up here in intensive remediation is little Lindsey, who in my class is able to perform at grade level. She's not that high compared to the rest of the class, but I was surprised .... Did she talk to any of you...she's a tiny little girl who talks like Minnie Mouse. You know, I ask her something and it's like 10 minutes later before she'll answer me. She's just slow as Christmas...not dumb or anything...

Mrs. Anderson: ...just kind of cocks her head to the side...

Miss Sheffield: She just looks at you and you about forget what your question was before she'll tell you what the answer is.... No wonder she did not do well on the timed assessments.

Miss McComas: Well, I can tell you that if mine were going to be DIBELed all the time, I would teach them how to do it correctly even though they already know how to spell...

Mrs. Whitman: You would teach to the test?

Miss McComas: I would tell them, "Don't say HAT, say /h/ /a/ /t/" even though they know it.

Mrs. Whitman: You know, we were just talking about back here [*gestures at the back of the table*] that you use a different vocabulary when you test that we don't use in the classroom. You know, we don't say "Segment sounds"; we say, "Talk like turtles." We do the phonemic segmentation but we don't say, "We're going to separate the phonemes." We're going to say it like this.... You know, I bet if you looked at half these kids and said, "Talk like a turtle," they would've known exactly what you're talking about, but we don't use this other vocabulary in the classroom...And you know, Mrs. James said to use the vocabulary that's used on the assessment, use that in your classroom, but up until now, we weren't allowed to give the test or know what was on the assessment, so we weren't given the vocabulary.

Mr. Coleman: In the past when I didn't give DIBELS, I thought—these kids know these letters and sounds. We go through it everyday. We say, "A apple /a/" and "B book /b/," and they can apply it in the classroom with reading, but when they see the letters by themselves, that's automatically what they do. If they're timed then that's against them too, so I've started kind of like Mrs. James was saying, "Sometimes you're asked for the sound—let's just say this with the sounds." Then we do our flash cards or we do whatever ...just pulling out the sounds because sometimes "we're asked just for the sounds." I try to go over it with them, but before I didn't know that that was something I needed to be doing. They have the knowledge—it's just not being appropriately extracted from their brains.

Miss McComas: We had kids do that—say "A apple /a/" and that slowed them down so they couldn't identify very many letters during the time...

Mr. Coleman: So they got a lower score. But you can't stop them... you can't tell them not to do it. You just gotta let that bright little kid sit there and say "B book /b/ C cat /k/" and you know the whole time you're thinking, "Not good, not good...you're going to miss 30 minutes a day of reading instruction to go to remediation for letter names even though you know them, and an hour after school in intensive intervention...."

Mrs. Whitman: And you know as soon as we start talking about kids we're concerned about, the principal and psychologist say, "How'd they do on DIBELS? You know, bad, good, what does it matter when we have kids who don't test well on it for lots of reasons...is it the first step in labeling a kid?

Researcher: [*aside*] Researchers have been evaluating whether DIBELS accurately identifies students needing support in first grade, whether DIBELS predicts achievement at the end of first grade, and whether DIBELS scores at the end of first grade actually predict which students are at risk of failing third grade state reading tests. The answer in all cases is "No!" DIBELS does not accurately identify students at risk in first grade [Doyle, Gibson, Gomez-Bellenge, Kelly, & Tang, 2008]; similarly, the Nonsense Word Fluency, Initial Sound Fluency, and Phoneme Segmentation Fluency have poor utility in predicting reading achievement at the end of first grade [Johnson, Jenkins, Petscher, & Catts, 2009]. And, the end of first grade DIBELS has limited utility in identifying which students are at risk of failing the state assessments at third grade [Salvador, Schoeneberger, & Tingle 2009]. In one state, for example, fewer than half the students who failed the state assessment were identified as at-risk on the DIBELS, suggesting that not only are students identified as needing intensive remediation when they do not, but students who *do* need extra support early in their school careers are not identified as at-risk. Teachers need to cast a critical eye on the claims of test developers and be vigilant about inappropriate inferences about students' abilities based on unidimensional measures of complex abilities.

Concluding Thoughts

Testing tools such as DIBELS, regardless of the "fidelity" of implementation, will always be co-constructed moment-by-moment between the test administrator and the student. The assumptions and dialogue embedded within the testing scenario may serve to create an event that is much less routine and reliable than previously imagined. Rather, it is an event that may exacerbate inequality for some students who may not fit "nicely" into the seemingly constrained mold required to perform adequately in particular testing situations. In this chapter, we have argued that a few short minutes of test administration can actually work to create students' literacy identities, both in terms of how the students view themselves and how they are viewed by the testing administrator and ultimately the institutional setting at large.

Though some researchers such as Mehan (1978) have provided valuable insights on the assessor/ student relationship and the implications that may arise from it, our hope is to add to this body of knowledge by making visible the specious assumptions about reading development that arise from particular kinds of tests and testing interactions. The outcome of such assessments contributes to the labeling of students and the limiting of opportunities available to them. Here we view testing administration through a different lens, that of performative text. Performance ethnography may provide a means of "expanding the definitions and assumptions of a range of social phenomena" (Madison, 2012, p. 166), and in this manner may become a "ubiquitous force in our social and discursive universe" (p. 166).

In the particular context of DIBELS testing, performance ethnography provides us with a forum that allows for the voices of the participants to be highlighted not just through extracts as would traditionally occur, but through the power of their actual words. These words open a space for thoughtful dialogue among professionals in the field on the critical subject of the power relations and inequalities that exist in many testing environments. Ultimately, our hope is to shed light on a practice that has become mundane and routinized, with dire consequences. By doing so, we may shift our stance from complacency to awareness and critical consumerism by provoking important questions about the uses and abuses of formative assessment as an instructional tool with implications for student identity and equality.

Questions for Dialogue

1. Think back on a testing experience that you had, either as the student being tested or as the tester. Rather than simply describing the experience in the first person, write and read aloud dialogue that allows us to more fully participate in the emotional impact of this experience. How does this experience, or the memory of the experience, complicate your position toward testing?
2. We have argued that performance is one tool with which to shed light on the importance of becoming critical consumers of materials, rather than just routinely and complacently administering tests such as DIBELS. How might you advocate for this notion of awareness in your school or district? How might you facilitate necessary dialogue to encourage discussions about power structures and inequality?
3. Throughout the performance, you were witness to negotiation between assessor and assessed, which resulted at times in the creation of a negative identity for the student involved. How might we do the opposite, and assist students in creating a positive literacy identity? What manner of assessments or testing interactions do you think might promote a more positive identity formation?

References

Conquergood, D. (2002). Performance studies. *The Drama Review, 46*(2), 145–155.

Doyle, M., Gibson, S., Gomez-Bellenge, F., Kelly, P., & Tang, M. (2008). Assessment and identification of first grade students at risk: Correlating the Dynamic Indicators of Basic Early Literacy Skills and an observation survey of early literacy achievement. In D. Compton, D. Dickinson, M. Hundley, R. Jimenez, K. Leander, & D. Rowe (Eds.), *57th yearbook of the National Reading Conference* (pp. 144–159). Oak Creek, WI: National Reading Conference.

Fuchs, L. S. (2004). The past, present, and future of curriculum-based measurement research. *School Psychology Review, 33*(2), 188–192.

Good, R., & Kaminski, R. (2002). *Dynamic Indicators of Basic Early Literacy Skills* (6th ed.). Retrieved from https://dibels.uoregon.edu/measures/files/admin_and_scoring_6th_ed.pdf

Goodman, K. (2006). *The truth about DIBELS: What it is-What it does.* Portsmouth, NH: Heinemann.

Gubrium, J., & Holstein, J. (2000). Analyzing interpretive practice. In N. K. Denzin & Y. S. Lincoln (Eds.), *Handbook of qualitative research* (2nd ed., pp. 487–508). Thousand Oaks, CA: Sage.

Johnson, E., Jenkins, J. R., Petscher, Y., & Catts, H. (2009). How can we improve the accuracy of screening instruments? *Learning Disabilities Research & Practice, 24*(4), 174–185.

Madison, D.S. (2012). *Critical ethnography* (2nd ed.). Thousand Oaks, CA: Sage.

McCall, M. (2000). Performance ethnography. In N. K. Denzin & Y. S. Lincoln (Eds.), *Handbook of qualitative research* (2nd ed., pp. 421–433). Thousand Oaks, CA: Sage.

McGill-Franzen, A., Solic, K., Payne, R., & Mathson, D. (2006, December 1). *Exploring the instructional utility of DIBELS as a screening and progress monitoring measure.* Paper presented at the National Reading Conference, Los Angeles, CA.

Mehan, H. (1978). Structuring school structure. *Harvard Educational Review, 48*(1), 32–64.

Mehan, H. (1979). What time is it, Denise? Asking known information questions in classroom discourse. *Theory into Practice, 18*(4), 285–294.

Mehan, H. (1992). Understanding inequality in schools: The contribution of interpretive studies. *Sociology of Education, 65*(1), 1–20.

Mehan, H., & Wood, H. (1975). *The reality of ethnomethodology.* New York: Wiley.

Pressley, M., Hilden, K., & Shankland, R. (2005). *An evaluation of end-grade-3 Dynamic Indicators of Basic Early Literacy Skills (DIBELS): Speed reading without comprehension, predicting little.* East Lansing: Literacy Achievement Research Center, Michigan State University.

Salvador, S. K., Schoeneberger, J., & Tingle, L. (2009, October). *DIBELS oral reading fluency predictive effectiveness for 3rd grade reading performance in Charlotte-Mecklenburg schools.* Charlotte, NC: Center for Research & Evaluation, Office of Accountability, CMS.

Chapter 5

Doing Time in ISS: A Performance of School Discipline

Katherine Evans

Introduction

Issues with student behavior have plagued schools, administrators, and classroom teachers for a long while. Historically, approaches to school discipline have alternated between highly punitive and more democratic (Evans & Lester, 2010). With the emergence of zero-tolerance policies in the mid-1980s, school discipline practices took on more punitive characteristics, with mandatory suspensions or expulsions for certain offenses (Rivkin, 2009). Current research on school discipline suggests that suspensions and expulsions not only are ineffective, but also negatively impact students academically, socially, and emotionally (American Psychological Association, 2008; Stinchcomb, Bazemore, & Riestenberg, 2006). Ferguson (2000) argued that classroom management often is simply about controlling students' behavior through the use of rules and subsequent consequences for breaking those rules. According to Ferguson, such discipline serves primarily to sort, evaluate, rank, and compare students based on their behavior, with the goal being "the production of people who are docile workers, self-regulated and self-disciplined" (p. 52) who conform to institutional norms. Discipline, then, serves as a tool for reinforcing social norms and rendering student bodies submissive, and punishment serves as the mechanism for addressing the violation of those norms (Foucault, 1977). Students who do not comply with normative or socially constructed rules about appropriate behavior often are excluded from schools or classrooms so that teachers can focus more effectively on those students who appear to be more motivated to learn (Noguera, 2003; Vavrus & Cole, 2002).

In the immediate aftermath of the Gun Free Schools Act (GFSA) of 1994 and the ensuing implementation of zero-tolerance policies, there was a sharp increase in school suspensions, followed by a wave of educational research that illustrated the negative impact, academically and socially, on students who were being suspended (see, for example, Casella, 2001; Skiba, Peterson, & Williams, 1997). In light of the evidence against removing the student from the school environment, schools began looking for alternatives to out-of-school suspension (OSS) for less serious behaviors; this prompted an increase in the use of in-school suspension (ISS). ISS generally involves the removal of students from their regular classrooms for a specific amount of time, during which they are "isolated from the general student body" and "expected to sit or study quietly for the duration of the punishment" (Theriot & Dupper, 2010, p. 209).

Although ISS was designed as an alternative to OSS, it was still perceived as punitive and, in many cases, continues to be exclusionary in that it excludes students from interacting with their peers and participating in learning opportunities. In one of the few studies that specifically examine the implementation of ISS, Troyan (2003) found that the educational services provided to students in ISS are vastly different from those in the regular classroom. Theriot and Dupper (2010) also argued that ISS is often configured in ways that produce consequences similar to OSS, such as lack of academic progress and increased social isolation (see also Christle, Nelson, & Jolivette, 2004; Hyman & Snook, 2000; Kupchik, 2010).

Very little research has specifically examined ISS as a form of school discipline; even less research has considered ISS from the perspectives of students. Thus, the purpose of this research was to understand ISS from the perspective of 13 middle school students in a school system in the southeast section of the U.S. The original study (Evans, 2011) included unstructured interviews focused on making sense of students' experiences in ISS. Desiring to move beyond mere descriptions of students' experiences, I chose to use performative writing as a way to engage with the reader/audience in ways that enact and embody those experiences of being in ISS (Madison, 2012). In this performance, then, the specific school disciplinary practice of ISS was examined from the perspective of those who have been at the receiving end of such practices, namely students. In drawing on the use of performative writing, I aimed to provide a space to "teach, incite, inspire, or provoke" (Bochner & Ellis, 2003, p. 507) a deeper understanding of those students' experiences with ISS.

Positionality

As a teacher-educator, I seek to promote classroom climates that facilitate the learning and well-being of *every* student. As a former middle and high school special educator, I have taught students who have been constructed by those in authority, sometimes by me, as "problem students," "discipline problems," or "delinquents." I have observed the impact of exclusionary discipline on their academic, emotional, and social lives. I believe not only that these students have opinions about their own experiences with school discipline, but also that they may have suggestions for improving related educational dilemmas. Further, as a researcher, it is my intention to provide opportunities for students to represent and define themselves, rather than to be defined by others. In a special edition of the journal *Theory into Practice* that focused on student perspectives, Lincoln (1995) called for more research that includes student perspectives, stating that they are "both the inheritors and the inheritance of the future" (p. 88) and should be considered "the primary stakeholders in their own learning processes" (p. 89). Since then, there has been a slight increase in such research (see for example, Brown, 2007; Cook-Sather, 2009; Fine & Weis, 2003). Unfortunately, however, student voices often remain excluded from educational research because of "intellectual paradigms that typically subtract, discredit, and disempower students' voices and experiences" (Rodriguez, 2008, p. 438). It was those student perspectives about ISS that I sought in this research; it is those perspectives that I seek to highlight in this performance.

Theoretical Framework

Situating this study within a framework of social constructionism (Berger & Luckmann, 1966), I oriented to rules and expectations as socially constructed and interpreted contextually by both the teacher and the students (Vavrus & Cole, 2002). When such interpretations vary between student and teacher, the students' interpretations are often disallowed, resulting in what teachers then construct as misbehavior (Thornberg, 2008). Further, as students' behaviors are constructed by teachers as deviant, inappropriate, and so on, the identities of students become reified into social categories (e.g., "the good kids and the bad kids," "the delinquents," or "tough cases"). Viewing school discipline and student behavior through a social constructionist framework opens the door for multiple perspectives and allows us to complicate notions of school discipline by including underrepresented voices. Choosing to engage in performative writing opens the door to consider the ways in which we view school discipline as mediated by our representations of school discipline, for if we are to "change the world, we must change how we write and perform it" (Denzin, 2003, p. 78).

Although the data from this research have been represented previously in more traditional academic formats (Evans, 2011), in this chapter I sought to present the findings in an experimental form. The use of the arts, including performance, as a way of representing research findings, allows us to transgress conventions, and serves as a "method for understanding one's own life, producing multicultural knowledge, evoking self-understanding" (Bochner & Ellis, 2003, p. 506). Through the use of performance, research findings potentially move "beyond the transcribed interview text and field note observations" to a place where the audience can understand the characters as "acting, interacting, touching and feeling, seeing and hearing, making sense of and representing their lives" through the performance (Roberts, 2008, n.p.).

With traditional academic texts, it is easy to flatten experiences, to oversimplify and reduce those experiences to themes described and defined by words alone; in those places, the "complex, finely nuanced meaning that is embodied, tacit, intoned, gestured, improvised, coexperienced, covert" is often "squeezed out" (Conquergood, 2002, p. 146). By involving the *words* of the participants, but also including nonverbal and aesthetic dimensions to the performance, I sought to provide the reader and/or audience with a chance to "understand, feel, and grapple with the experiences being expressed" (Bochner & Ellis, 2003, p. 509). Thus, as performers take up the script, adding their own interpretive layer to the text itself, there is an opportunity to experience those nuanced, often unattended-to layers of communication—the tone of voice, the gestures, the eye contact, and so on—that enhance our understanding of experiences (Bochner & Ellis).

In teacher-education classrooms, the infusion of theory and practice is often a source of tension; a great deal of theoretical information is passed along to pre-service teachers, at times without adequate experiences to which to relate the information. The use of performance within teacher education potentially provides a space for creating new meaning beyond simple definitions and theories; it provides a glimpse into the possible applications of such theories and allows for new ways of interpreting and developing understanding. Thus, rather than simply the dominant academic genre of knowing about something through observation and analysis, what Conquergood (2002) calls a "knowing from above," performances allow for a "knowledge that is anchored in practice and circulated within a performance community"; it is a knowing "from ground level, in the thick of things" (p. 146). Thus, as pre-service teachers perform this retelling of ISS, the possibility exists for them to experience the tensions of ISS by placing themselves, albeit to a limited degree, in the moments experienced by the student participants in this study.

Conquergood (2002) proposed that performance not only provides a "compelling alternative" to traditional research presentations, but also creates "an alternative space of struggle" (p. 152). Presenting the experiences of middle school students as a performance, I sought to convey "stories that create the effect of reality, showing characters embedded in the complexities of lived moments of struggle, resisting the intrusions of chaos, disconnection, fragmentation, marginalization, and incoherence" (Bochner & Ellis, 2003, p. 509). It is my intention to represent ISS as a complex space of struggle and resistance where the characters are attempting to make sense of what can be viewed as exclusion and marginalization. Within such places of struggle and opposition, however, there lies the potential for re-imagining the outcomes of such struggle—what Denzin (2003) calls "utopian alternatives" (p. 38).

As a teacher-educator, it is my conviction that we must not only prepare teachers for what exists in current educational climates and contexts, but also foster their ability to envision what might be, and how they might play a role in moving toward that utopian alternative. It is in these places of liminality (Denzin, 2003), the spaces between what is and what could be, that many of the tensions of schooling exist. Within teacher education, performances can be taken up as a way to "create oppositional utopian spaces, discourses, and experiences within our public institutions" (Denzin, p. 8). Thus, in this performance, my aim is not only to provide a space for students often labeled "behavior problems" to speak back to those identities, but also to suggest utopian alternatives for their behavior-related interactions with teachers and administrators within school settings. For example, one possible alternative to punitive disciplinary practices is to adopt more therapeutic approaches that assist students not only behaviorally, but academically and emotionally as well (Nevetsky, 1991). In the following script, I draw attention to the students' accounts of other school personnel who employed a different way of interacting with them, in a sense, speaking back to the unfair treatment that many of them discussed. This possibility of engaging in more therapeutic approaches is represented by the guidance counselor, Mrs. Nyce. Her presence in ISS, mentioned in several participants' interviews, represents a "utopian alternative" for the implementation of ISS, one in which students are listened to, respected, and helped to develop problem-solving skills related to their behavior, as well as their interactions with teachers.

Thus, as I created this text, I drew upon the words of the participants in order to construct what their experiences in ISS were like, but I also referenced their responses to a specific question about what they would like for their teachers to know about school discipline. Through their accounts of ISS—both what it was like to be in ISS and what it was like to get written up and sent to ISS—I constructed a performance of what is, and included, where appropriate, glimpses into what might be.

Data Sources

This study took place in a midsize school system in the southeast with students who met the following criteria: (a) participants were currently enrolled in a middle school in the county; thus, they ranged in age from 10 to 15; (b) each participant had been suspended through an in-school suspension (ISS) program at least twice during the 2009–2010 school year for a minimum of 5 days; and (c) participants had been in ISS during the previous month. After securing both parental consent and student assent, 13 participants, consisting of 6 black males, 1 black female, 5 white males, and 1 white female, were interviewed. These 13 participants had been suspended between four and 14 times, for terms of 8 to 37 days.

The total number of days of school missed due to time spent in ISS was 186, for an average of 14 days per participant. Consistent with extensive research on disproportionality in school discipline (Fenning & Rose, 2007; Mendez & Knoff, 2003), the black males in this study were suspended at a higher rate than their white counterparts; the 6 black males were suspended 57 times for a total of 114 days, compared to the 5 white males, who were suspended 28 times for a total of 52 days, a detail that I attempted to maintain in the construction of the script. I conducted open-ended interviews with each of the 13 students, either before school or during lunch; the interviews, lasting between 9 and 56 minutes, were digitally recorded, and were transcribed for analysis. Each participant selected a pseudonym that was used throughout the interview, ensuring that their identity remained anonymous to all but me. In addition to the interview transcripts, my own researcher notes, including observational data, were collected for analysis.

Data Analysis

An initial layer of data analysis followed an interpretivist approach to phenomenology (van Manen, 1990) and yielded a thematic structure revolving around students' experiences with getting written up and spending time in in-school suspension. Further, I developed verbal portraits (Polkinghorne, 1989) of each student's experience with in-school suspension. In creating the following performance text, I primarily drew from students' descriptions of their time in the ISS room, as well as the verbal portraits of each participant. As I created the performance, I followed suggestions made by Saldaña (2003). I began by analyzing data from the students' verbal portraits, focusing on those interview excerpts that described ISS and the events that unfolded while they were there. Through this analysis, I developed six student characters that are composites of the original participants.

I added other characters based on students' descriptions. In that I did not interview classroom teachers, guidance counselors, or the ISS teacher, those characters are represented as they were presented by the student participants, creating an interesting tension for me as a researcher regarding representation (Madison, 2012). However, in that my intent was to provide a space for the student perspectives about school discipline, I chose to create characters based on students' retelling, drawing on Saldaña's (2003) suggestion that characters can be created by both what the characters say about themselves and what others say about them.

Next, using students' descriptions of their time in the ISS room, I constructed a list of the rules for ISS that they discussed, a physical description of the ISS room, and an account of the activities that they participated in while they were in ISS. Because much of the students' discussions of ISS oriented around time, I chose to construct the performance around time as well, using "chronological linearity" (Saldaña, 2003, p. 220) as a way of representing their experience. It is important to note that the use and control of time has been an historical mechanism for controlling behavior and promoting discipline (Foucault, 1977); thus, organizing the performance chronologically allowed me, and the reader/audience, to focus on how time was experienced as a part of that disciplinary mechanism. I began by constructing a timeline of a day in ISS, creating a template of a day with accounts of their interactions with one another, with the ISS teacher, and with other adults, as well as accounts of the activities they participated in while in ISS. This resulted in a chronological, albeit creative, reconstruction of their day.

Finally, with the chronological sequence in place, I developed interactions between the students and the ISS teacher, adding a visit from a classroom teacher and a guidance counselor, based on students' accounts of other adults who sometimes come into the ISS room. This polyvocal performance, then, includes the voices of six students, the ISS teacher, the guidance counselor, and one classroom teacher. At various points throughout the performance, each of the characters engages the audience in a monologue, providing a more personal connection between the character and the audience (Saldaña, 2003). The interactions and the monologues were creatively constructed through participants' accounts of interactions they had with various teachers in the school, with each other in the ISS room, with the ISS teacher, and with me as the researcher.

As I analyzed the data, I chose to pay particular attention to the importance that the students assigned to their academic progress; it was a recurring theme for almost all of the participants in the study. For some students, ISS was beneficial, allowing them to get caught up on assignments and thus pull up their grades; for other students, ISS prevented them from being in the regular classroom and thus impeded their learning. This was true for the majority of students, who noted that the teachers did not always send assignments to the ISS room. By hinting at some of the possible alternative imaginings of ISS, I question some of the taken-for-granted notions of school discipline and explore some of the complexities of maintaining safe schools where learning opportunities are fostered, while the needs and voices of students who often are not afforded such learning opportunities are also honored.

Performance Suggestions

In the following performance, textual data and observational research notes were used to compose a chronological retelling of students' experiences in ISS. The following script is presented as one possible rendering of such a retelling. Acknowledging that there are other possible renderings, I propose that the script be performed as written, and also, in keeping with Boal's (1985) forum theater, that it might be beneficial to pre-service teachers to interrupt the script at places, allowing for reinterpreting, renegotiating, and reconstructing various moments of the text (Mienczakowski, 1995). For example, stopping the action after James is assigned an extra 2 days of ISS could allow teachers to re-imagine how that scenario might have played out differently. Further, it might be interesting to see the script performed with a mixed group of teachers and students, allowing adequate time for discussion during and after the performance. Finally, the role of the narrator is crucial in moderating the time. In that the notion of time is a key element of the script, allowing the audience and actors to experience the passage of time, while not allowing the action to wane, is a critical component of the performance.

Doing Time in ISS

Characters

James: an eighth-grade black male who has spent 37 days in ISS.

Jeffrey: a seventh-grade white male who has spent 10 days in ISS.

Jonathan: a sixth-grade black male who has spent 16 days in ISS.

Josh: a sixth-grade black male who has spent 25 days in ISS.

Matt: an eighth-grade white male who has spent 8 days in ISS.

Stewey: a seventh-grade white male who has spent 9 days in ISS.

Mrs. Wolfe: the ISS teacher, in her mid-60s. According to district policy, she is not required to be a certified teacher; she is only required to have a high school diploma.

Mrs. Nyce: the guidance counselor, in her mid-40s, who seeks to help the students in ISS make better decisions about their behavior.

Mr. Wise: the seventh-grade math teacher, who visits ISS to check on his student(s) and to ensure that they have their assignments.

Narrator: The narrator emphasizes and reads each of the listed times. The narrator also reads any parts that are not explicitly assigned to one of the above characters. The narrator is responsible for monitoring the performance to ensure as much silence as possible—without losing the audience—in order to illustrate the amount of silence experienced in the ISS room.

Performance Notes

Throughout the script, actor instructions and performance suggestions are placed in brackets. These should not be read aloud; they serve as guidelines to help the performers. The time stamps before narrator lines can be read aloud to demonstrate the passing of time.

Doing Time in ISS

Setting

The ISS room is a regular-sized classroom; there are no windows. One of the walls in the room is painted black. On the wall in the front of the room is a large clock with a large second hand that ticks loudly; in the silence in the room, it sounds even louder, marking time as the students endure their stay in the ISS room. In the room are 12 cubicles—desks with wooden walls on three sides such that each student is unable to see the other students in the room. In one corner, there is a computer workstation. On another wall is a poster with a list of rules; according to one student, there were 13 rules, according to another, 27. The 14 rules that students discussed explicitly in the interviews are listed in Appendix A. They could be displayed as part of the performance set. The following scene opens on a Thursday morning at the end of May.

The ISS Day Begins

8:23 a.m.
Narrator: Several students, along with Stewey and Matt, are gathered in the hallway outside the in-school suspension room, talking excitedly about the end of the school year. The audience is aware of their animated conversations, but is not able to hear what they are talking about.

8:26 a.m.
Narrator: The first bell rings, alerting students that they should be making their way to their first-period classes. Two students, Jonathan and Jeffrey, are already in their seats in the ISS room. Jonathan is organizing his belongings and getting his desk ready for a day's worth of work; Jeffrey is already on page 4 of a new book he is reading about U.S. military history.

8:29 a.m.
Narrator: Matt and Stewey make their way into the ISS room; they hang up their backpacks and grab some supplies to take to their desks; Josh rushes in and heads straight to his seat. Matt and Stewey are leaning back in their seats, talking to each other.

Matt: So what are you doing in here today?

Stewey: Man, there is no tolerance in the eighth grade right now. All I did was, we were playing around, horseplay, you know, and I hit someone in the face. We were just messing around.

Matt: You're lucky you didn't get sent home the rest of the year.

Stewey: Yeah, I probably woulda, but Principal Kendall knew it was just an accident.

8:30 a.m.
Narrator: The tardy bell rings and the door to the ISS room slams. The students stop talking immediately. Jeffrey, deep in concentration reading his book, is startled by the loud slam; Matt and Stewey sit up in their chairs quickly. The ISS teacher, having gotten the attention of the students in ISS, now calmly begins to instruct them about their day.

[*Mrs. Wolfe sits at her desk and instructs the students.*]

Mrs. Wolfe: Welcome to ISS. We will begin by making sure that you know what is expected of you today. You are to remain in your seats at all times and stay quiet. You will have one bathroom break in the morning and one in the afternoon. We go to lunch at 10:30. You eat in silence. While you are in here today, there is to be no idle time and no sleeping. You are to be working on your schoolwork. If you do not have work from your teachers, I will supply you with work to do.

8:31 a.m.
Narrator: There is a knock on the door. The ISS teacher notices a student standing outside the door peering in. She ignores the knocking and continues to give instructions.

[*Mrs. Wolfe looks at James with a frustrated look but ignores him, leaving him outside the door.*]

Mrs. Wolfe: The first thing you will do is copy the ISS rules. They are listed on the wall over here. [*points to a list of rules written on the wall*] So get out a sheet of paper and begin writing... [*Her voice trails off as attention is turned to the knocking on the door, which is getting louder.*]

Matt: Mrs. Wolfe, I don't have any paper.

Mrs. Wolfe: Well, you will have to borrow some. It is not my job to provide you with paper. And from now on, be sure to raise your hand before speaking.

Jeffrey: Here man, I got some. [*hands Matt a stack of loose-leaf paper*]

8:32 a.m.
Narrator: The knocking on the door gets louder.

James: [*standing outside the door yelling*] Hey, let me in!

Mrs. Wolfe: [*gets up to open the door and speaks very sternly*] You are tardy; perhaps you should come back another day.

James: But I asked you if I could go to the restroom and you said I could.

Mrs. Wolfe: [*raising her voice*] I gave you no such permission.

James: [*raising his voice louder*] You were in the office talking to the secretary and I asked and you said, "Just go." So I went.

Mrs. Wolfe: James, you are tardy; that will get you 2 more days. [*moves aside so that James can enter the ISS room*] Now go sit down and get your work out before 2 days becomes 3.

James: [*mumbling under his breath*] This is so unfair. [*sits down with a loud sigh and throws his book bag loudly on the desk*]

8:35 a.m.
Narrator: Mrs. Wolfe continues to instruct the students about the rules.

Mrs. Wolfe: [*now standing next to the list of rules*] I was saying, the rules are written on the wall. You should copy those on your paper and then you should get to work on your classwork.

8:42 a.m.
[*Students should be writing at their desks. The Narrator should pause several seconds/minutes before reading in order to illustrate the time passing.*]

Narrator: Students are still copying the rules; one student, finished, raises his hand.

[*Josh raises his hand but does not wait to be called on.*]

Josh: Um, Mrs. Wolfe, none of my teachers sent me any work. Do you have a book I could read?

Mrs. Wolfe: [*rolls her eyes, takes a deep breath, and stands up*] I will get you some work together. [*She turns to a filing cabinet next to her desk and begins pulling out worksheets. As she gives Josh instructions, she piles a list of worksheets on his desk.*] Josh, here is a list of 25 vocabulary words. First, you need to look up each word in the dictionary and then write the words 20 times each. Then, here are a couple math worksheets to complete. Then, there are a couple of essays—this one on the history of the American flag, this one on how to properly drape a coffin—you can copy those. Then here is a page of sentences; the verb in each sentence is wrong. You need to write each sentence, replacing the verb with the correct form. That should get you started. [*turning to the rest of the class*] Does anyone else need any work to do?

[*The students all look down at their desks.*]

Josh: [*looks up from the pile of work at Mrs. Wolfe*] Um, Mrs. Wolfe, I'm missing a bunch of work in Mrs. Carpenter's class. Can I go find out what I'm missing in there and work on that instead?

Doing Time in ISS

Mrs. Wolfe: [*returns to her desk as she is talking*] No Josh, the rules are clear; no leaving the ISS room to go get work. If you didn't get the work yesterday, that's your fault.

Josh: But they didn't send my work.

Mrs. Wolfe: That's too bad. Now get to work before I add more sheets to that stack.

9:00 a.m.
Narrator: [*waits as long as possible before beginning to read*] Jonathan raises his hand and clears his throat to get Mrs. Wolfe's attention.

Jonathan: Mrs. Wolfe, it's 9:00. It's time for me to get on Skype for Mrs. Thurber's class.

Mrs. Wolfe: Okay. Just make sure you put the headphones on.

[*Jonathan stands and goes to the computer workstation.*]

Narrator: In the corner of the ISS room, Jonathan logs onto Skype, where a student from Mrs. Thurber's Language Arts class accepts his request to join the class. He is unable to talk to the other students, but he can see what is going on in the classroom and he can hear her instruction about today's lesson on the use of metaphor in creative writing. A student from Mrs. Thurber's class knocks on the ISS room door and brings Jonathan an organizational chart that the students are using for the lesson.

[*The rest of the students are sitting at their desks. James, Josh, Matt, and Stewey are writing; Jeffrey is reading a book. Mrs. Wolfe stands and begins walking around the room, monitoring students to ensure they are working. She stops at each desk to see what they are doing. When she gets to Jeffrey's desk, she pauses.*]

Mrs. Wolfe: Jeffrey, what are you working on?

Jeffrey: I'm reading this book on military history.

Mrs. Wolfe: [*reaching down to close the books*] Put those books away. Let me get you a grammar worksheet. [*walks to the filing cabinet and opens a large binder with worksheets, pulling one out and taking it back to Jeffrey's desk.*] You need to be working in ISS, not reading for fun. [*Jeffrey, protesting a little, takes the worksheet and begins working. Mrs. Wolfe makes her way back to her desk and sits down.*]

[*Time should be allowed to pass.*]

Matt: [*raising his hand, but not waiting to be called on*] Mrs. Wolfe, I need some help with my math work.

Mrs. Wolfe: Come up here, please.

[*Matt stands and walks to Mrs. Wolfe's desk.*]

Narrator: Matt walks to the ISS teacher's desk and shows her the linear equation problems he is working on; she does not know how to help him with it.

Matt: Can I go see Mrs. Johnson and get her to explain it to me?

Mrs. Wolfe: No Matt, you cannot leave the room.

Matt: Can I write her a note and have you put it in her mailbox?

Mrs. Wolfe: I'll put it in her box on our way to lunch.

9:30 a.m.
Narrator: [*Time should be allowed to pass before the Narrator begins.*] Mrs. Wolfe stands up and calls on Stewey.

Stewey: Yes ma'am?

Mrs. Wolfe: It's time for your morning bathroom break; you may go one at a time. Stewey, you may go first. [*Stewey stands and leaves the room; each of*

Doing Time in ISS

the students stands and takes their turn. When the students are finished, Narrator should pause before reading.]

9:45 a.m.
Narrator: The ISS teacher stands to take her bathroom break. As she leaves the room, the guidance counselor, Mrs. Nyce, comes in.

[*Mrs. Wolfe stands and leaves the room as Mrs. Nyce is entering the room. They smile at each other as they pass. When Mrs. Nyce is in the room, she sits on Mrs. Wolfe's desk and looks at each student before talking.*]

Mrs. Nyce: Hello gentlemen, how are you all doing this morning?

[*Several students murmur responses; the others keep their heads down. As the conversation progresses, students one by one turn and face Mrs. Nyce.*]

Jonathan: [*turning around in his chair to face Mrs. Nyce*] I'm doing alright, Mrs. Nyce. Just trying to get my work done.

Josh: [*looking at Jonathan and then at Mrs. Nyce*] At least your teachers sent you work!

Mrs. Nyce: Josh, you don't have any work? Your teachers didn't send stuff for you to do?

Josh: I've been in here so much this year and my teachers never send my work.

Mrs. Nyce: Did you go and ask them to send your assignments to ISS?

Josh: I asked Mrs. Lofton and she said she would send something and Mrs. Carpenter was out yesterday, so I didn't get to talk to her. Mr. Jeffers just told me to study for our test tomorrow.

Mrs. Nyce: [*picks up a notepad and scribbles a note to herself*] I'll see if I can talk to your teachers today and get them to send some assignments. Does everyone else have things to do?

Matt: I had some math, but I didn't get anything from my other classes.

Jeffrey: Me neither, Mrs. Nyce. [*gets out his military history books again and begins reading*]

Mrs. Nyce: [*scribbling some more notes*] Okay, I'll see what I can do about talking to teachers about getting your assignments sent down here. So, have you guys thought about what you're doing in here? What happened?

Jonathan: I got written up for talking; I like to talk and move and I got ADHD and all, and when I don't take my medicine, I usually get in trouble.

Matt: I didn't do nothin', Mrs. Nyce. I dropped my pencil and I asked the teacher if I could get it and he said no, so I asked him to get it for me and he wouldn't; so I sat there for a couple of minutes later, and then I got up and got my pencil. So he sent me to ISS.

Josh: [*turning to Matt*] Like what were you supposed to do? Sit there and not do your work?

Stewey: [*adjusting his chair so he can look at Mrs. Nyce*] I just wish teachers would try to be a little bit more, like, think about it a bit more before you write somebody up out of impulse, like instinctively out of anger, because sometimes they really won't do something or they really haven't done anything, but they end up getting punished for it.

James: [*rolling his eyes and shaking his head*] I'm tired of getting into trouble. It's just bull crap. It's little stuff you shouldn't write students up about, like a cell phone being out. Don't write a student up for a cell phone being out. Just tell them to put the cell phone up. You know? Now in a couple of days, if it happens again, then call the parents and if the parents don't do anything, then you should write them up, but it's just little petty stuff.

Mrs. Nyce: Do you think the teachers expect you to know what the rules are?

Doing Time in ISS

Josh: Yeah, but sometimes they write us up just cuz they in a bad mood; they already mad cuz the class was already being disrespectful. And then I get there late and talk one time and I'm the one get written up.

Mrs. Nyce: So are there some things you can learn, about your own behavior or about how to get along with some of your teachers, that might help you stay out of ISS in the future?

10:15 a.m.
Narrator: Before the students have a chance to respond, the ISS teacher returns from her break. As Mrs. Wolfe enters the room, Mrs. Nyce stands to leave. On her way out the door, she looks at the students and smiles.

Mrs. Nyce: Hang in there, guys. Get your work done, if you have it, and learn a lot. I'll see what I can do about getting your assignments to ISS. Let me know if you want to talk further about anything we talked about today. [*turning to Mrs. Wolfe, she smiles and nods*]

Mrs. Wolfe: [*begins walking around the room to monitor students. Noticing that Jeffrey has his military history books out again, she walks over and takes the books, stacking them on the cabinet behind her desk*] Jeffrey, you can stand by your desk for the next 15 minutes until time for lunch. When we return from lunch, you better find some work to do or I will find some for you. Do you understand?

Jeffrey: [*stands by his desk with his hands behind his back*] Yes ma'am. Can I work on some word searches that I brought from home?

Mrs. Wolfe: [*sitting down at her desk and opening a book to read*] That will be fine.

Jeffrey: [*turning to face the audience*] So basically, I'm supposed to sit in here, bored out of my mind. This is just pure torture to us kids cuz we're missing out on our learning time. It's just taking us out of our learning so the teachers don't have to put up with us. Then, I get yelled at for not doing work, but I can't do nothing because I have no work to do. I end up getting zeros on all the assignments, but it ain't my fault.

[*Jeffrey is still standing by his desk; the other students are all writing at their desks. Occasionally they look at the clock on the wall. The Narrator waits several minutes before reading, in order to illustrate the passing of time.*]

10:30 a.m.
Narrator: The students are all watching the clock carefully, knowing it is approaching time to go to lunch. At 10:30 on the dot, the ISS teacher commands them to stand up and get in a straight line.

Mrs. Wolfe: [*standing and walking to the door*] When you are all standing quietly with your hands behind your back, we will proceed to the cafeteria. [*waits while the students line up and lock their hands behind their back*] Remember that you are only allowed to get white milk, and no buying chips. When you get your tray, I will assign your seat. [*turns and walks out of the room with the students following her*].

Matt: [*whispering to Jeffrey as they walk down the hall*] Hey, you got any extras of those word searches to do? I did my math already and my other teachers didn't send any work and I ain't got nothing to do. I don't wanna have to copy words out of the dictionary again.

Jeffrey: [*whispering back*] Yeh man, I'll hook ya up when we get back to the room. Just keep it between us. This is my third day in here and I ain't got many left.

Mrs. Wolfe: [*pausing upon arriving in the cafeteria*] Remember, no talking while you eat. You have 20 minutes.

Narrator: Students go through the line and get their lunch and are told where to sit. They eat in silence.

[*The Narrator waits before reading again.*]

11:55 a.m.
Narrator: The ISS teacher, who has been standing talking to the lunch workers, announces that the students should put up their trays and line up.

Doing Time in ISS 143

[*Students move to put up their trays and get in line.*] As they begin walking back, Josh sneaks in a conversation with Jonathan.

Josh: Hey, you have Mr. Jeffers for science, right? Can I borrow your science notes when we get back in the room so I can study for that test tomorrow?

Jonathan: Sure. I'll try to pass them to you when she's not looking.

Josh: Thanks. I cannot stand to do another one of those stupid worksheets.

Mrs. Wolfe: Josh, are you talking in line? You'll stand beside your desk for 15 minutes when we return to the room.

Josh: [*turning to the audience, sounding exasperated*] So aggravating! I'm so tired of all this. Maybe if I was in here for a reason, I might learn something, but I don't even belong in here. These two girls was messing with *me* and I'm the one who gets in trouble. And now, I gotta sit in here for a small, small reason doing stupid work. I been in here 25 days this year and I bet I've written that American flag story 25 times. There's a big ole book of English worksheets; why she keep giving me the same one over and over? At least I get to stand up for a few minutes when we get back to the room.

11:57 a.m.
Narrator: Back in the ISS room, Mrs. Wolfe instructs the students, except Josh, to sit down and get back to work on whatever they were working on before lunch.

[*Josh is standing by his desk. The other students are all writing at their desks.*]

12:10 p.m.
Narrator: [*waiting before reading*] There is a quiet knock on the door; an adult opens the door and looks at Mrs. Wolfe, who is sitting at her desk reading.
[*Mr. Wise enters the room hesitantly and looks at Mrs. Wolfe.*]

Mr. Wise: Um, Mrs. Wolfe, I just came by during my lunch to check on Jeffrey. Is that okay?

Mrs. Wolfe: Sure, Mr. Wise.

Mr. Wise: [*pulling up a chair next to Jeffrey and whispering*] How's it going? I brought you some math work [*handing him a textbook and some worksheets*]. Turn to page 137; you need to do 1 to 42. Do you know how to do these?

Jeffrey: [*looking at the page and smiling*] Um... I know how to do *these*, but not the ones with the words.

Narrator: A conversation ensues between Mr. Wise and Jeffrey about the assignment. Mr. Wise asks some questions, helping Jeffrey connect the word problems to the work they had been doing in class. Jeffrey begins to work on the assignment and Mr. Wise stands to leave.

[*Mr. Wise and Jeffrey converse pleasantly before Mr. Wise stands.*]

Matt: [*turning to Mr. Wise*] Mr. Wise, can I ask you a quick algebra question?

[*Mr. Wise stops and walks to Matt's desk and leans over to look at Matt's work. Matt opens up a folder and pulls out a worksheet.*]

Narrator: Matt pulls out his work from earlier and points to a problem that he didn't understand. Mr. Wise asks him a couple guiding questions, to which Matt replies:

Matt: Oh, yeah, I got it. Thanks! [*turns around and begins working on his math again*]

Narrator: Mr. Wise again turns to leave.

Josh: [*turning toward Mr. Wise*] Hey Mr. Wise, can you find Mrs. Lofton and ask her *please* to send some work for me down here! She didn't send anything today and I ain't got nothing to do.

Mr. Wise: [*making his way to the door and turning to answer Josh*] I'll see if I can find her, Josh.

12:30 p.m.
Narrator: [*waits before reading, to indicate the passing of time*]: Mrs. Wolfe stands to take her lunch break. [*Mrs. Wolfe stands and leaves the room.*] As she leaves, she instructs the office personnel to keep an eye on the ISS students. Occasionally, they will peak their heads in and check to make sure that the students are working, but for a few minutes, the students are left virtually unattended.

James: [*leaning back in his chair and throwing up his hands*] I hate that woman. She is so rude!

[*Students sit up and turn in their chairs in order to have a conversation—all except for Jeffrey, who puts his head down on his desk.*]

Jonathan: [*turning toward James*] She ain't that bad; you just shouldn't be late. She's strict and likes when you follow her rules and stuff.

Matt: There's too many of her rules! And she'll write you up and assign you more days for nothin'!

Stewey: I think she's funny; when no one's in here, she makes jokes and all. She's just in a bad mood today.

Jonathan: Yeh, she's kinda nice to me.

Josh: That's cuz she like you. She be nice to people she likes. If she don't like you, she yell at you all the time.

James: I know! She hollers at you like you is a dog. I just don't like that. You yell at me and I'm just going to yell back at you. I'm sure she's a nice lady; she's just got a snoozy attitude.

[*The students continue this conversation. Stewey stands up to stretch his legs, walks to the door and realizes that Mrs. Wolfe is in the office talking to the secretary; he rushes back to his desk.*]

Stewey: Quick, she's coming back. Get quiet everyone.

12:48 p.m.

Narrator: Mrs. Wolfe returns to find the students quietly sitting at their desks; most of them appear to be working. Mrs. Wolfe walks back into the room, stands at the door, and looks around the room suspiciously. She notes that the students appear to be working, but then she sees Jeffrey with his head down. She goes to her desk and picks up a large encyclopedia and then walks quietly to Jeffrey's desk. Raising the book and releasing it, it falls loudly to the floor, abruptly waking him up. Jeffrey sits up groggily.

Mrs. Wolfe: [*yelling loudly*] You do not sleep in ISS! It is rule number 6. Now I want you to stand up by your desk for 15 minutes. Maybe that will help you wake up. If you fall asleep again, you will get another day in here. Do you understand? [*Mrs. Wolfe walks back to her desk and sits down.*]

Jonathan: [*turning to the audience*] It's lots better when there's only a couple of us in here, or when you're like in here by yourself. Mrs. Wolfe, she'll let you get up and talk to her for a few minutes or stretch your legs or whatever. Some days, she's really nice and funny, but when there's a bunch of people in here, she's all in a bad mood and yells all the time. Sometimes, we leave with headaches cuz of how much she yells. Today's one of those days.

Jonathan: [*turning to Mrs. Wolfe and trying to cheer her up*] Did you go walking on the track again today, Mrs. Wolfe?

Mrs. Wolfe: [*looking up at Jonathan and nodding*] I sure did. It is such a beautiful day outside.

Doing Time in ISS

James: [*muttering almost to himself, but loud enough to be heard*] We should be able to go outside after lunch too and get some exercise. It ain't right that we have to be cramped in this room all day without any chance to move around.

Mrs. Wolfe: Well, it was your choice to get put in here, James. Maybe you'll think about that next time.

James: [*turning to the audience*] Does she even know why I'm in here? One of my teachers called me gay and I mouthed off at him. So, I get written up for being disrespectful; he gets nothing. I think teachers should get written up too. If I could, I would just change everything around at this school. I wouldn't have ISS; I wouldn't have it at all. No, I don't believe in it. I think it's the worst thing ever. If I were the superintendent, I would change a whole bunch of things such as freedom in the school. I don't feel we have freedom at all.

1:14 p.m.
Narrator: [*waits before reading to indicate the passage of time. Mrs. Wolfe is reading at her desk. The students are all writing, except for Jonathan, who is staring off into space, apparently daydreaming.*] Jonathan raises his hand and waits for Mrs. Wolfe to notice and call on him.

Mrs. Wolfe: Yes, Jonathan?

Jonathan: Mrs. Wolfe, I'm finished with all the work that my teachers sent. Do you have anything that I can work on?

Mrs. Wolfe: [*stands up and reaches into the filing cabinet*] I have a crossword puzzle; it's about Abraham Lincoln. Would you like to work that?

Jonathan: Sure. [*stands and walks to the front of the room to get the sheet of paper*] Thank you. [*returns to his desk and sits down and starts working on the puzzle*]

Stewey: Mrs. Wolfe, can I get on the computer? I'm finished with most of my work, but I need to type up this report that I wrote for social studies.

Mrs. Wolfe: Sure Stewey.

[*Stewey stands and walks to the computer station.*]

Stewey: [*turning to the audience*] This is what I like about ISS; I'm failing like three classes right now, but with all the worksheets that I got made up today from all my classes, I bet I'll be able to pull my grades up to like Bs and a C, just from doing all this makeup work. Some kids are just, like, I hate ISS; it's boring. It is boring, but I get my work done and it brings my grades up, and so I'm good with that. [*Narrator waits a while before beginning to read again, to indicate the passing of time. During this time of waiting, Stewey is typing at the computer and the rest of the students are writing, all except for Josh, who is studying for his science test.*]

1:52 p.m.
Narrator: The room is quiet except for the ticking of the clock. All the students are writing, except for Stewey, who is typing, and Josh, who is reading from a stack of papers.

Mrs. Wolfe: [*looking up from the book she is reading*] Josh, you need to be working.

Josh: [*turning around in his chair to look at Mrs. Wolfe*] I am working, Mrs. Wolfe. I'm studying for a test I have tomorrow in science.

Mrs. Wolfe: But you need to be working. I need to see your pencil on that paper.

Josh: But I don't need to write anything; I just need to study my notes.

Mrs. Wolfe: Don't argue with me; get to writing. There is no idling in here. See rule 4. Do you need something else to do?

Josh: [*turning back around in his chair*] No ma'am, I'll just copy my notes.

Mrs. Wolfe: Good thinking, young man. [*returns to reading her book*]

Doing Time in ISS 149

2:08 p.m.

Narrator: [*waits a while before reading*] The door bursts open and one of the assistant principals motions the ISS teacher to come to the door. [*Mrs. Wolfe stands up and walks to the door.*] They stand whispering just outside the ISS room. Their conversation seems very animated. In a few minutes, the principal ushers a young female student into the room. He is carrying her backpack, and points to a cubicle in the back of the room. The student sits down, immediately puts her head down on the desk, and goes to sleep.

[*Mrs. Wolfe seems visibly upset by the new student. Instead of returning to her desk, she walks around the room, keeping a wary eye on the girl. Jonathan, also looking uncomfortably at the new student, has finished his crossword puzzle. Noticing that Mrs. Wolfe is watching the new student, he begins to fold his crossword puzzle into an origami fish. The other students at least appear to be writing, occasionally staring off into space, looking visibly tired of sitting all day.*]

2:24 p.m.

Narrator: [*Narrator waits to begin reading, to indicate the passage of time.*] There is a knock on the door and a student comes in the room with a history textbook and some worksheets. He indicates that he has some work for Jeffrey.

Mrs. Wolfe: [*walks to the door to get the assignment for Jeffrey and then takes it to his desk, reading the instructions as she walks*] Well, Jeffrey, here's your work from Mrs. Kilgore. It says to read chapter 17 and answer the questions at the end of the chapter. Then do these worksheets.

Jeffrey: [*looks at the worksheet and textbook and states sarcastically*] Well, that's just great. I won't get finished before it's time to go home.

Mrs. Wolfe: At least you got your work so you can do it tonight for homework and not get zeros on it. [*As she says this, she points to Jeffrey and then walks to the front of the room.*]

2:48 p.m.

Narrator: [*waits to begin reading*] Mrs. Wolfe begins to clean up the room.

[*Mrs. Wolfe walks around the room, pushing in extra chairs and picking up some paper off the floor.*] She instructs the students to finish up whatever they are working on.

Mrs. Wolfe: Be sure to turn in the work you have done for your classes. Make sure your name and your teacher's name is on each page. I will put that work in your teachers' mailboxes.

Matt: [*not raising his hand*] What about all of the worksheets that you gave us?

Mrs. Wolfe: You can stack them on the corner of your desk and throw them away on your way out—unless you think your teachers will give you any extra credit for them. It could be worth a try, you know? [*turns her back to the class while she cleans up her own desk*]

Matt: [*turning to the audience*] Aagghh. All that writing and stuff, you know, it makes your day longer. Just another day of busy work, while getting further and further behind. ISS makes me mad because, you know, I really like to be with my friends and I like to learn stuff and I pretty much like to be in the classroom and learn stuff and uh, extend my knowledge for my future and stuff, because I want to go to college, like really bad, and I was going to try really hard next year and try to get honors classes in high school. To be in ISS and not be able to learn stuff, you know, it really makes me mad. [*Matt turns back around and runs his hands through his hair, frustrated.*]

3:00 p.m.
Narrator: [*waits to begin reading*] The bell rings and the students get up quickly and run out of the ISS room. Jonathan, lingering behind the others, leaves an origami fish on Mrs. Wolfe's desk.

Questions for Discussion

1. From your own perspective, what is the purpose of ISS? What is the purpose of school discipline? Based on the characters in this performance, do you think that purpose is being fulfilled?
2. Did you ever spend time in in-school suspension when you were in school? If so, what was your own experience with ISS? What did you

notice in the performance that was similar or dissimilar to your own experience with ISS?
3. How do you think classroom teachers should approach school discipline? Should ISS be a part of a discipline plan? If so, how should it be implemented?
4. What questions did the performance evoke about your own ideas about school discipline? What emotions did the performance elicit?

References

American Psychological Association. (2008). Are zero tolerance policies effective in the schools? An evidentiary review and recommendations. *American Psychologist, 63*(9), 852–862.
Berger, P. L., & Luckmann, T. (1966). *The social construction of reality: A treatise in the sociology of knowledge*. New York: Anchor Books.
Boal, A. (1985). *Theater of the oppressed*. New York: Theater Communications Group.
Bochner, A. P., & Ellis, C. (2003). An introduction to the arts and narrative research: Art as inquiry. *Qualitative Inquiry, 9*(4), 506–514.
Brown, T. M. (2007). Lost and turned out: Academic, social and emotional experiences of students excluded from school. *Urban Education, 42*(5), 432–455.
Casella, R. (2001). *At zero tolerance: Punishment, prevention, and school violence*. New York: Peter Lang.
Christle, C., Nelson, C. M., & Jolivette, K. (2004). School characteristics related to the use of suspension. *Education and Treatment of Children, 27*(4), 509–526.
Conquergood, D. (2002). Performance studies: Interventions and radical research. *The Drama Review, 46*(2), 145–156.
Cook-Sather, A. (2009). "I am not afraid to listen": Prospective teachers learning from students. *Theory into Practice, 48*(3), 176–183.
Denzin, N. K. (2003). *Performance ethnography: Critical pedagogy and the politics of culture*. Thousand Oaks, CA: Sage.
Evans, K. R. (2011). *Suspended students' experiences with in-school suspension: A phenomenological investigation*. (Unpublished doctoral dissertation). The University of Tennessee, Knoxville.
Evans, K. R., & Lester, J. N. (2010). Classroom management and discipline: Responding to the needs of young adolescents. *Middle School Journal, 41*(3), 54–61.
Fenning, P., & Rose, J. (2007). Overrepresentation of African American students in exclusionary discipline: The role of school policy. *Urban Education, 42*(6), 536–559.
Ferguson, A. A. (2000). *Bad boys: Public schools in the making of black masculinity*. Ann Arbor: University of Michigan Press.
Fine, M., & Weis, L. (2003). *Silenced voices and extraordinary conversations: Re-imagining schools*. New York: Teachers College Press.
Foucault, M. (1977). *Discipline and punish: The birth of the prison*. New York: Vintage Books.
Hyman, I. A., & Snook, P. A. (2000). Dangerous schools and what you can do about them. *Phi Delta Kappan, 81*(7), 489–498.

Kupchik, A. (2010). *Homeroom security: School discipline in an age of fear.* New York: New York University Press.

Lincoln, Y. S. (1995). In search of students' voices. *Theory into Practice, 34*(2), 88–93.

Madison, D. S. (2012). *Critical ethnography: Method, ethics, and performance.* Los Angeles: Sage.

Mendez, L. M. R., & Knoff, H. M. (2003). Who gets suspended from school and why: A demographic analysis of schools and disciplinary infractions in a large school district. *Education and Treatment of Children, 26,* 30–51.

Mienczakowski, J. (1995). The theater of ethnography: The reconstruction of ethnography into theater with emancipatory potential. *Qualitative Inquiry, 1*(3), 360–375.

Nevetsky, J. (1991). At-risk program links middle school, high school programs. *NASSP Bulletin, 75,* 45–49.

Noguera, P. A. (2003). Schools, prisons, and social implications of punishment: Rethinking disciplinary practices. *Theory into Practice, 42*(4), 341–350.

Polkinghorne, D. (1989). Phenomenological research methods. In R. S. Valle & S. Halling (Eds.), *Existential-phenomenological perspectives in psychology* (pp. 41–60). New York: Plenum Press.

Rivkin, D. H. (2009). Decriminalizing students with disabilities. *New York Law School Law Review, 54,* 909–952.

Roberts, B. (2008). Performative social science: A consideration of skills, purpose and context. *Forum: Qualitative Social Research 9*(2), n.p.

Rodriguez, L. F. (2008). Struggling to recognize their existence: Examining student-adult relationships in the urban high school context. *Urban Review, 40,* 436–453.

Saldaña, J. (2003). Dramatizing data: A primer. *Qualitative Inquiry, 9*(2), 218–236.

Skiba, R. J., Peterson, R. L., & Williams, T. (1997). Office referrals and suspension: Disciplinary intervention in middle schools. *Education & Treatment of Children, 20*(3), 295–316.

Stinchcomb, J. B., Bazemore, G., & Riestenberg, N. (2006). Beyond zero tolerance: Restoring justice in secondary schools. *Youth Violence and Juvenile Justice, 4*(2), 123–147.

Theriot, M. T., & Dupper, D. R. (2010). Student discipline problems and the transition from elementary to middle school. *Education and Urban Society, 42*(2), 205–222.

Thornberg, R. (2008). "It's not fair"—Voicing pupils' criticisms of school rules. *Children & Society, 22,* 418–428.

Troyan, B. E. (2003). The silent treatment: Perpetual in-school suspension and the education rights of students. *Texas Law Review, 81*(6), 1637–1670.

van Manen, M. (1990). *Researching lived experience: Human science for an action sensitive pedagogy.* Albany: State University of New York Press.

Vavrus, F., & Cole, K. (2002). "I didn't do nothin'": The discursive construction of school suspension. *The Urban Review, 34*(2), 87–111.

Appendix A

ISS Rules
1. No talking. If you need help, raise your hand and I will call on you to ask your question.
2. If you talk without permission, you will be required to stand next to your desk for 15 minutes.
3. You must stay in your seats throughout the day. If you get out of your seat, you will be assigned another day.
4. No idling. You must be working the entire time you are here. If you have failed to get your work from your classroom teachers, work will be provided for you to do.
5. You may not leave the room to go get work from your teachers or to get forgotten materials or supplies.
6. No sleeping. If you put your head on your desk, you will be required to stand by your desk. If you fall asleep, you will be assigned another day of ISS.
7. Do not ask to go to the bathroom. You will have one bathroom break in the morning and one in the afternoon.
8. Do not ask to get water. You may get water when you go to the bathroom.
9. No food or drink in the ISS room. If you are caught with food, another day of ISS will be added.
10. You may not chew gum in the ISS room. If you are caught with gum, you will be required to stand by your desk for 30 minutes.
11. No candy in ISS. If you get caught with candy, you get written up and have to do another day.
12. Lunch is at 10:30. You will spread out in the cafeteria during lunch. You will have 20 minutes to eat.
13. No talking during lunch. If you talk, another day will be added.
14. For lunch, you may not have chocolate or strawberry milk and you may not buy chips.

Chapter 6

Education Is a Small Part of the Life I Have to Live

Allison Daniel Anders, Kafele Jahi Khalfani, and Amy E. Swain

Introduction

Tentatively and eloquently, Urrieta (2003) invited his readers to reflect on the complexity of identity, labels, and the power to name an experience, a life, and a death. He shared a story of about the death of his paternal grandmother, who died from a brutal beating by women who lived in her pueblo. In sharing this, Urrieta resigned himself to the inevitability of analysis an outside reader would render. He wrote:

> To the outside observer, or reader, the act of analyzing the causes of such an event is inevitable, but to those of us for whom this was a real person, the emotions triggered by such memories are quite different and more complex than a synthesis or analysis. As I wrote this, I was alone and I cried. I wanted to holler, demanding a justice never served .... As I've presented this history at professional conferences my voice quivers, but I hold back my tears and a painful feeling of suffocation fills my chest. Part of the anguish comes from the *testimonio* itself and part of it from guilt because I am not sure that my audiences understand the pain involved when the story is told. (p. 155)

Urrieta's work taught me (Anders) to read with my heart and not just my mind. It taught me to question my privilege as a reader and my propensity to analyze stories instead of experiencing them. It taught me to be careful, and to invite care when representing a lived experience that is not my own. As you read this chapter, I (Anders) invite you to remember that the script is based on the tellings of lived experiences. As you read, there may be moments when you search for the how or why of these experiences. If you work to analyze and synthesize what is on these pages, I caution you against sedimentation of thought.

In 2000 I began work as an evaluator on a team that was tasked with assessing the effects of an education program in North Carolina correctional facilities, a program now called the Incarcerated Individuals Program (IPP). The program included college courses, a course on employability, and a course on cognitive behavioral intervention. Most of the program participants were 18- to 24-year-old students who had either completed their GED or received a high school diploma, and were within a few years of their release date. During two of the years I was on the team, I completed a series of in-depth interviews with nine out of the dozens of students the team interviewed over the years. These interviews informed the tenor of the script. Each name in the cast represents a composite of interviews, field notes, and observations in school spaces. Each interaction represents a recounted experience from one of students (Saldaña, 2011). The students shared their experiences courageously and selflessly and this text would not exist without them. If you do not know someone who has been to prison, I invite you to work against what it is you think you know about who goes to prison and why. If your brothers and sisters, mothers and fathers, friends, and loved ones are not in these pages, I hope you will read with your breath and your heart. As you do, know that this text may never join the imagined community of which you are a part, yet it is a part of mine, and I share it carefully.

In the production of this text, I was most aware of the anguish I carry regarding these tellings of lived experience. My positionality affects my work, from coding to analysis and representation (Noblit, Flores, & Murillo, 2004). As Noblit (1999) wrote, it's tough to get out of our own way as readers and researchers. Though writing against myself is a commitment to which I return again and again, I fail to accomplish it here. This representation is one of many. It is partial and positional, and therefore, personal; the language performed for me by the students and the language of my interpretation limited this representation. Layers of discourse and analysis reveal and reproduce my able-bodiedness, my whiteness and racisms, my gender and expressions, my status and economic privilege as a middle-class graduate student at the time of the interviews and as an assistant professor teaching at a predominantly white institution now. Though you may take up the experiences of these students as words in your voice, know that the speech here comes from moments they have lived. The men and women who make up Luce, Justice, Citlali, and Belysa are real people, as are the men and women who make up Mrs. Rigsdale, Mrs. Fox, and Mr. Eaton. I ask you to seek the particularities of experience as you read, as we all have particular lives to lead, and no life, and alas no death, is exactly like another (Abu-Lughod, 1991; Noblit, 1999). Finally, if you think you know these lives, if you think you know these deaths, I ask you to think about what you are doing about them. There are prison abolition movements to join, racial justice work to fortify, economic, social, and cultural rights to pursue, government assistance programs to repair, after after-school programs to support, and education policies to rewrite.

Education Is a Small Part of the Life I Have to Live

Characters
Belysa: Justice's African American grandmother

Citlali: Luce's Mexican/Italian older sister

Justice/Young Justice: an African American/Native American/Puerto Rican male student, at 18 years old and 6 and 11 years old, respectively

Luce/Young Luce: a Mexican/Italian male student, at 18 years old and 6 and 11 years old, respectively

Mrs. Rigsdale: an African American elementary school teacher

Mrs. Fox: a Latina middle school teacher

Principal Eaton: a white male middle school principal

Shahidi: an African American female student

Stanley: a white male student

Tye: an African American female student

Correctional Officer: an African American male

Act One, Scene 1

Stage right: A wide sidewalk winds around the corner of brick apartment building. A streetlight and a light over the entrance to the building glow as dusk falls. Outside the building three African American men stand on the corner, and a group of 6-year-old African American and Chicano boys, including Young Luce and Young Justice, play near the entrance of the building. Young Luce arranges small rocks in a row and balances a stick on them. One by one, the boys pull a rock from under the stick. As Young Luce pulls a rock, the stick hits the ground. The other five scatter across the stage as Young Luce tries to tag each one. Laughter fills the space. Young Luce

Education Is a Small Part of the Life I Have to Live

catches Young Justice first. They burst into laughter. Together they catch the other four boys. Gasping for breath through their laughter, they all return to set up the rocks and stick again. In a small kitchen on the second floor of the apartment building, Belysa lights four candles along the kitchen counter and two on the table. She takes from one of the cabinets a loaf of bread and makes sandwiches.

Center stage: Cue light on Justice. Justice wears a gray jacket. He glances stage right.

Justice: I was like 6 or 7 when I saw my gran'ma lighting candles in the house, because we had no lights. That's definitely under the poverty line. I knew it was bad. My gran'ma couldn't do it all. My mama wasn't too steady. I had to buy my own school clothes, school shoes, paid my own lunch. Back then, my dad was a kingpin. Ran half the city. I never saw him, though. He got locked up when I was 3. Been locked up 12 years. I'm the only boy in the house. I've got three sisters. We're really tight. When they got scared they came to me.

Stage right: Belysa leans out the kitchen window.

Belysa: Justice!

Young Justice: Coming gran'ma!

Center stage:

Justice: [*looks at the audience*] I was a rock in a hard place.

[*Young Justice passes the men outside his apartment building. He climbs one flight and enters the kitchen.*]

Belysa: Justice, I want to talk to you.

Young Justice: Yes ma'am.

Belysa: [*sits facing Young Justice*] I know you know the streets teach people things in order to survive.

Young Justice: Yes.

Belysa: And some folks don't think they need anything else. You know, you can live day to day and survive. You'll be happy.

[*Shallow laughter drifts through the kitchen from the men on the corner.*]

Belysa: So-called happy.

Young Justice: So-called happy?

Belysa: Happy with a limited situation—folks not realizing they're not truly happy. The streets has a way of giving people temporary, small amount of happiness, and they get satisfied.

Young Justice: Where's mama? She left? Didn't she? [*Young Justice stands.*] She never stays! Why won't she stay?

Belysa: She wants to be steady for you, your sisters, Devisha, but she's struggling right now.

Young Justice: When is she coming back?

Belysa: As soon as she can.

Young Justice: But you don't know? [*pause*] She goin' to get locked up? Luce's dad left and he got locked up.

Belysa: Your mama's not Luce's daddy. [*touches Young Justice on the shoulder*] You know, folks who get locked up, 90% of the time, they don't have a family. They turn to—

Young Justice: Gangs. I know, I know. [*turns away from Belysa*] Leave the streets alone.

Belysa: They turn to the streets for that sense of belonging. You belong here in this house with this family. You are my pride and joy, Justice. And I love you and your mama. Right now, she's having a hard time, but I'm not going anywhere. [*Young Justice falls into her arms for a hug.*] I'm right here. I'm right here.

Young Justice: Why won't she stay?

Belysa: [*holding Young Justice*] She's strugglin', suga'. She's strugglin'. Now, go round up the girls.

[*Young Justice exits and returns with four girls. They sit on chairs around the table. The youngest two climb into their chairs and kneel on their knees to eat. They are all younger than Young Justice. As Belysa gives each of them a sandwich, she touches each one on the head. Belysa sits down to eat with them.*]

Act One, Scene 2

Center stage: Cue light on Luce. He stands with his hands on his hips. He wears a white t-shirt and gray pants. He looks at the men outside Justice's window.

Luce: I didn't like drugs. I wore a DARE patch on my pants. I was quiet, bad sometimes. I tried to be smooth. It was hard growing up. Hispanics called me "white boy" because my father was Italian. White kids called me "wetback." Everyone said, "Oh, he's from Third Street." My mom, she made sure that I understood where I came from though, that I'm a descendant of the Aztecs. She told me stories of what our ancestors have been through, what we stand for. [*Luce looks stage right.*]

[*Dim light.*]

Stage right: Cue light on Citlali as she walks past the men outside the apartment building. She has a shopping bag under her arm. She calls to Young Luce.

Citlali: Luce, ven acá!

[*Citlali walks into the apartment building. She climbs two flights. Young Luce follows her, skipping steps up the stairs. Citlali opens the door and enters the kitchen. Bright blue curtains hang at the window and artwork decorates the refrigerator. Family photographs adorn the walls. Citlali enters her bedroom. As she falls on her bed, colorful pillows tumble to the floor beside a neat row of seven pairs of shoes.*]

Citlali: Come in here! Where've you been?

[*Young Luce puts a soda and a bag of chips on the dresser.*]

Young Luce: I was getting somethin' to eat.

Citlali: What's wrong?

Young Luce: Nothin'.

Citlali: Here, I want you to try this on. I picked it out for you.

Young Luce: You keepin' me fresh.

Citlali: [*laughing*)] Put it on. Let me see.

[*Young Luce takes his t-shirt off and puts on a button-down shirt Citlali has taken from the bag.*]

Young Luce: Kinda preppy?

Citlali: It looks good. You don't like it?

Young Luce: No. I like it.

Citlali: You don't act like you like it. What's wrong?

Young Luce: Nothin'. I like it, alright?

Citlali: Sit down.

[*Young Luce sits in front of her at her dresser. Citlali looks at him in the mirror. Young Luce is quiet. Citlali grabs her hair gel and spikes Luce's hair.*]

Citlali: What's wrong? You're upset. I can see it.

Young Luce: Nothin'. Just some white kids at the store.

Citlali: [*nervous*] From the neighborhood?

Young Luce: Naw, from the other side of the Boulevard. They kept blockin' my way, callin' me "fucking wetback," sayin' "Speak English. Speak English." I speak English!

Citlali: I want you to stay away from the Boulevard. Don't cross it again. You know mama says to go to the store on Ninth.

Young Luce: I don't want to go down to Ninth. All I wanted was a soda and a bag of chips. We should be able to go there. [*Young Luce opens his soda.*]

Citlali: You know it's on the other side of the Boulevard. You gotta stay outta their way. You just gotta ignore them. People don't realize what they do with their mouths. They try to jump you?

Young Luce: Naw, some of Uncle Tony's brothers came up the Boulevard, and they took off. Tony watched me cross back.

Citlali: Whites with whites, blacks with blacks, Mexicans with Mexicans. In the park, in the streets, in school, anywhere. Don't mess with 'em. You're just not going to see it: a Mexican with a white person. [*Young Luce looks at Citlali in the mirror.*] Okay, you might see every once in a while, but I guarantee you, it'll be once in a black moon.

Young Luce: A black moon?

Citlali: Once in a black moon. [*Citlali spikes the rest of Young Luce's hair away from his head.*] Yeah. Cause we get blue moons almost every night, don't we?

[*Lights fade.*]

Act One, Scene 3

Stage left: Cue light on a first grade classroom. Four rows of five desks face a green chalkboard, the teacher's desk, and a table of pans and mixing bowls. Two children stand very still at every other desk, with two small pans and a small bowl in front of them. Young Justice and Young Luce stand next to Young Justice's desk, the fifth desk in the fourth row. Mrs. Rigsdale stands at the front of the room.

Mrs. Rigsdale: Quiet! Right now. [*The children stand very still.*] We will not continue to step 4 until everyone is silent. Everyone. I want your listening ears open, your watching eyes forward, and both hands on your desk. Has everyone completed step 3? [*No one moves.*] We have completed step 3. Now, step 4. Count your noodles. You need three.

[*Young Justice raises his hand. Mrs. Rigsdale turns and writes step 4 on the board.*]

Young Justice: Our noodles are stuck together. [*to Young Luce:*] What do you do?

Young Luce: I don't know.

Young Justice: [*hand raised still*] We didn't do the step right.

Mrs. Rigsdale: Quiet, Justice. You need to be listening.

Young Luce: Listening to what? She's not even saying anything. She's writing on the board.

Young Justice: [*to Young Luce*] They're stuck.

Mrs. Rigsdale: Count three noodles.

Young Justice: [*raises his hand*] Wait.

Young Luce: [*looks at Young Justice raising his hand*] She doesn't care. She's just ready to go home for the day.

Young Justice: [*stretches his hand high*] I couldn't get them apart.

[*Mrs. Rigsdale walks to the desk where Young Justice and Young Luce stand.*]

Mrs. Rigsdale: This is incorrect. Your noodles are not side-by-side.

[*Mrs. Rigsdale shakes her head and takes some of the noodles from the pan and sets them in front of Young Justice.*]

Mrs. Rigsdale: Peel these apart. Luce, help.

Young Justice: I tried to.

Mrs. Rigsdale: Give 'em to me. Class, wait just a moment. [*Mrs. Rigsdale takes them, puts them in the pan, and ladles sauce from the bowl on them. She hands the bowl back to Young Justice.*]

Mrs. Rigsdale: Doesn't your mother cook? [*Mrs. Rigsdale returns to the front of the room.*]

Young Luce: She knows you live with your gran'ma. She didn't have to say that.

Mrs. Rigsdale: Now that everyone has completed step 3, step 4: everyone ladle again.

Young Justice: Why she gotta make us feel like we're doing something wrong? I just wanted her help. I couldn't get the noodles apart.

Young Luce: I just want some lasagna. I'm hungry.

[*Mrs. Rigsdale watches Young Justice and Young Luce. Young Justice ladles sauce into the pan.*]

Young Justice: [*smiles*] Yeah, me, too. Okay. Step 4. Done.

[*Young Luce glances at Mrs. Rigsdale.*]

Young Luce: You know, she doesn't like us.

Young Justice: I don't like her.

Mrs. Rigsdale: Justice and Luce, quiet! You two are starting to run your mouths. You failed to complete step 2 because you were not paying attention. You are in first grade now and you need to be listening. Things wind up happening when you don't pay attention.

[*Mrs. Rigsdale places an "x" next to "Justice" and "Luce" on the class list. She turns to face the class.*]

Mrs. Rigsdale: Justice and Luce need to work on opening their listening ears and keeping their mouths shut.

Young Luce: Man, she's an ogre.

Young Justice: She's got her ways.

Young Luce: She's got a temper. She's hateful.

Mrs. Rigsdale: Luce, Justice, what did you say?

[*Young Justice and Young Luce do not respond.*]

Mrs. Rigsdale: What did you say?

Young Justice: You're an ogre.

Young Luce: Justice!

Mrs. Rigsdale: Follow me right now. Class, I'll be right back. [*To Young Justice and Young Luce:*] Let's go.

[*Young Justice and Young Luce follow her into the hallway. Mrs. Rigsdale stops and turns to them.*]

Mrs. Rigsdale: You two've got prison cells with your names on them. You're gonna end up just like your daddies.

[*Light fades.*]

Act One, Scene 4

Center stage: Cue light on Young Justice and Young Luce. who sit on top of the desks from elementary school.

Justice: We spent a few days in-school suspension for that.

Luce: Mrs. Rigsdale "did not approve" of some of the language you used for "a first grade child."

Justice: She had a hot temper. She expected first graders to stay quiet at all times. No compassion.

Luce: Compassion? She was heartless. She didn't care about any of us. You know she talked my mama into holding Citlali back.

Justice: Oh yeah? Why'd she hold her back?

Luce: "To help her in the long run"? Mama let Citlali start school when she was 4 cause of when her birthday was, but Rigsdale held her back. It was bad. Everyone called her "dummy."

Justice: I know Citlali didn't take any of that.

Luce: She did and she didn't. She's all tough at school but she'd come home crying. She hated to go to school. She cried every morning. They hurt her feelings so much, my mama had to bribe her a charm a day to go to school.

Justice: A charm a day?

Luce: You know those, those little charm necklaces were in style, those little, ugly plastic charms, you know what I mean? And if we made good grades, it was a Happy Meal or something for both of us, you know, something real special.

Justice: Citlali still in school?

Luce: Yeah, she graduated with honors last May. You know they gave her that hardship transfer when—

Justice: When your mama took off?

Luce: Yeah, she went to Snow Field, night classes. She's taking a couple of courses out at the community college now. She said Snow Field really helped her. She got all this one-on-one attention out there. Two, three, four teachers were in each class. If you had a question, a teacher would come over and sit right next to you, show you exactly what's going on. Mad attention. [*Luce looks stage left.*] Hey, you remember Mrs. Fox?

Justice: Ah man. There you go—Mrs. Fox.

Luce: She was a real nice lady, always had a smile on her face, like she was happy to see us. And her library.

Justice: She had a pile of books. She let us read anything we wanted. I'd pick up a big book and she'd say: [*imitating Mrs. Fox*] "You can do anything if you put your mind to it. You wanna read that. Let's read it."

Luce: Yeah. I read so many books in there. Books I never would've read.

Justice: [*still imitating Mrs. Fox*] "That's good, Luce, very good, very good." [*smiles*] You wanted to impress her.

Luce: You didn't? You know, no one paid me much mind when I made bad grades in elementary school. They said, "He doesn't care." "He's dumb." But Mrs. Fox turned on a switch. She'd listen when I had a question, explain stuff. She helped me read. She'd stay after when I didn't understand.

Justice: Yeah. She treated us like grown ups, didn't sugarcoat things. She stood up for us. Tried to keep me outta trouble.

Luce: Outta trouble? You punched that white boy right in front of her. What was his name?

Justice: [*looking at his right hand*] Stanley.

Luce: Yeah, Stanley. Hey you remember Tye and Shahida? No more beautiful things walkin'. Pretty. Pretty as the devil.

Justice: Yeah, they were. I remember them. Hangin' out.

Luce: Puppy love. [*Luce looks stage left.*]

Stage left: Cue light on Mrs. Fox's classroom. Desks are in five groups of four, pairs facing one another. Artwork covers the walls. In the corner is a library nook with beanbags and pillows piled on soft carpet. Books are on the shelves next to the pillows, stacked in neat piles on the floor, and in baskets along the edge of the carpet. Tye and Shahida stand next to Young Justice and Young Luce, talking. Stanley crosses the room quickly and stands in front of Young Luce and Young Justice. The hallway to the classroom is covered with bulletin boards.

Tye: Want to eat lunch outside today?

Young Justice: Okay. [*looks at Stanley and then Young Luce*] We'll catch up with you outside.

Shahida: [*looking at Tye*] We can eat inside?

[*Center stage: Luce stands*]

Luce: Here comes Stanley.

Stanley: [*to Young Luce*] Where do you wanna eat, Chihuahua? Yo Quiero Taco Bell?

Young Luce: Man, don't say that.

Luce: [*to Justice*] Why's he gotta be like that? I never bothered him. Barely ever said anything to him.

Stanley: [*to Young Luce*] Yo Quiero Taco Bell!

Luce: That's all he had? Really? Man, Mexicans don't even eat at Taco Bell.

[*Young Luce looks at Tye and Shahida.*]

Young Luce: [*to Stanley*] Look, I feel you comin' at me in a racist way. I appreciate it if you didn't do that.

Justice: [*to Luce*] You were such a nice fuckin' kid. Polite. Mrs. Fox taught you well. [*looking stage left*] Still he gives you no respect.

Tye: He thinks he's the baddest boy walkin'.

Stanley: That's right. The baddest. [*looking at Justice*] Untouchable.

[*Justice stands.*]

Luce: [*to Justice*] He doesn't even know what's comin'. If we'd been in the cafeteria I would've hit him in the head with my tray by now.

Young Justice: Man, let it go. Nobody's trying to face up to you.

Luce: Look at you, Justice, bringin' about the peace.

[*Stanley steps toward Young Luce. Luce steps toward stage left.*]

Stanley: Yo Quiero Taco Bell!

Tye: Stop it, Stanley!

Stanley: Yo Quiero Taco Bell!

Education Is a Small Part of the Life I Have to Live

Young Justice: [*to the girls*] We'll meet you outside.

[*Tye and Shahida exit down the hallway offstage.*]

Young Justice: You don't gotta be over everybody, Stanley.

[*Young Justice and Young Luce step past Stanley and exit the classroom into the hallway.*]

Stanley: You know what, Justice? You stink. Always wearin' the same raggedy clothes. [*Stanley follows them into the hallway. Justice takes a step toward stage left. Justice and Luce stand next to each other.*] Same pair of pants, same shirt, every day? You don't have any other clothes?

Young Justice: Man, enough. Be smooth.

Luce: He's just mad messin' with everybody, 'cause he got no friends.

Young Luce: [*touches Young Justice's shoulder*] Let's go, Justice.

Stanley: Why don't y'all roll on outside with that stink. The Chihuahua's ready for Taco Bell now

[*Mrs. Fox enters downstage at the end of the hallway.*]

Young Justice: [*raising his voice*] Stanley! Shut up!

Stanley: Shut up? [*pushing Young Justice.*]

Mrs. Fox: [*walking faster*] Boys?

[*Stanley shoves Young Justice into Young Luce. Young Justice and Young Luce lose their balance.*]

Mrs. Fox: Stanley, step back. Right now. Justice, Luce, you alright?

[*Stanley does not move. Young Justice gains his balance and turns to face Stanley. Mrs. Fox helps Young Luce.*]

Stanley: [*steps toward Young Justice*] What? You gonna do something?

[*Center stage: Luce touches Justice's shoulder as Young Justice hits Stanley's chin with his fist. Stanley falls to the floor. He begins to cry, holding his hand to his mouth.*]

Luce: And that's what you call Justice.

Mrs. Fox: Justice! Damnit.

[*Mrs. Fox grabs the box of tissues off her desk from inside the classroom and returns to Stanley, Young Justice, and Young Luce. She and Stanley begin walking downstage.*]

Mrs. Fox: Let's go.

[*Young Justice and Young Luce follow. Mrs. Fox looks over her shoulder at Young Luce and Young Justice, and then in the direction of Luce and Justice at center stage as she and the boys exit downstage.*]

Justice: [*to Luce*] You were smooth with it. But that boy, no little girls liked him, you're right. And he wasn't likin' that. He just needed to be smooth, not bad.

Luce: He just needed to be smooth? Smooth? Man, he was a racist cracker. [*Justice laughs.*]

Act One, Scene 5

Stage left: Cue light on Mrs. Fox who waits outside the principal's office. Young Justice and Young Luce exit from the office.

Mrs. Fox: Justice, will you wait here? I want to talk to the principal before he calls your gran'ma. Luce, you can head to lunch, okay?

[*Young Justice sits in one of the two chairs along the wall. Young Luce departs. Mrs. Fox enters the office and sits down.*]

Principal Eaton: You can't help him. Justice knocked Stanley's tooth out. I know, [dismissively *waving his hand*] Stanley's no good, but we can't have students fighting. Period. You know the DR on student behavior.

Mrs. Fox: I know the discipline response policies include expulsion for a fight, and I'm asking you not to expel Justice.

Principal Eaton: I can recommend expulsion, and I am within my rights to do so.

Mrs. Fox: Stanley has been taunting the kids in my class all year. You know that. He was in here 2 weeks ago. He targets Justice and Luce in particular. He knows what upsets them.

Principal Eaton: Mrs. Fox, my options are limited here. The DRSB is clear. You know that regardless of who started the altercation, fighting that results in serious physical injury requires off-site, long-term suspension or expulsion. It's a 5.10 because Justice knocked Stanley's tooth out.

Mrs. Fox: A 5.10? Justice is a good student. He's getting As and Bs. He does well in his classes. He needs our support, our help, not a reputation.

Principal Eaton: Are you suggesting we set up a support-team meeting in preparation for his return?

Mrs. Fox: No. An s-team meeting? I'm referring to the fact that his cousin, Devisha, was just murdered. He needs our support. He doesn't need to be evaluated for special ed. He had a fight. I'm not worried about his learning.

Principal Eaton: None of that means he might not benefit from testing. You know, a fight like this can be a red flag. You're not a school psychologist or a social worker. You're a teacher, and I expect our students to behave responsibly and with restraint at all times. Justice is in middle school now.

Mrs. Fox: Restraint. And what about verbal restraint? Do we have the same expectation?

Principal Eaton: The DRSB addresses harassment. Persistent harassment is a category 4 violation that results in off-site short- or long-term suspension. Persistent harassment based on actual or perceived age, disability, gender, gender expression, [*pause*] personal appearance, race, sexual orientation, status as a victim of an intrafamily offense, religion, matriculation, [*takes a breath*] or place of residence—all category 4 behaviors.

Mrs. Fox: So Justice faces expulsion, but no matter how many times Stanley bullies other students, because persistent harassment is only a category 4 behavior he will only be suspended?

Principal Eaton: We have a history of productive communication, here, Mrs. Fox, let's not jeopardize it now. I suspect Luce and Justice will have other unpleasant encounters, face other bullies.

Mrs. Fox: Unpleasant encounters?

Principal Eaton: They need to learn to deal with it.

Mrs. Fox: It?

Principal Eaton: Yes.

Mrs. Fox: We deal with it every day, sir.

Principal Eaton: [*pauses*] Then they need to learn to refrain from fighting when it happens.

Mrs. Fox: They're 11 years old, sir. They're trying to figure out who they are, where they fit into this world. Luce gets it from all sides from white kids, black kids, other Chicanos. And Justice faces extreme poverty. Stanley rips open those wounds open, again and again.

Principal Eaton: Mrs. Fox, I appreciate your concern, and I am well aware of how old these boys are. Now, I don't want to keep you from your work any longer. [*He shifts his attention to papers on his desk.*] If you would, please drop Justice off at ISS on your way back to your classroom. Thank you for sharing your concern.

[*Light fades.*]

Stage left: Cue light Mrs. Fox as she exits the principal's office. Mrs. Fox looks at Young Justice and sits down next to him.

[*Lights fade.*]

Act One, Scene 6

Stage right: Cue light Mrs. Fox and Young Justice in Belysa's kitchen. Open books are on the table. Mrs. Fox takes folders from her bag and opens one. She places worksheets next to the books and sits next to Young Justice.

Mrs. Fox: Are you doing okay today?

Young Justice: I'm okay.

Mrs. Fox: You don't look okay. I know you're thinking about Devisha. Is there anything I can do for her family? Do her folks live nearby?

Young Justice: [*looks at Mrs. Fox*] She lived here. My gran'ma took her in when her mama was killed.

Mrs. Fox: Oh. I'm so sorry. How's your gran'ma holdin' up?
Young Justice: I don't know. She's been strugglin'. She's real sad. Everybody keeps crying. My sisters, too. Gran'ma's plannin' the funeral. They're all at the church right now.

Mrs. Fox: I know it feels unfair, and it is. I won't tell you I know when it will feel better. But if you need me, I'm here. I'm here for you.

Young Justice: I've been trying to help out. Gran'ma wants me to focus on my studies. But I can't.

Mrs. Fox: It makes sense your attention's not on school.

Young Justice: It's not. It's not on school or learning right now.

Mrs. Fox: Only one of these worksheets is due Friday. You wanna go over it tomorrow?

Young Justice: Mrs. Fox, he made me snap. It was like a reflex. He won't stop saying stuff. He thinks it's funny. I've never hit someone like that before. I didn't mean to knock his tooth out.

Mrs. Fox: I know you didn't.

Young Justice: But I've heard it. I've heard it from teachers. "He's from Third Street. He's gonna be just like his daddy."

Mrs. Fox: You're doing very, very well at school.

Young Justice: Don't try to sugarcoat nothin', Mrs. Fox.

Mrs. Fox: I'm not. You are doing well, but I know you're sad about Devisha and worried about your gran'ma and your sisters.

Young Justice: They look to me; you know what I mean? My sisters they look to me when they're scared. My gran'ma's been looking for work. They keep cutting her hours. She's been takin' care of all of us since my mama left. She's the strength of all of us. But she can't do it all.

Mrs. Fox: She can't do it all?

Young Justice: You know what I mean, she's workin' as hard as she can, but she can't do it all.

Mrs. Fox: I care about you so much. And if I could keep you from fights at school, from racist kids, from losing Devisha, I would. I wish I could. You deserve better. But I can't. This is a hard place to live. I know you know it's not easy. [*pauses*] I want you to know you can call me anytime, okay? Call me.

Young Justice: Okay.

Mrs. Fox: Please. Will you do something for me? [*Young Justice looks at Mrs. Fox.*] I want you to be careful, okay? Be careful.

[*Light fades.*]

Act Two, Scene 1

Center stage: Cue light on a prison dormitory, rows of bunk beds with white sheets. Luce sits on the top bunk. Justice stands.

Justice: They found Devisha in the park. Her throat was cut. [*Justice takes off his gray jacket. He wears a gray jumpsuit with a white t-shirt underneath.*] Mrs. Fox helped me make it through the end of seventh grade. She came to my house and made sure I was doing things I needed to do. Every day she stopped by after school.

Luce: And when you got back you had Stan running from you. He was scared of you. You were the baddest boy walking.

Justice: I made a 97 on those end-of-the-year tests, and my gran'ma got these letters askin' if I might want go to another school. She gave me the decision to make. I wanted to stay in public school.

Luce: You wanted to stay with your people.

Justice: I wanted to stay with my friends.

Justice: [*to the audience*] But then everything really went downhill. It just all went away. Gran'ma lost her job and my little sister got sick.

Stage right: Light follows Young Justice as he paces in front of his house. Justice watches from center stage.

Justice: Day by day, it looked scary. My mind was made up: I was not going to go out there and sell drugs. I was going to better myself, get good grades, stay in school. I thought about it every night. But then I started skipping school. I started to work.

[*Young Justice stops at the corner outside his apartment building and leans against the wall.*]

[*Light fades.*]

Act Two, Scene 2

Stage right: In Belysa's kitchen there are new appliances on the kitchen counter, a new refrigerator, and new chairs and table. A picture of Belysa, Young Justice, his three sisters, and his cousin is framed on the wall. Young Justice enters with two bags of groceries and puts them away quietly. He covers a plate of leftovers and cleans the kitchen counter. He pulls a blanket over Belysa, who is asleep in the living room, and checks on his sisters, who are asleep in a tidy row of three twin beds. He returns to the kitchen and pours a glass of water. Young Luce knocks on the door.

Young Luce: Hey man. What's up? Where've you been?

[*Young Luce sits down.*]

Young Justice: Around. I've been helpin' out.

Young Luce: You gonna come to school?

Young Justice: I come to school, man.
Young Luce: Not like you used to. You hoping you'll get in trouble, so you'll have an excuse to stay home?

Young Justice: I'm taking care of my gran'ma and my sisters and paying the bills.

Young Luce: I get it. My uncle's is like a drug house. I could work, but I'm going to school.

Young Justice: You don't get it. There was no food, no lights, no grocery money, no lunch money, nothin'. What was I supposed to do?

Young Luce: Man, it's really bad at school.

Young Justice: It's bad here.

Young Luce: No, I mean, I don't really hang with nobody besides you and some of my brothers. You know, I'm cool with everybody, but it's not the same.

Young Justice: Man, going to school's not gonna fix my problems. We got nothin'. I gotta help out. Devisha's dead. Her mom's dead. Our moms split. Dads locked up. We're outta their hands!

Young Luce: What if we take it a whole different way? You know what I mean? A corporate job or something. $20 an hour. Legal.

Young Justice: When, Luce? In 5 years when we graduate from high school? In 2 years when we get work permits? Yeah right. We're gonna be flippin' burgers or pumpin' gas.

Young Luce: This is not your way of life, Justice.

Young Justice: Way of life? What about your uncle? He hasn't been providin' for you and Citlali?

Young Luce: It might be my uncle's. But it's not yours.

Young Justice: [*raising his voice*] How can I come home to an empty refrigerator and not fill it? I'm not letting them go hungry.

Young Luce: I'm not asking you to.

Young Justice: But you are.

Young Luce: [*blows into his hands and begins pacing*] It's getting colder. You gonna be able to keep the heat on? I can always ask my uncle to—

Young Justice: No. We're good, Luce. I got it.

Young Luce: You got it? You're not comin' to school.

Young Justice: I'm too busy, too tired. I get home at 2 or 3, man. I shower, sleep a couple of hours, get up, catch the bus if I can, try to stay awake through lunch, maybe make it to English, then I gotta start walking back. I can't be in school and in the streets.

Young Luce: Let me talk to my uncle?

Young Justice: I'm not taking handouts and your uncle isn't givin' any. It's just the way it is. It doesn't mean it's for a lifetime.

Young Luce: [*stops pacing and looks out the window*] I'm gonna walk with you tonight, alright?

Young Justice: Naw, man. It's gonna be brick outside. You don't wanna be out there.

Young Luce: I'm walking with you.

Young Justice: You should stay home.

Young Luce: I'm gonna walk with you.

[*Light fades.*]

Act Three, Scene 1

Center stage: Cue light on Luce walking toward his bunk. He hops on the top bunk.

Luce: I'm gonna be valedictorian. [*Justice walks into the pod and sits on his bunk.*] I'm gonna be valedictorian.

Justice: What?

Luce: The teachers told me I'm valedictorian. I'm gonna give the speech.

Justice: Luce the bookworm?

Luce: I thought it was a joke at first, too, but they told me my score was highest of all the GED classes this year.

Justice: So, you're really writing a speech?

Luce: Yeah. And I'm gonna write it for all of us.

Justice: All of us?

Luce: You know, for us, from the neighborhood. Chicanos. Hispanics.

Justice: I'm Puerto Rican, man, Indian—

Luce: Dude, I know, Indian, and black. We've accomplished things in here. You know? Getting a GED, taking college courses.

Justice: [*smiles and grabs his book, notebook, and pen*] You comin' to sociology or are you gonna work on your speech?

Luce: I'm comin'.

[*Justice and Luce walk through corridors toward stage left.*]

Stage left: Cue lights an African American correctional officer in a navy blue uniform and a navy cap. He stands behind a podium at the end of the corridor, before a metal door. Justice and Luce walk the yellow line on the floor until they reach the podium.

Luce: They called me a young scholar.

Justice: They called you what?

Luce: Yeah. Young scholar.

Correctional Officer: Hold up. We got Count.

Luce: What? Man.

Justice: What's goin' on?

Luce: The Count's not right.

Correctional Officer: Step back against the wall.

[*Justice and Luce step back and lean against the wall.*]

Justice: We've got class tonight in school.

Correctional Officer: No one's going anywhere until the Count is clear.

Justice: [*opens his book*] You should write about our class.

Luce: What do you mean?

Justice: You know, some people without a background in sociology, they might think that we're able to do just what we want in society.

Luce: Right. Dr. Martin always talkin' about capitalism and wealth, poverty, and poor schools.

Justice: And poor nutrition and poor housing.

Luce: Low unemployment.

Justice: No employment.

Luce: Straight mom or gran'ma, nobody else. Daddy most of the time locked up or just gone. Government assistance that's not enough for self-sufficiency. All that determines whether you're successful in life or not. Right? You believe that?

Justice: Everybody's not going to be successful. They could, I mean, if the U.S. wanted to, if they wanted to stop crime they could stop it. Drugs. Selling. Everything. It's like a 360; everything is needed to make this one big complete circle. It's a shame how they throw crime in the mix to make it all work. [*looks at correctional officer*]

Luce: Prisons for profit. Slave labor. 49 cents a day in the cannery. 100 degree heat. It's crazy. It's not like we can go anywhere. We can't strike. Just imagine the big things we don't know. Things with the government we don't even know about.

Justice: Man, it's all for show, correctional education. It's about the labor. You know, they're trying to make it look good in here. Give us some education programs, access to a GED class, but they're puttin' us to work. Who wouldn't run that racket? We're free labor. They call prison a revolving door, but they make it a revolving door. It's just a program that's been going on for years, centuries. [*to the correctional officer:*] Do you know if we're gonna make it to go to class?

Correctional Officer: You know it can take 2 hours. The Count's still not clear.

Luce: You know, I feel you, but I'm not coming back. My mind's made up. I think about it every day. I have a nephew. He's a reason for me not to fail. I'm determined. I gotta do this for him. It's not about me anymore. It's about the kids.

Justice: We don't have kids, Luce.

Luce: Naw, I mean, kids out there. A lot of guys in here have kids out there. You know, there's only so many Hispanic guys here. I want to make like a statement to let people know that just 'cause we're Hispanic and some of us don't speak English doesn't mean that we're not smart, that we're stupid. I've met artists and people who speak two or three different languages.

Justice: You writing your speech right now, professor?

Luce: We're not in here to just to fill in the profile that we're trouble makers. We weren't born here. [*Luce holds up his sociology book.*] This shows that we can accomplish things even though we're in here. Some of these guys couldn't read when they got here. They read now. It's been a stepping stone.

Justice: Yeah, they discovered books in prison, that's a good thing. It's always good to gain more knowledge in anything, you know, but that don't necessarily mean it's going to help. People gotta eat, take care of their kids, keep a roof over their heads. How are they supposed to do that?

Luce: But you were "AG" all those years, in all those CP classes in high school.

Justice: Yeah, so? College prep wasn't payin' the utility bill. And they didn't want us out there anyway. No matter how many Mrs. Foxes we get, we're not ever gonna fix that. I was in "AG" classes, but I was the only black guy in there. And that's all those white people ever saw. The teachers recognized it, too.

Luce: Yeah, I was the only Mexican in my class. Every time my homeroom teacher turned around, she looked at me. I don't know why. She looked at me like I was an alien or something. I guess she wasn't used to seeing a person who looks like me. They looked at us like they expected trouble. I'd never had people do that before. It felt awkward.

Justice: High school was a whole different game.

Luce: What d'you mean high school was a whole different game? You were there 39 days.

Justice: You know, we were way out past 36th Street. The school was huge. More people. Tons of students. They gave you work, but if you had questions, too bad.

Luce: You were pretty much on your own, huh?

Justice: Yeah. There were like 30 of us in the whole school. And it's not like if you fell asleep, anyone was gonna wake you up and tell you what's goin' on.

Luce: Yeah, the students just wanted me to tell stories about where we grew up.

Justice: What'd you tell 'em?

Luce: Nothin'. I mean, I was always in ISS or the front office.

Justice: What you mean? What were you doin' there?

Luce: Answerin' phones, sorting the mail, deliverin' messages. Runnin' the show! You know, after so many write-ups, you get ISS. So, I'd be late on purpose, and I'd do better in in-school suspension than in the classroom. I'd do a day's worth of work in 2 hours. I made better grades in ISS.

Justice: So you purposely got in trouble? That's crazy.

Luce: In the second 9 weeks, not that you were there, I had 3 weeks in school suspension, and in 2 days I had done all the work, all As and Bs. And they let me come in the front office and help out the rest of the time. I always got distracted in the classroom. I couldn't concentrate. In the classroom, you know, the teacher was always like, "Oh, hold on, she needs help first." I would wait, but I couldn't get the attention I needed, you know what I mean? I'd stop tryin' on my own and start talkin' to my friends. Maybe I wasn't determined enough? I used to like school. I don't know what changed.

Justice: Naw, you got work done. You just went to ISS to do it. You know that's fucked up?

Luce: I didn't have your book smarts.

Justice: You do now.

Luce: Man, I didn't know I was smart until I got to prison.

[*Lights fade.*]

Act Three, Scene 2

Center stage: Cue light on Luce.

Luce: [*faces audience*]
I go home December 11th
I'll be home for Christmas

with Citlali
and my nephew.
I can't wait.
I'm nervous.
Scared.
Real scared.
But I'm ready
to get in a better place,
a better situation in life.

When mama started doing bad
and left us
it was hard times.
Citlali and I had to move into my uncle's.
Mama had kept us fresh
and I wanted to keep up in the race.
I couldn't be the turtle.
But I had to be the turtle.
I wanted to be the rabbit.
I had to be the rabbit.

Justice wouldn't let me deal.
He flipped my cash for me
but he wouldn't let me work with him.
He told me the money was more addictive than the drug.
He was right.
I worked with my uncle,
I got a taste of the money
and it was on from there.

I just want to make sure my nephew realizes
that I support him,
that no matter who puts us down,
that he knows we are proud people.
We are smart.
We are descendants from the Aztecs.
I want to see him take opportunities.
It's about him.

I want to enable him to see
all the paths he can take.

And my mind's made up.
I can't come back.
They're only two things to choose:
either you go back out there and get it right,
or you come back.
Or you can die.

I'm not too good to work at McDonald's.
I don't want to flip burgers,
but I will because I need an income.
I picked up trash here,
so I'm not too good to work there.
I did my upholstery here,
so there's probably a job I could get:
upholstery.

I might try to enroll in community college.
I was talking to an officer
about someone he knows
who could help me enroll.
You know.
I'm just ready to further my education
really.

I'd like to start a program
a non-for-profit
to talk to kids
when
where
everything starts
in elementary school,
in middle school,
in detention,
in the streets,
help them, tell them

what prison is really like.
I feel like it would have made a difference in my life.

[*Light dims.*]

Center stage: Cue light on Justice.

Justice: [*to the audience*]
Society molds your life for you.
Rehabilitation.
It's a hopeless cause.
The administration doesn't care if you change.
They know you can't do anything about it.
Prison education is all for show.
Trying to make something look good.
Make it look like a rehabilitation facility.
When in all actuality, we already know,
It's a revolving door.

They say you gotta bury the past and move on
but how can you?
When society won't let you?
I'd like to study legal theory
or science.
I could go out there,
put on a pair of glasses,
pair of slacks,
and a tie,
cut my dreads off,
take it a whole different way.
But they're gonna ask.
I see you have all this education
and a felony on your record?
I have three strikes against me:
I'm black,
I'm male,
I'm a felon.
I can't see going to flip no burgers,

getting paid $5 an hour,
getting paid $200 a week—
that was never even enough to pay the rent.

I'm trying to better myself
all these college classes,
but regardless of the education in here,
there isn't too much I can do out there
except what I have been doing.
Education is a small part of the life I have to live.

My gran'ma died while I've been in here.
I couldn't be there for her.
I missed her funeral.
At night I'm up crying about her
my sisters
my family.
I'm a grown man,
and I'm crying at night.
She was the strength of all of us.
I didn't even get to say goodbye.

My sisters are all still in school
doin' good.
The oldest is workin'
through the co-op program at school
for the grocery store on Ninth.
She wants to go to the university.
I want to help her do that.
I want to be there for my sisters.

It's sad, but the streets,
it's all I see.
Since I was 12,
I was hustling, selling dope,
comin' home at 2 or 3,
takin' a shower, goin' to school.
I'm not saying it's going to last a lifetime,

But it's all I see.
It's just a way of life.
I've still got time.

[*Light fades.*]

Method

In *Ethnotheatre* Saldaña (2011) articulated distinctions between research and art, and for us, the movement from interview transcripts to script production demanded a multilayered process. In this section, we describe some of this layering. The representation in this chapter began with in vivo coding and sociologically constructed coding, narrative analysis (Clandinin & Connelly, 2000; Coffey & Atkinson, 1996), and ethnopoetic representation (Glesne, 2006; Norum, 2000) in the first iterations of this research (Anders, 2007, 2011; Anders & Noblit, 2011). In seeking to transform these forms of understanding into a script, we worked together as researchers and a screenwriter across the following process. We first read the narrative analyses and poetic representations again. Second, we sketched two composite narratives, which informed the speech and action of Young Justice/Justice and Young Luce/Luce. We then created scenes that reflected both the repeated sentiment that "education is a small part of the lives that many live" and lived experiences with education, with references to elementary school, middle school, high school, and a college course in prison. Based on the aims of this particular iteration, we chose deliberately to include experiences of school in the action and body of text. Next, we generated ideas about conflict from the data, and worked to include conflict in explicit and implicit ways. To do so, we returned to the original interview transcripts to understand the nuances of relationships with friends, family members, and teachers to analyze language, the articulations of internal struggles, and political exposition about poverty, race, prison, and correctional education. Saldaña (2011) might call this process the act of character and plot development. The two composite narratives were created from actual incidents students had described at school and in their neighborhoods. The first version of the script reflected verbatim speech from interview transcripts. Then, just as we returned to early analyses, we returned to the literature on youth, school leaving, school push out, incarceration, for-profit prisons, and prison abolition. Additionally, we spent time reviewing current public school discipline policies and special education practices.

We moved then to the most recursive process in building the script—revising and refining language of speech and language of memory from lived experiences. The reasons for this are threefold. First, we approached the project as one in which we would "write to know" (Goodall, 2000). That is, although we had sketched the arc of the script with two composite narratives, we did not know in what moment, or with what moment, it would end. Through writing, we came to know the multiple possibilities of representation. Second, as two white female researchers and an African American male screenwriter, we were aware of our immediate effect on the text as editors. The first versions of the script were faithful to the transcripts (verbatim) in order to capture the tenor of the interviews. As we edited, however, we aimed to achieve a truth that reflected the constraints of an interview study versus, for example, an ethnography. Though we sought pace and dramatic tension, we used the students' own words as much as possible, wherever possible. We wanted to represent the original materials as much as we could, even as we sought to create a certain pace for the script and dramatic tension in and across scenes.

The script's foundations are built on the lives and truths of the students who became Luce and Justice. Our goal was to reach future teachers, new teachers, and veteran teachers with this text. This was a challenge for us, as it meant trying to write against our (Anders's and Swain's) embodiments of whiteness and female gender as researchers. If we speak through our bodies and our experiences, then speech and the language we use to interpret experience is situated by our bodies. How might we write as white women about white supremacist capitalist patriarchy (hooks, 1999) and the whitestream practices of public schooling using data saturated with experiences of racism, and neoliberal policies dominated by whiteness, to an audience of teachers—the majority of whom are also white and female? We question whether it is possible, even as we work against our racisms. We present one attempt here. Though we strive to challenge majoritarian narratives and to defy denials of racism (Solórzano & Yosso, 2008; Krog, 1998), as Bell (1992) warns, we risk reifying that which we work against. This work is situated in the neoliberal and whitestream landscape we critique as we are already always situated by the historical and political contexts of our lives (Grande, 2004). It does not exist outside of it. In our pursuit to deconstruct the spectacle of poverty, the stereotype of thug, the hysteria around the idea of a "criminal," we may contribute the regime of a single story (Adichie, 2009; Ferguson, 2000)—reductionist reenactments too often celebrated in Hollywood. Third, those working with performative texts and ethnodrama might name this part of our process working with the development of lines and plot. We hesitate to use that language here. For us, such language created distance we did not want between what we knew to have been lived experience and what someone else might call with detachment: character development or plot.

Last, we wrote nine versions of the script, revising scope, setting, narratives, stage direction, and language, and incorporating feedback from multiple sources: anonymous reviewers from three reader theater workshops Gabriel and Lester facilitated, and colleagues in foundations of education and higher education who are committed to challenging systemic inequities facing targeted youth. Also, we invited feedback from one of the original participants with whom Anders keeps in touch.

The process of dramatizing lived experience versus coding lived experience is one of the most profound differences between art and research for us. The theorizing in the script came from the production of language and scene. It was in the process itself; it was not separate from a process called analysis. We hope that as you read the script you encountered the complexity these children navigated growing up, and that if you found answers to questions you may have been asking that they were multiple and reflected a world much bigger than one child, one teacher, or a single story of explanation. Every story is always partial.

Finally, we offer gratitude to the men and women who participated in the Incarcerated Individuals Program and shared their time with us. The words on these pages would not exist without their narratives about what school was like for them growing up. We thank Rachael Gabriel and Jessica Nina Lester, as well, for their courage to bridge spaces of understanding across politics and schools.

Questions for Dialogue

1. Rules appear in various iterations throughout the script, beginning with the rules of the game stick, and continuing with school rules, rules of the street, rules in prison. Discuss and contrast the role and function of these rules. What is the difference between rules that protect or create order and rules that push out or criminalize?

2. How do the various representations of rules across the script compare with the ways in which teachers are so often encouraged to create behavior management plans, or to set clear expectations with clear consequences?
3. Consider the interaction between Mrs. Fox and Mr. Eaton regarding Young Justice and Stanley. What, if anything, could have been done differently?
4. Mrs. Rigsdale named Luce and Justice as "bad" early in their educational experience (first grade). Discuss the possible implications of the first grade construction of "bad boys" and "criminality" for the boys and their classmates. What was her interpretation of the boys' behavior? And what was the boys' interpretation of her behavior? What, if anything, could have happened differently between them?
5. Consider the descriptions and actions of Mrs. Fox. What do you imagine were her goals and motivation for her work with her students? What separated her from other teachers in Justice's and Luce's memory? How do you think she defined success with students she taught?

References

Abu-Lughod, L. (1991). Writing against culture. In R. G. Fox (Ed.), *Recapturing anthropology: Working in the present* (pp. 137–154). Santa Fe, NM: School of American Research Press.

Adichie, C. N. (2009). *The danger of a single story* [Video recording]. United States: The Sapling Foundation. TED Conferences, LLC.

Anders, A. D. (2007). *Revisiting the panopticon: Educational narratives from incarcerated youth.* (Doctoral dissertation). Available from Dissertations and Theses database (UMI No. 3257541).

Anders, A. D. (2011). Circuits of dominance in education and poverty: Control logic and counternarrative. *The Urban Review, 43*(4), 528–546.

Anders, A. D., & Noblit, G. W. (2011). Understanding effective higher education programs in prisons: Considerations from North Carolina's incarcerated individuals program. *Journal of Correctional Education, 62*(2), 77–93.

Bell, D. (1992). *Face at the bottom of the well: The permanence of racism.* New York: Basic Books.

Clandinin, D. J., & Connelly, F. M. (2000). *Narrative inquiry: Experience and story in qualitative research.* San Francisco: Jossey-Bass.

Coffey, A., & Atkinson, P. (1996). *Making sense of qualitative data: Complementary research strategies.* Thousand Oaks, CA: Sage.

Ferguson, A. A. (2000). *Bad boys: Public schools in the making of black masculinity.* Ann Arbor: University of Michigan Press.

Glesne, C. (2006). *Becoming qualitative researchers: An introduction.* Boston: Pearson.

Goodall, H. L. (2000). *Writing the new ethnography.* Lanham, MD: AltaMira Press.

Grande, S. (2004). *Native American social and political thought.* Lanham, MD: AltaMira Press.

Habermas, J. (1988). *Theory and practice* (J. Viertel, trans.). Boston: Beacon Press.

hooks, b. (1999). *Black looks: Race and representation.* Cambridge, MA: South End Press.

Krog, A. (1998). *Country of my skull: Guilt, sorrow, and the limits of forgiveness in the new South Africa.* New York : Three Rivers Press.

Noblit, G. W. (1999). *Particularities: Collected essays on ethnography and education.* New York: Peter Lang.

Noblit, G. W., Flores, S. Y., & Murillo, E. Jr. (2004). Introduction. In G. W. Noblit, S. Y. Flores, & E. G. Murillo, Jr. (Eds.), *Postcritical ethnography: Reinscribing critique* (pp. 1–52). Cresskill, NJ: Hampton.

Norum, K. E. (2000). School patterns: A sextet. *Qualitative Studies in Education, 13*(3), 239–250.

Saldaña, J. (2011). *Ethnotheatre: Research from page to stage.* Walnut Creek, CA: Left Coast Press.

Solórzano, D. G., & Yosso, T. J. (2008). A critical race counterstory of race, racism, and affirmative action. *Equity & Excellence in Education, 35*(2), 155–168.

Urrieta, L., Jr. (2003). Las identidades también lloran, identities also cry: Exploring the human side of indigenous Latina/o identities. *Educational Studies, 34*(2), 14–168.

Chapter 7

We Hear What We Know: Racial Messages in a Southern School

Kimberly J. Howard

"We hear what we know.... My kids are working toward hearing each other.... There are such diverse groups in my room. I talk to them different ways, and they are learning to accept that."—Tyrell Watters, black special-education teacher

"I try to get them to realize that everybody should be treated the same."—Sunday Thomas, white third-grade teacher

Introduction

Previous research that has explored how teachers make sense of race has focused heavily on pre-service teachers (e.g., Castro, 2010; Lensmire & Snaza, 2010; Lowenstein, 2009; Milner, 2007, 2008); far less work has explored how in-service teachers make sense of race in their classrooms (e.g., Earick, 2009). Research is needed to explicate the ways in which race influences the day-to-day interactions of teachers and students in the school community. As Webb (2001) pointed out, "helping teachers understand their own assumptions and beliefs about other ethnic and racial groups will go a long way in helping teachers understand how their pedagogy can be better adjusted to meet the needs of all children" (p. 251). Furthermore, Nasir and Hand (2006) identified a need for researchers to consider local environments for understanding race, culture, and learning, and they called for research that contributes to a deeper understanding of the ways in which teachers perceive broader issues of power and how they relate to classrooms.

To address the need for further research about teachers' understandings of race, the performance text in this chapter was created with data from a larger ethnographic case study. This project explored the intersections of *place*[1] and race, and how teachers made meaning of and performed race in a primarily white southern school, Redmen Elementary.[2] In this chapter, I focus specifically on exploring the *racial messages*, or the "implicit and explicit racial lessons that are taught and learned in schools" (Lewis, 2001, p. 782), that are sent to and by teachers. The goal of this script is to give examples of ways in which racial messages are connected to the geographic places in which they are told.

Coming to This Work

I am both an ESOL (English for Speakers of Other Languages) teacher and an educational researcher. As a teacher-researcher, I am uniquely positioned in dual roles: one, as a researcher looking at academic theories that aim to explain how race impacts the daily lives of teachers and students in schools, and two, as an ESOL teacher at Redmen Elementary. For the past 5 years, I have worked beside teachers and students—real people, with names and faces. My experiences as a practicing teacher have influenced this ethnographic study, from my research questions to my methods and my choice to represent this work as a performance.

Redmen Elementary is located in a state in the southeastern region of the United States. The area of Redmen, located just outside of Big City, is part of Farmers County, and is in the process of becoming its own municipality. Redmen Elementary School's population has doubled in the last 10 years, with a noticeable racial demographic change. Within a 10-year period, Redmen Elementary has gone from 88% white and 12% black to 74% white, 15% black, 7% Hispanic, and 4% Asian/Pacific Islander or Native American (National Center for Educational Statistics, 2012).

In the 5 years that I have worked at Redmen Elementary, I have heard some people speak of Redmen as home, whereas others have referred to it as racist. Most everyone agrees that it is changing. Through this lived experience in a place that some view as comforting and others view as threatening, I have realized that educational theories about race must do a better job of speaking to the evolving and multidimensional racialized experiences of key actors in public schools, specifically teachers. For this reason, I came to view performance as a way to both conduct and represent research (Denzin, 2003) in a way that speaks to the layered realities of how and why race matters in teachers' professional lives.

Theoretical Framework

In order to explore the racial messages that teachers both gave and received in Redmen Elementary School, I used a theoretical framework that drew mainly from critical race theory (Ladson-Billings & Tate, 1995; Lewis, 2001). At the same time, I added a lens that included concepts from critical geography (Creswell, 2004; Helfenbein & Taylor, 2009) in order to examine notions of place. Finally, I drew upon performance theory (Alexander, 2005; Butler, 2003; Conquergood, 2006; Madison, 2007) to better understand human actions as cultural performances. Though the complexity of each theoretical orientation cannot be captured within the confines of the space provided here, I briefly highlight the major premises of these distinct theories and examine how each was utilized in my study.

Critical Race Theory

Critical race theory (CRT) aims to disrupt, expose, challenge, and change racist policies that disenfranchise marginalized groups of people and practices that maintain the status quo (Ladson-Billings & Tate, 1995; Milner, 2008). Five basic tenets form the basis of CRT in education: (a) the centrality and intersectionality of race and racism; (b) the challenge to dominant ideology; (c) the commitment to social justice; (d) the centrality of experiential knowledge; and (e) the use of an interdisciplinary perspective (Solórzano, 1997).

CRT framed the way that I analyzed teachers' talk about and performances of race by providing a framework for understanding how race shapes and informs actions and interactions at a personal and structural level. It further supported the importance of counter-narratives and experiential knowledge. Additionally, CRT led me to utilize performance as a way to (re)present counter-narratives of black teachers and to name practices and language that challenge popular racial messages of colorblindness, such as denial, meritocracy, ambivalence, and goodwill (Blaisdell, 2005; Bonilla-Silva, 2003; Lensmire, 2008; Vaught & Castagno, 2008).

As both researcher and practitioner, I am committed to working toward creating more socially just[3] learning environments for students. For this reason, I used the tenets of CRT to inform the questions I asked from the outset of my study, as well as how I collected and analyzed data and created a performance text (Denzin, 2003). More specifically, as CRT scholars suggest, I aim to make my work challenging yet accessible to practitioners in the pursuit of social justice. Finally, CRT encourages an interdisciplinary approach toward research; in this study, though CRT largely drove my questions, methodologies, and (re)presentation of research, it also made room for me to draw upon critical geography and performance theory.

Critical Geography

Critical geographers hope to "reveal complicated connections between place, meanings, and power" (Creswell, 2004, p. 27), and put "issues of race, class, gender, sexuality, and a host of other social relations at the center of this analysis" (Creswell, 2004, p. 29). Helfenbein and Taylor (2009) explained that critical geography "insists on the addition of spatial analysis beyond the merely discursive" (p. 236). They asserted that:

> Although valuing and acknowledging the important work in recognizing the ways in which language helps to construct spaces, a Critical Geography seeks to then take the oft-neglected next step of analyzing how those spaces change, change over time, and impact the lived, material world. (pp. 236–237)

My work is informed by critical geography in that I aim to map connections between the sociocultural makeup of the school's community (e.g., demographic change, economic shifts) and the ways in which it is connected to teachers' racial messages at Redmen Elementary.

Performance Theory

Performance, a relatively recent way of understanding research subjects' words and (re)presentations in qualitative research, has multiple definitions (Denzin, 2003). In this study, I took up the notion of performance in three important ways. First, I used performance as a way to understand identity as performative. Butler (2003) described the performative nature of (racial or gender) identity as publicly regulated by social norms. Thus, I understood teachers' performances of race as informed by the social norms that regulated the school context of which they were a part, rather than simply individual choices. Viewing performances of race in this way provided a lens with which to analyze the structural rules, regulations, and social norms that shape social interactions. Further, this perspective allowed me to acknowledge personal agency and subjectivity, while leaving room for possibilities of change.

Second, I used performance theory to reflect on my role as a teacher-researcher. As an ESOL teacher who co-taught with mainstream teachers in multiple classrooms, my observations were layered, and performances in themselves. In this study, I reflected (in concrete terms, in my research journal and analytic memos) on *how* my performance as a teacher, white researcher, friend, and co-worker influenced observations and interviews.

Finally, performance theory was also used to create a performance text (Alexander, 2005; Denzin, 2003). My decision to (re)present findings through performance was motivated by my belief, like Madison's (1998), that "...performance becomes the vehicle by which we travel to the worlds of subjects and enter domains of intersubjectivity that problematize how we categorize who is 'us' and who is 'them' and how we see ourselves with 'other' and different eyes" (p. 282). Viewing performance in this way illustrates how performative texts have the potential to capture and allow others to experience the complexity of teachers' racial messages.

Method and Representation

Performance methodology. A performance-oriented lens informed how I collected, analyzed, and (re)presented data in this project. Conquergood's (2006) concept of *co-performative witnessing,* which was further explained by Madison (2007), helped me to organize and understand observing in the school in which I worked. Co-performative witnessing means to be "radically engaged and committed, body-to-body, in the field...a politics of the body deeply in action with Others" (Conquergood, personal communication, cited in Madison, 2007, p. 826), or said another way, "to be inside the breath and pulse of cultural performance as a feeling, sensing, being, and doing witness" (Madison, 2007, p. 829). Teachers' racial messages are an abstract concept in many ways, but co-performative witnessing made room for a depth of insight that would not have been possible from interviews or observations alone.

Being a teacher in Redmen Elementary for 5 years meant that I was not simply observing from the outside. I was inside, and invested in this school; thus, I heard more than verbal statements. I noticed the subtle ways that issues and attitudes were expressed because I was part of insider conversations. I experienced the same pressures that teachers faced from their school community, and the challenges inherent in the everyday practice of teaching. I, too, had multilayered relationships with students and their parents. Because of this, I was able to ask questions that might otherwise have been hidden from view, as I looked at the participants as performers within layers of ideologies, social constraints, and political positions that influenced the racial messages that were sent and received.

My 5 years of sustained engagement with the school as a full-time teacher and educational scholar, roles that sometimes coincided and sometimes ran contradictory paths, supported my position that researchers should engage in co-performative witnessing. For example, as you will see in Act Three of the performance text, I moved between my identities as an ESOL teacher, researcher/observer, colleague, and in some cases, friend. Each of these identities, while perhaps limiting at times, also allowed me to participate in an ongoing dialogue that shed light on intentions, interpersonal and professional constraints, and unplanned observations in different venues.

Study Design, Data Gathering, and Analysis

The design of this study was an ethnographic case study. "Ethnography is the work of describing a culture" (Spindler & Spindler, 1987, p. 3), or a study of "what people do, what people know, and the things people make and use" (Spradley, 1980, p. 5). In this study, I was particularly interested in understanding the intersections of the place of Redmen Elementary and the teachers' culturally mediated racial messages. Drawing from the ethnographic work of Jan Nespor (1997), I framed the place of Redmen Elementary as "an intersection in social space, a knot in a web of practices that stretch into complex systems beginning and ending outside the school" (p. xiii).

Given my theoretical framework, I understood the school, uniquely situated in the area of Redmen, as fundamental to understanding the teachers' racial messages. My view of Redmen Elementary as a web of social interactions required more than simply describing the context of the school. Rather, I centered my questions on how the area of Redmen and the teachers' racial messages were intertwined in time and space, and in this particular place of Redmen Elementary. Thus, I framed this work as an ethnographic case study because I investigated what teachers do and know, and how they use cultural resources to make meaning of race for themselves, each other, and their students.

The study was conducted in a large predominantly white elementary school in the southeastern region of the United States. Participants were chosen through *intensity sampling,* or "excellent or rich examples of the phenomenon of interest, but not highly unusual cases" (Patton, 2002, p. 235). Five teacher-participants were selected based on the following criteria: teaching core subjects; representing the school's racial diversity among teaching staff (black and white); representing diversity in grade levels taught; and displaying a willingness and having experience in working with racially, ethnically, and culturally diverse students. These teachers were selected[4] by community nominators because they were most likely to be able to express ideas about the study's focus on race based on their experience and reported success in working with racially diverse students.

Before beginning formal data collection for this study, I was a graduate student and an ESOL teacher for 3 years. In my fourth and fifth years of teaching at Redmen Elementary, I collected formal data for the project over a 14-month period. Primary data sources included a total of 15 semi-structured interviews with 5 teacher participants (each teacher was interviewed three times), two focus groups with the 5 teacher participants (one with the white teachers and one with the black teachers), and 20 semi-structured observations of these teachers' classrooms. Additionally, I collected 14 months of field notes, visual data (photographs), and observations of teachers' meetings. Finally, I conducted seven interviews with diverse community representatives. I selected these community representatives based on community nominations that indicated that these people would be able to offer insight about racial and cultural changes in the Redmen area over time. Thus, each community representative was a long time (30 years or more) resident of the Redmen area.

I used performance analysis to construct a performance text (Denzin, 2003) based on events and dialogues recorded in the data described above. In order to analyze data, I conducted a pattern analysis, where data were reduced, displayed, and interpreted to draw conclusions (patterns) from the data (Miles & Huberman, 1994). As I analyzed data for racial messages (Lewis, 2001) from observations, interviews, and field notes, I found the following patterns of racial messages sent and received by teachers: (a) in the classroom, (b) (in)visible, (c) the school place as a mold, and (d) we hear what we know. I used performative mapping, or "a collage-style performance that occurs through performed dialogue" (Leavy, 2009, p. 153) to create a performance text that focused on the themes specifically addressing racial messages.

Given the breadth of data, I had to significantly reduce the data. I selected examples of dialogue that appeared in my data and represented the four themes. Some study participants were represented directly in the script (e.g., Tyrell and Millie); however, although themes and data from each participant either directly or indirectly informed the text, not all of the participants were individually represented in the script. Instead, composite characters were created and indicated by generic pseudonyms "Ms. A" or "Ms. B."

Positionality

I am an ESOL teacher, a mother of biracial (black/white) children, and a white female in an interracial relationship. In the course of this study, I have become a confidant to participants who are also colleagues. For this reason, I am limited by my views and others' views of me, while at the same time I am able to see and hear more because of my diverse public and private identities. This duality has, for me, become part of the process of co-performative witnessing (Madison, 2007). Because of my layered personal and professional identities, I am aware of the contradictions and constraints that teachers may embody, regardless of their intentions.

In order to address this subjectivity, throughout the study I kept a research journal in which I documented my own biases (e.g., "I have a strong aversion to the Confederate flag that to me represents racism and hatred") and decisions about the research process itself (e.g., "Is it ethical to record this conversation?"). Before beginning this study, I conducted an autoethnographic study about my own racial identity in which I analyzed written data that represented 12 years of personal reflections (Howard, 2012). This project created a space for me to name my own past and present ideology as it pertains to race—an understanding of racism that had been limited to individual actions and beliefs, but has evolved into an understanding of racism as systemic—and recognize the multitude of factors (e.g., (de)racialized discourse, geographic location) that influence and impact how racial messages are both given and received. I acknowledge, nonetheless, that I still carry with me the limitations of being a privileged white female. Thus, this performance text is but one possible rendering of stories that could be told and retold in many different ways.

The performance text that follows, *We Hear What We Know*, is intended to be performed by a group. The opening dialogue begins by painting a picture of the multidimensional layers of this school place and its community through the words of four very differently positioned community members. This is intended to set the stage for the audience to picture the kind of place that Redmen Elementary has been and is today. Act One, "I Just Don't See How It Affects Us Here," (re)presents an observation of a fifth-grade classroom where I worked as the ESOL teacher with a small group of students.

This scene captures my observations of a single event and actual dialogue, and (re)presents my first theme, racial messages in the classroom. This act (re)presents patterns that I observed in the classrooms and in the interviews with white teacher participants. Act Two, "It's Here All the Time!," draws upon data collected from interviews and the focus group with black teacher participants. These quotes reflect these participants' explanations of the ways in which their bodies symbolized racial messages that were often beyond their control within the school community. This act correlates with the second theme, "(in)visible," because as the participants explained, they were simultaneously hyper-visible and invisible at the school. Act Three, "Our Multicultural School," (re)presents the theme of the school place as a mold, using direct quotes and actions from an observation of a team of third-grade teachers. This scenario demonstrates that despite a lack of explicit conversation around the concept of race at this school, race does in fact shape how people are categorized in this place. These categorizations had an impact on how students were grouped and understood by teachers. The final act, "You Live in America and You Don't Celebrate Thanksgiving?," illustrates the theme "we hear what we know." It (re)produces events and conversations from several classroom observations, interviews, and teacher meetings. This final act demonstrates how teachers send and receive racial messages to other teachers and students based on their background knowledge.

The performance text has 13 characters, but it is possible to assign multiple parts to the same actors for smaller groups. There are no props needed, but readers should read the director's notes in italics for explanations of the scene or characters' actions. The script is written so that actors can read from their seats in a circle or from chairs lined up facing a larger audience. The text is intended to be performed in different ways, and will be understood differently by audience members. These differences in understanding should support the notion that we are all "co-performers in each other's lives" (Mienczakowski, 2000, p. 2), and that racial messages, even when experienced in tandem, can have multiple readings.

We Hear What We Know

Characters

Narrator: this voice sets the scene in each act

Kimberly: a white female ESOL teacher and researcher, age 31

Tonya: a white female retired teacher from Redmen Elementary, born in Redmen, age 58

Willow: a white female parent in a biracial Latino/white family, born in Redmen, age 31

Otis: a black male janitor at Redmen schools, born in Redmen, age 80

Jaime: a white female district office leader, born in Farmers County age 61

Tyrell Watters: a black male teacher, born in a southern state, age 27

Millie Blackwell: a black female teacher, born in another state in the South, age 58

Ms. A: a white female teacher (composite character)

Ms. B: a white female teacher (composite character)

Ms. C: a white female teacher (composite character)

Janeth: a Mexican immigrant female, fifth grader, English Language Learner

Maya: an African American female fifth grader

Khan: a Vietnamese male fourth grader, English Language Learner

Introductory Dialogue

Narrator: The script begins with monologues describing this place called Redmen. All characters speak from their seats, representing voices from the community.

Kimberly: Redmen is...

Tonya, Willow, Otis: Home

Willow, Tyrell, Millie: Racist.

Tonya, Willow, Otis, Jaime, Tyrell, Millie: Changing.

Kimberly: Tell me about Redmen.

Tonya: When I started school, everybody who lived here was just like me. We were all white. We were all middle-class. Our families all had large parcels of land. And you know, we, everybody was just exactly like me. It was like, overnight we got all the businesses and industries, the restaurants, the gas stations. It was just a small, little, rural, everybody-was-just-alike kind of place. And there are a lot of people who wish that it were still that way.

Kimberly: Tell me about Redmen.

Willow: When I was growing up, even though the teachers and staff were not supposed to be racist, I think they were. It wasn't a big deal back then if you were racist, because everybody was racist. When more races moved in, it started a new conversation. The people who've always been here, the ones whose bloodlines go way back, they hate it.

Kimberly: Tell me about Redmen.

Otis: I grew up sharecropping, and when I was coming up it was blacks was to theyself, and whites was to theyself. It wasn't like it is now, all mixed.

Kimberly: How about school?

Otis: I went to a little school called Valley View. It didn't go no higher than seventh grade. I had one teacher, and she taught all the way from first through seventh. So that's where I got my education. Well, at that time it ain't like the schools is now, the only high schoo' was Bates Academy High School in Farmers and you didn't have no transportation, no way of getting' down there, and so all I was able to get is seventh-grade education.

Kimberly: Tell me about Redmen.

Jaime: When I first came to the district office in 1994, as far as school size, a graduating class of 50 or 60 was big at that time. Redmen was just sort of sleepy, very country I suppose. Redmen has changed so, so much. It's going from extremely rural to beginning to urbanize a bit, and becoming a bedroom community of Big City. It's certainly become more . . . more diverse and I'm sure that creates some struggles in that area.

Act One: I Just Don't See How It Affects Us Here

Narrator: This scene, representing how many of the white teachers in the study dealt with racial messages in the classroom, begins with Kimberly and Ms. A talking as they walk into the school building in the morning.

Kimberly: Good morning.

Ms. A: How's school going? Are you almost done? What's your project about again?

Kimberly: Well, it's about race and ethnicity and how it affects what we do here as teachers.

Ms. A: Huh, well, personally, I just don't see how that affects us here. Good luck with that. Have a good day.

Kimberly: You too. Tell Janeth I'll be by later today to help her with that test.

Narrator: Later that morning, Kimberly is in Ms. A's fifth-grade classroom working with Janeth on a grammar test given by the teacher. There are 19

We Hear What We Know 207

white students, four black students, and two Latino students in the class. The scene begins as the class is reviewing their spelling words list as a whole group.

Ms. A: Okay, how many syllables does culture have in it?

Janeth: [*raises her hand*] What is culture?

Ms. A: Well, it's where you are from. Where are you from. Janeth?

[*everyone is silent for 5 seconds*]

Ms. A: It's what your beliefs are.

Maya: What's my culture? African Am—

Ms. A: No. It's like Protestant and Jewish. Like during the holidays, we celebrate differently.

Maya: Can Jewish people be Christian?

Ms. A: Well, maybe. Okay, any other words you don't know? [*whispering to Kimberly:*] I don't want to get into that debate! [*loudly to the class:*] Okay class, we'll discuss each of your cultures in the next couple of weeks. It will be part of your homework.

[*Maya and Janeth moan*]

Ms. A: Don't worry. It will only take 5 seconds! Your parents have to do more work than you.

Act Two: It's Here All the Time!

Narrator: This scene, demonstrating the theme "(in)visible," takes place in a focus group with the black participants, Millie and Tyrell, and the researcher, Kimberly. They are sitting around a table at a restaurant, talking.

Kimberly: What does a teacher need to know in order to teach here?

Millie: You have to have a "yes sir" mentality. This community runs the school even though they say it doesn't. This school is back in time. I feel like it's probably . . . the mentality of these people today, if I didn't know better, it would be the 50s, not even the 70s. This place is like the 50s without the lynching. Well, the lynching is different. They lynch you with their mouths. They destroy you with what they say, and especially, really it's like their intent is to force you out. You have to be strong enough to stand, and you can only stand with God. Racism is not dead.

Kimberly: How do you know racism is not dead?

Tyrell: Last year, I got called into the office and a lady from the district office was there about to fire me. She said she got a letter from a parent saying I hit a kid and said a racial slur. To this day, I've not seen that letter. But the parents have that much power.

Kimberly: A racial slur?

Tyrell: I don't know who it was, just some kid walking down the hall with a bloody nose from outside. And I said, "What happened to your nose?" He said, "I was playing basketball." And I said, "Were you playing basketball, or were you PLAYING basketball?" And he said, "I was playing basketball." And I said, "Well, can you play?" And that was it. That was the racial slur.

Kimberly: How do you explain that? How do you deal with that?

Tyrell: [*points to self*] You don't see this everyday in Redmen. You don't see THIS! So now, I keep to myself more, and I don't talk to kids I don't know. Last year I had to fake that funk so bad, and finally I told myself, "You don't need to be miserable," so I just do my job. I say to my administrators, no matter what you call me in here for, you are never going to be able to say I'm not teaching.

Act Three: Our Multicultural School

Narrator: This scene (re)presents the theme "the school place as a mold." A group of white female third-grade teachers at the end of the 2010–2011 school year are in a teacher meeting. They have student information sheets and are working on sorting students into classes for the following school year. Kimberly attends the grade level meeting as a representative for the school's writing committee. The teachers include Kimberly in the conversation and also go about the business of sorting students for the next school year.

Ms. B: Oh, Kimberly, you are the perfect person for this conversation. We were just talking about race sorting. We don't know what to do with some of these kids.

Kimberly: What do you mean?

Ms. A: What do we do with these mixed kids?

Ms. B: Like what do you do with this kid? She's mixed, but she's light-skinned and you could never tell, so I put her as white. So what pile does she go in? Is she African American, or white, or other? What are your kids?

Kimberly: Well, it depends on what you are doing with this information and who is telling you to categorize these kids, I suppose.

Ms. A: Well, like I have one, she's mixed. She has dark skin, so I guess I'd say she's black. And I have another one who is light. She is mixed with something, but. . . I'm not sure what. Can we just look at them and decide?

Ms. B: I don't know why we have to do this anyway. Why it matters so much.

Ms. C: I'm just uncomfortable with this whole thing. I don't want any part of it. Not any of it.

Kimberly: Okay, well, I'm going to sit in the back of the room and observe how you guys do this, okay?

[*Ms. A, Ms. B, and Ms. C nod their heads yes*]

Ms. B: We need to pass out all the minority students equally.

Ms. C: I don't understand why we're sorting them this way.

Ms. B: The races crap is stupid. Like Kinu, he's from France, but his parents are from Sri Lanka. Try explaining that to a third grader. And this one has dark hair, and her mother speaks Spanish, but she's not Mexican because that offends her.

Ms. A: Can we just switch white for white and black for black? I'm just southern, that's all.

Ms. B: Is it racist to call someone a Mexican?

Ms. A: I'm going to put this one down as African American because she's Jamaican and she has dark skin. Is that right?

Ms. C: Are we offending you, Kimberly, because your husband is black?

Ms. A: Come to think of it, I actually have two Jamaican kids in my room. One is lighter though. He looks mixed, and I think his dad is still in Jamaica. But I'm going to put him down as "other" because the girl is darker than him. Is that wrong?

Narrator: The teachers continue passing out student information sheets as if they were playing cards. The next day in the hallway, Kimberly meets Ms. B, the grade-level chair, and asks her for some clarification on the sorting process.

Kimberly: Why did you guys start with race to figure out how to sort these classes?

Ms. B: I'm not the one that said race matters.

Kimberly: Who did?

Ms. B: The principal.

Kimberly: And what did she say about race?

Ms. B: The first thing she said was there aren't many African Americans at this school. In fact, she's never been at a school with this few African Americans, so we need to make sure we evenly distribute them into classes. She said, "Heck, we have everything else, so just kind of distribute them evenly," and then she said then make sure that there are an even amount of boys and girls, low-medium-high students, and stuff like that.

Kimberly: But did she tell you why?

Ms. B: I've never really gotten the reason behind it. I mean, it seems to be racially motivated. She said that this is the way it's always been done. She wants all the homerooms to look basically the same, to be a "melting pot." [*pauses for 5 seconds*] Why is it, why did we do that? We passed out all the minority students based on their race and didn't consider their personality or what they need.

Act Four: You Live in America and You Don't Celebrate Thanksgiving?

Narrator: This scene exemplifies the theme "we hear what we know." It begins on the Monday afternoon before Thanksgiving, when a group of teachers are meeting to create a mission statement for the school's writing curriculum. The mission statement is supposed to be based on a collection of statements that the entire faculty, organized into small groups, composed the previous week. This act begins midway through the meeting, when the conversation about the mission statement is already in progress.

Ms. C: Well, I think we need to include something about diversity.

Kimberly: While I agree with you 100%, it should be a priority, I never saw "diversity" or anything like it on any of the statements that any group came up with. We need to make a statement that we are going to be willing to be accountable for, and no one said "diversity," so I don't know how we can put it in there. I'm not saying we can't, we just need to be careful about how we do it because no one wrote it, so we don't know if it's one of our major beliefs. What do we mean by "diversity" anyway?

Ms. C: Well, all any teacher has to do is look around her classroom and see that diversity is something that is important at this school. And if we are interested in individual children's interests, we need to look at diversity.

Narrator: The meeting continues, and there is no final decision amongst the group about including the word "diversity" in the mission statement. The next day, Kimberly is walking to her fourth-grade classroom when she passes Ms. C, who is ushering her long line of kindergarteners down the hall. The children are wearing Indian head-dresses and Pilgrim hats made from construction paper.

Kimberly: Good morning. Where are you guys going?

Ms. C: We are on our way to the Pilgrim and Indian Feast. Aren't they cute?

Kimberly: Have fun!

Narrator: Kimberly continues on to the fourth-grade class, where she works with students on writing. She has a writing conference that day with a Vietnamese English Language Learner, Khan, who is having trouble with the assigned writing.

Ms. B: Class, I want you to pretend that you are a turkey, and convince someone why they shouldn't eat you for Thanksgiving dinner.

Khan: [*looks at Kimberly, puzzled*] What a turkey?

Kimberly: [*quickly sketches a turkey on a paper*] It looks like this. Do you know what that is?

Khan: Oh. Yes. What thank giving?

Kimberly: Well, it's a holiday. Actually, this Thursday is Thanksgiving. We remember the people who came to America from Europe, and the Native Americans who tried to be friends with them. But the most important thing you need to know now is that it is a tradition to eat turkey on Thanksgiving. So let's make a graphic organizer about why people should not eat you. Remember you are a turkey. Can you think of anything?

Khan: I too skinny!

Kimberly: Good. What else?

Khan: You be sick.

Kimberly: Okay.

Ms. B: Kimberly, how is Khan doing?

Kimberly: He's having some trouble, but we're working on it. He doesn't really know what Thanksgiving is all about, so I have to give him some background.

Ms. B: Oh. That reminds me, I was in a meeting with another ESL student and his mom the other day. His mom said, "I don't celebrate Thanksgiving." I couldn't believe it. I mean, you live in America now. You should be thankful that you live here.

Kimberly: Well, she didn't say that. She just said she didn't celebrate the holiday.

Ms. B: Well, my mom wasn't from here, but we grew up celebrating it anyway, because she was thankful to live here in America.

Questions for Dialogue

1. In the Opening Dialogue, in what ways might the monologues be different if given a different racial demographic and/or placed in a different geographical location?
2. In Act One, in what ways did Ms. A's belief that "race doesn't really affect me here" impact her students?
3. In Act Two, "It's Here All the Time!," what professional (and/or personal) risks do Tyrell and Millie face based on their racial identities?
4. What impact do teachers' understandings about race have upon students in "Our Multicultural School" (Act Three)? What role do teacher leaders and administrators play in sorting students into classrooms?

5. How do the different teachers in Act Four, "You Live in America and You Don't Celebrate Thanksgiving?," understand and approach "diversity" differently?

Notes

1. I use the term *place* to invoke the notion that all spaces are socially informed and function to limit, allow, and inform social interaction (see also Creswell, 2004; LeFebvre, 1991; Massey, 1997; Soja, 1999).
2. Pseudonyms for names of places are used throughout.
3. I define *social justice* as a concerted effort to promote justice for humankind, particularly those who have been disenfranchised in society.
4. All of the school's 50 certified classroom teachers were invited to participate. Thirty-two teachers indicated that they would consider participating. A list of 32 potential participants was given to two community nominators (one white male and one black female) who regularly observe teachers. I asked the community nominators to name two teachers from each of three levels (kindergarten and first, second and third, and fourth and fifth)—one "excellent" and one "average" teacher of students from diverse racial, ethnic, and cultural backgrounds. No black teachers were named. Four white teachers were cross-listed by the respective community nominators as "average" by one nominator and "excellent" by the other, meaning the two community nominators had different opinions about the same teacher. These four white teachers were then asked to participate in the study; three of them agreed to participate. Two black teachers were also selected for the study based on the criteria of representing the school's racial diversity (there are only three black classroom teachers at the school).

References

Alexander, B. (2005). Critically analyzing pedagogical interactions as performance. In B. K. Alexander, G. L. Anderson, & B. P. Gallegos (Eds.), *Performance theories in education: Power, pedagogy and the politics of identity* (pp. 41–62). Mahwah, NJ: Lawrence Erlbaum Associates.

Blaisdell, B. (2005). Seeing every student as a 10: Using critical race theory to engage white teachers' colorblindness. *International Journal of Educational Policy, Research & Practice, 6*(1), 31–50.

Bonilla-Silva, E. (2003). *Racism without racists: Color-blind racism and the persistence of racial inequality in the United States*. Lanham, MD: Rowman Littlefield.

Butler, J. (2003). Performative acts and gender constitution: An essay in phenomenology and feminist theory. In C. McCann & K. Seung-Kyung (Eds.), *Feminist theory reader* (pp. 415–427). New York: Routledge.

Castro, A. J. (2010). Themes in the research on preservice teachers' views of cultural diversity: Implications for researching millenial preservice teachers. *Educational Researcher, 39*(3), 198–210.

Conquergood, D. (2006). Rethinking ethnography: Towards a critical cultural politics. In D. S. Madison & J. Hamera (Eds.), *The Sage handbook of performance studies* (pp. 351–365). Thousand Oaks, CA: Sage.

Creswell, T. (2004). *Place: A short introduction*. Malden, MA: Blackwell.

Denzin, N. K. (2003). *Performance ethnography: Critical pedagogy and the politics of culture*. Thousand Oaks, CA: Sage.
Earick, M. (2009). *Racially equitable teaching: Beyond the whiteness of professional development for early childhood education*. New York: Peter Lang.
Helfenbein, R. J., & Taylor, L. H. (2009). Critical geographies in/of education: Introduction. *Educational Studies, 45*, 236–239.
Howard, K. J. (2012). Unbecoming . . responding to colorblindness: An autoethnography. In F. Briscoe & M. Khalifa (Eds.), *Becoming critical: Oppression, resistance, and the emergence of a critical educator/researcher*, New York: SUNY Press.
Ladson-Billings, G., & Tate, B. (1995). Toward a critical race theory of education. *Teachers College Record, 97*(1), 47–67.
Leavy, P. (2009). Performance studies. In *Method meets art: Arts-based research practice* (pp. 135–178). New York: Guilford Press.
Lefebvre, H. (1991). *The production of space*. Cambridge, MA: Blackwell. (Original work published 1974 as *La production de l'espace*).
Lensmire, T. (2008). How I became white while punching de Tar Baby. *Curriculum Inquiry, 38*(3), 300–322.
Lensmire, T. J., & Snaza, N. (2010). What teacher education can learn from blackface minstrelsy. *Educational Researcher, 39*(5) 413–422.
Lewis, A. (2001). There's no "race" in the schoolyard: Color-blind ideology in an (almost) all-white school. *American Educational Research Journal, 38*(4), 781–811.
Lowenstein, K. (2009). The work of multicultural teacher education: Reconceptualizing white teacher candidates as learners. *Review of Educational Research, 79*(1), 163–196.
Madison, D. S. (1998). Performances, personal narratives, and the politics of possibility. In S. J. Dailey (Ed.), *The future of performance studies: Visions and revisions* (pp. 276–286). Annandale, VA: National Communication Association.
Madison, D. S. (2007). Co-performative witnessing. *Cultural Studies, 21*(6), 826–831.
Massey, D. (1997). A global sense of place. In T. Barnes & D. Gregory (Eds.), *Reading human geography* (pp. 315–323). London: Arnold.
Mienczakowski, J. (2000). Ethnodrama: Performed research: Limitations and potential. In P. Atkinson et al. (Eds.), *Handbook of ethnography* (pp. 468-476). London: Sage.
Miles, M. B., & Huberman, A. M. (1994). *Qualitative data analysis*. Thousand Oaks, CA: Sage.
Milner, R. (2007). Race, narrative inquiry, and self-study in curriculum and teacher education. *Education and Urban Society, 39*, 584–609.
Milner, R. (2008). Critical race theory and interest convergence as analytic tools in teacher education policies and practices. *Journal of Teacher Education, 59*(4), 332–346.
Nasir, N. S., & Hand, V. M. (2006). Exploring sociocultural perspectives on race, culture, and learning. *Review of Educational Research, 76*(4), 449–475.
National Center for Educational Statistics. (2012). Common core of data CCD. Retrieved from http://nces.ed.gov/ccd.
Nespor, J. (1997). *Tangled up in school: Politics, space, bodies, and signs in the educational process*. Mahwah, NJ: Lawrence Erlbaum Associates.
Patton, M. (2002). *Qualitative research and evaluation methods*. Thousand Oaks, CA: Sage.
Soja, E. (1999). Thirdspace: Expanding the scope of geographical imagination. In D. Massey, J. Allen, & P. Sarre (Eds.), *Human geography today* (pp. 260–278). Cambridge, UK: Polity Press.

Solórzano, D. G. (1997). Images and words that wound: Critical race theory, racial stereotyping, and teacher education. *Teacher Education Quarterly, 24*, 5–20.

Spindler, G., & Spindler, L. (1987). *Interpretive ethnography of education: At home and abroad.* Hillsdale, NJ: Lawrence Erlbaum Associates.

Spradley, J. P. (1980). *Participant observation.* Toronto: Wadsworth/Thompson.

Vaught, S. E., & Castagno, A. E. (2008). "I don't think I'm a racist": Critical race theory, teacher attitudes, and structural racism. *Race, Ethnicity, and Education, 11*(2), 95–113.

Webb, P. T. (2001). Reflection and reflective teaching: Ways to improve pedagogy or ways to remain racist? *Race, Ethnicity, and Education, 4*(3), 242–253.

Chapter 8

Our School: College-Going Scripts of Students in an Early College High School

James A. Brooks

Introduction

One contemporary initiative in the United States aimed at preparing high school students for college, particularly underrepresented students, is the Early College High School Initiative. Beginning in 2002, the Bill and Melinda Gates Foundation funded this initiative in seven early college high schools across the United States as a way of blending secondary and post-secondary education. As Kirst (2004) pointed out, the transition from high school to college is a critical period for underrepresented students. Early exposure to college and college-level work, a central aim of the Early College High School Initiative, helps those who will be the first in their families to attend college to see themselves as succeeding in college (Gullatt & Jan, 2003). By 2009, more than 200 early college high schools had opened across the U.S. (Berger, Adelman, & Cole, 2010), each of them small and autonomous (Edmunds et al., 2010), and each aimed at bridging the gap between secondary and post-secondary education. In 2011, there were 230 early college high schools in 28 states (Vargas & Miller, 2011). The initiative is coordinated and supported by Jobs for the Future, a nonprofit organization dedicated to creating a skilled workforce.

Early college high schools have been designed to prepare students to attend college. There is intentionality regarding the size of the schools, the location, and admission into the program. The schools are small by design; they are most often located on community college and university campuses; and the students admitted are typically those underrepresented in college (Jobs for the Future, 2008). Because this is a relatively new initiative, little research exists about the effectiveness of early college high schools in preparing students for college, except for limited quantitative reporting done by groups implementing or funding early college high schools. Consequently, the nuanced variables that might facilitate the transformation of students remain undocumented.

The way in which institutional structures challenge and support students who aspire to attend college should be examined by educational leaders to provide a more complete view of what makes the early college high school experience unique. This study explored how participation in a college readiness program such as the Early College High School Initiative interacts with other discourses to shape students' perceptions about college and about themselves as college-goers. Examining the dominant discourse in such a program could reveal how it differs from the discourses found in traditional high school programs, and consequently, how the experience may or may not impact college-going. Because the Early College High School Initiative is so intentional at reinforcing a strong message about college-going, one might wonder to what extent students in an early college high school are able to imagine and articulate the many post-secondary opportunities available to them, outside of the discourses to which they are exposed.

An examination of the narratives that circulate in early college high schools is necessary for educational leaders to more fully understand the phenomenon of college-going within that setting. This examination represents an intentional stepping back to create a complicated picture of a program that is beginning to serve as a model for U.S. school reform. By troubling the phenomenon under study, I sought to challenge assumptions and raise issues that otherwise might have remained unaddressed. The timing for this kind of scrutiny is relevant because the Early College High School Initiative is gaining favor as a strategy for the reform of secondary education (Vargas & Miller, 2011). Before the initiative goes to scale across the country, educational leaders should examine the initiative more closely. Such scrutiny is complicated by the high-profile funding the initiative receives; it is difficult for educational leaders to critically examine the specifics of a program that has such cachet. As an educational leader, I believe that those at the implementation level of a program should have opportunities to voice ideas and concerns. In this study, the varied voices of participants illustrate discourses that may complicate the picture, offering a more nuanced portrayal of this college-readiness initiative than currently exists in the literature.

Data Sources

In this chapter, I drew upon a qualitative case study that employed a focused ethnographic (Jeffrey & Troman, 2004) methodology. Data sources included interviews of the seven teachers, one counselor, and principal of an early college high school; observations of classes, seminars, and daily school routines over the course of 5 weeks; and documents, including 150 pages of student journal writing. This methodology allowed me to gather from multiple sources, providing a richness and depth that might not have been possible otherwise.

Representation

I constructed extracts from this focused ethnography (Jeffrey & Troman, 2004) as a layered account, a "polyphonic narrative" (Mienczakowski, 1995, p. 365) that gave voice to the varied stories of my participants in the form of an ethnodrama (Saldaña, 2003). I created vignettes that "phenomenologically reenact lived-experiences" (Norris, 2009, p. 34). I did not choose to represent my data in this alternate format for the sheer novelty of expression, but because, as Saldaña (2003) maintained, doing so allowed the participants' stories to be told in the most vivid and engaging way possible.

Further, the notion of scripts (Abelson, 1996; Bieber & Worley, 2006; Rubin & Berntsen, 2003; Steiner, 1990) has been a central metaphor in this study. The school narratives and family narratives that the students of the early college high school negotiate are scripts that reflect both the lives they have lived and the lives that the early college high school envisions for them. I have chosen to offer the data and its interpretation and analysis as a script as well—a script that integrates the discourses observed in this particular early college high school and alludes to the way in which students may become authors of their own life narratives (Baxter Magolda, 2001).

In keeping with the practice of verbatim theatre (Hammond & Steward, 2008; Paget, 1997), I used the words of participants, for it is in a character's own words that reality can be found (Smith, 1993). In using the "words, stories and advice" (Mienczakowski, 1995, p. 367) of first-generation college students, their teachers, and administrators, I sought to provide a stage for their stories to be enacted beyond the way in which educational research is traditionally communicated, one in which the voices of students and practitioners who work with them daily are present (Tierney, 2004). Using the benchmark that Saldaña (2003) suggested, I aimed to create an "entertainingly informative experience for an audience, one that is aesthetically sound, intellectually rich, and emotionally evocative" (p. 220).

Initial coding analysis of the data collected in this study revealed that participants had shared conflicts, both internal and interpersonal, related to their experiences in an early college high school. Conflict is paramount to dramatic writing (Goldstein, 2002). These conflicts represent the major themes in the data. In vivo coding pointed me to the components of the data that best illustrated those themes, what Saldaña (2003) calls "the juicy stuff" (pp. 184–185). Dramaturgical codes (Saldaña, 2010) gave me insight into characterization, motivation, and conflict, and into applying them to the family narratives and institutional narratives that the students in the early college high school were negotiating.

Following thematic analysis, the patterns that were noted included: (a) the way in which the small size of the early college high school impacts student learning and relationships with teachers; (b) the metaphor of family that students and teachers use to describe their experience at this early college high school; (c) the lack of academic preparation of the students admitted into the program; (d) the barriers to becoming ready for college that students face; (e) the emerging identities of adolescents heretofore not destined for college; (f) the family narrative, or life script, reinforced at home; (g) and the institutional message of college-going enacted at the early college high school.

Our School

Characters

Researcher: a doctoral student and high school English teacher

Ms. A.: a tenth-grade English teacher

Mrs. B.: a ninth-grade English teacher

Mr. C.: a math teacher

Mr. D.: a science teacher

Mr. E.: a math teacher

Mr. F.: a social studies teacher

Mrs. G.: the school guidance counselor

Mrs. H.: the principal

Austin: a tenth grader who originally did not want to attend the early college high school

Hector: a tenth grader who does not have legal immigration status

Iliana: a tenth grader who feels pressure from her immigrant parents to succeed in school

Brittany: a tenth grader who lives with her grandmother

Brennan: a ninth grader who dreams of a good education and a job he enjoys

Cody: a ninth grader who was labeled a troublemaker at his middle school

Gabby: a ninth grader who does not understand why she is referred to as "first-generation"

Various parent voices

As the lights come up, some of the actors are already on stage in a tableau. The seven high school teachers interviewed in the study are positioned stage right. Theirs is the dominant voice not only in this narrative, but also in the everyday operation of the early college high school; consequently, they occupy a greater amount of space on the stage. The principal and counselor are off-stage for now. The early college high school students are represented by seven actors who for the moment are in the dark in the space not occupied by teachers, at stage left. Because the family discourse has been communicated in the data via students and teachers only, the parents are represented by off-stage voices. The Researcher narrates the action and offers commentary in the form of research and analysis, citing research throughout the drama. The citations that document the research are not intended to be read by the Researcher.

Researcher: [*Walking from the dark upstage area into the light down stage*] This play is called *Our School*. I call it *Our School* as a nod to Thornton Wilder's play *Our Town* (1960), in which the everyday occurrences in a small New England town are elevated to reflect larger life themes. The title is also a reference to the shared ownership and collaborative spirit that teachers and students in the school have expressed.

Our School is a case study of a small school in the rural southeastern United States drawn from what researchers refer to as a focused ethnography (Jeffrey & Troman, 2004). In some ways, you will find *Our School* familiar. School is a familiar setting for all of us. We have all experienced school as students, and popular media has continued to propagate images of what schooling is like in America. There are things, however, that set *Our School* apart.

[*The lights slowly begin to rise on stage. Teachers and students appear on stage and arrange chairs to establish the setting.*]

While the school and the players remain anonymous, the players' expressions are in their own words. This portrayal of qualitative research data borrows from the tradition of *verbatim theatre* (Hammond & Steward, 2008; Paget, 1997) in which the voices of participants are honored above mine. Their words have been drawn from teacher interviews, classroom observations, and school documents to create this ethnodrama, and their words have been used verbatim. The characters represent neither all the students across the country who attend early college high schools nor all the teachers who teach in them, but they reflect the composite attitudes and perceptions of the teachers and students I came to know in *Our School*. This play is my version of the many possible stories that could be told.

[Researcher walks through the chairs and desks that have been arranged on stage.]

Our School is not a traditional school by most contemporary Western educational institution standards. We won't find desks in ordered rows, there's no football team, no homecoming court; there are only six teachers. *Our School* is situated on the campus of a community college where students are also concurrently enrolled. The students recruited to attend are those often underrepresented on college campuses. Most of the students are first-generation college students, with neither parent having earned a college degree.

[Researcher takes his place in front of the classroom and begins to speak like a teacher.]

Teachers are required to teach each day using methodologies that are prescribed by the funders of the Early College High School Initiative[1]: collaborative group work, writing to learn, groups, questioning, classroom talk, and scaffolding. While some teachers in a traditional education setting might find this pedagogical structure restrictive, the teachers in *Our School* appear to find the structure supportive. As one teacher put it, "the teachers here can stress the importance of thinking more than they might in a traditional class; it's not just necessarily teaching them the content, but teaching them to be thinkers."

Researcher: The students are coming in now...

[*The seven students have backpacks or books. They change position, arranging themselves into an informal tableau. As their names are called they indicate they are present and mime interaction.*]

Ms. A.: [*calling roll*] Hector…

Researcher: Hector is the oldest of three children. His family came to this community seeking seasonal work in the apple orchards. Because Hector does not have legal status, the early college high school is his only opportunity to attend college. Pending passage of the DREAM Act[2], Hector's education will end with the associate's degree he can obtain through this high school program.

Ms. A.: [*continues calling roll*] Brittany…

Researcher: Brittany lives with her grandmother. Her mother dropped out of high school and was not equipped to care for her. She sometimes sees her on the weekends. Her mother is more like a friend than a parent. She talks about taking classes at the community college one day, but she hasn't followed through with that.

Ms. A.: [*continues calling roll*] Austin…

Researcher: Austin didn't want to come to the early college high school at first. He missed his friends and would like to have played sports. His father insisted that he apply. Austin's father is a high school graduate; he has worked his way into a supervisory position at a local furniture factory.

Ms. A.: [*continues calling roll*] Cody…

Researcher: Cody always seems to be in trouble. His teachers wonder about his home life. His parents are uninvolved. Cody's middle school teacher thought the early college high school would be a fresh start for him; they hoped he would escape some of the peer pressure he was dealing with at his old school. Mrs. B. taught Cody's parents. She had hopes that they would attend the community college, but she's nearly certain that they didn't.

Ms. A.: [*continues calling roll*] Gabby…

Researcher: Gabby is from a large family. She is often overshadowed at home by siblings needing more attention, but has come to develop an identity at school as a strong student. Her teachers have taken a special interest in her. Gabby's mother dropped out of high school when she became pregnant. Her father finished high school and has struggled since to support his growing family.

Ms. A.: [*continues calling roll*] Iliana…

Researcher: Iliana's family are immigrants and have been fortunate to find work in the community. Her education is a high priority for her family; in fact, they are resting many hopes on how education will give her a different life than they have had without any formal post-secondary education. Sometimes that puts a lot of pressure on her.

Ms. A.: [*continues calling roll*] Brennan…

Researcher: Brennan is the oldest of three children. His parents are hard-working folks and want a better life for their son. They recently lost their jobs when a local textile factory closed. Without education and training, his parents are struggling to find jobs. Brennan's father must complete his GED before he can take advantage of retraining through the community college.[3]

Researcher: The students in *Our School* come from middle schools across the district; for many, it is a second chance at learning, a way to escape the labels they have been given. These labels represent the range of subjectivities (Orbe, 2004) with which the students must contend.

[*The students deliver the following lines in a choral reading style, raising their heads to face the audience as they deliver their first line—labels that they have brought with them from middle school and from home, labels that other people have given them. The lights come up on each student as he or she speaks, until the entire stage left area is lit.*]

Students: [*alternating, with a slight pause between each*] goof-off... slacker... good for nothing... goody two-shoes... reserved... laid-back... procrastinator... goth... prep... redneck... lazy... underachiever... low... unmotivated... undisciplined... impulsive... nerd... gifted... shy... very, shy... athletic... gamer... bright... first-generation college student...

Gabby: [*stepping forward*] I took it wrong when my teacher said to me that this school would be perfect for me since I would be the first person in my family to go to college. First-generation college student? I thought she was insulting me.

[*On the backdrop, the words they say fill the screen in various fonts, sizes, and shapes.*]

[*The lights fade on students, leaving Researcher in light.*]

Researcher: It's break time now.

[*Students disperse to form a new tableau in silhouette: some on cell phones, some using laptops, and those closest to center stage grouped around the teachers closest to them.*]

Researcher: The students will be using their i-Pods or checking their e-mail accounts or updating their Facebook pages. That's ok here. Students have unfiltered access to the Internet at *Our School*, unlike their friends at the traditional high schools in the system.

Mrs. B.: [*to Researcher, moving toward him to offer additional information*] School is the only place that many of these students have access to the Internet. *Our School* is sensitive to that. One father told me that he drives his daughter to the end of the driveway to access a neighbor's wireless Internet. [*moves back toward students who gather around her*]

Researcher: You'll also find that students will use this time to seek out teachers, like Mrs. A., with whom they have forged close relationships.

[*The principal, Mrs. H., enters from stage right, well-dressed and confident. As she speaks the lights slowly dim on the teachers and students on stage. Mrs. H. takes center stage in a spotlight.*]

Researcher: The principal of *Our School* began her career in education later in life after working in public relations and marketing, perhaps explaining her polish. Mrs. H. is well-dressed, the very model of professionalism. She became an educator after being a full-time mother for a number of years. She is well-traveled and comes from a different socioeconomic background than perhaps all the students in *Our School*.

Mrs. H.: [*in a well-prepared manner that suggests that she has had many opportunities to deliver this information before*] *Our School* provides a small learning community of students the opportunity to earn both a high school diploma and an associate degree at no cost to students and their families. It is a 5-year school which enrolls approximately 60 ninth graders each year. *Our School* is located on a community college campus where students are enrolled in both honors-level high school and college courses.

Since 2002, the partner organizations of the Early College High School Initiative have started or redesigned more than 230 schools in 28 states and the District of Columbia. The schools are designed so that low-income youth, first-generation college goers, English language learners, students of color, and other young people underrepresented in higher education can simultaneously earn a high school diploma and an associate's degree or up to 2 years of credit toward a bachelor's degree—tuition free.

Here in the building we have banners from schools local, Ivy League, and military, and there might be one from Texas up there. I went to the University of California at San Diego; that's where I started. [*nervous laughter*] But you know, we think that's important; we have posters up. We have them looking at careers. We have them do self-assessments. Currently our sophomores are doing a special project on college-going that is built into their course of study; it's integrated as a project. Our freshmen have two mandatory college visits.

Researcher: [*to audience*] You may have some questions. I'll ask one on your behalf. [*as audience member, raising hand to ask his question*] Besides the college visits and research project about colleges, what does *Our School* do to emphasize college-going for these students?

Mrs. H.: I really believe that the professionals that work in this building take pride in what they do each day, and we're motivated by the mission here. We want very much to fulfill that. And yes, it is our employment and we do have a paycheck at the end of the month, but I believe that we go above and beyond; I *know* we go above and beyond, and that comes from an intrinsic motivation to support the mission of the school and to see it through to the success that we believe that we can have.

[*On the backdrop there is a collage of college banners, university mascots and logos.*]

Researcher: [*asking a question as an audience member again*] I wonder why Bill Gates seems to be driving this initiative. Is the fact that he is wealthy and that his foundation is able to fund whatever initiatives he supports a good reason for him to be allowed to set America's education agenda?

[*Mrs. H. pauses, has no answer*]

[*The lights dim and Mrs. H. exits stage right.*]

Researcher: The teachers and students in *Our School* are relatively unfamiliar with the political and social implications of their school. The students sense that they are part of something new. For students who have had negative experiences with school, something new is appealing.

Our School 229

The students have applied to attend *Our School*. They were all interviewed as part of that selection process—not to select the brightest or the most promising, but those who might fall through the cracks in traditional high schools. For many it was scary and intimidating.

[*The lights slowly come up on Austin. The Researcher assumes the role of interviewer and steps toward him.*]

Austin: The first question they asked me was…

Researcher: What is your favorite book?

Austin: I said, *Enders Game*, and they said—

Researcher: I really like that book.

Austin: After that, the interview went fine.

Researcher: Ironically, one of the major themes in the book is the dichotomy between children and adults and the conflict that rises from these power structures. In the novel, Andre Wiggin, known as Ender, is being recruited into a school, the Battle School. Valentine, Ender's sister, tells him that she doesn't think it is possible for him to define his own path.

[*An image of the book cover is projected on the screen.*]

Austin: [*reading from the novel*] "Welcome to the human race. Nobody controls his own life, Ender. The best you can do is choose to fill the roles given you by good people, by people who love you."

[*Citation appears on the screen: Card, 1985, p. 219*]

Researcher: Austin's passage is significant because the early college high school sets students on a path toward college. Some students are there because their parents or teachers think they should be. Like Ender, they had little choice in whether they would attend the early college high school. By the end of the first year, most report that they are glad to be there. Another part of the book deals with identity and bears some examination in relation to this study, as well.

Austin: [*reading from the novel*] "Perhaps it is impossible to wear an identity without becoming what you pretend to be."

[*Citation appears on the screen: Card, 1985, p. 231*]

Researcher: For some of the students at the early college high school the identity of hard working student or a student who is college-bound is a new identity. It is the hope of the staff of the early college high school that eventually that identity will become the student's own.

Brittany: [*to audience*] When I was being interviewed I was afraid I would say something wrong and that I wouldn't be good enough. I don't like to talk about me. I feel uncomfortable bragging on myself. [*to Researcher*] The only person that brags on me is my Nanna.

Researcher: What would your Nanna say about you, Brittany?

Hector: I didn't realize how much I didn't know about myself. They asked so many questions about me. I was really nervous, and I was afraid I wouldn't get in.

Gabby: When I got interviewed I was scared, but then I felt comfortable talking to them because they were friendly. The interview made me feel important.

Brennan: Some of my family said I shouldn't go to this school. My brother said, "what if you don't get accepted?" I wanted to apply because no one in my family has ever been to college, and I wanted to achieve that for my family. My father nearly cried when I got my acceptance letter. He said he always knew I could do it. I guess they just saw my inner self and saw that I had potential.

Researcher: What these students don't know is that there were 70 openings at *Our School* this year and only 69 applicants. Besides those students who expressed interest on their own, middle school teachers and counselors recommended students for the program. The interview was merely a formality. *Our School* is only in its second year of operation. Teachers anticipate a time when more students apply and when admission can be more selective.

Striplin (1999) points outs that many students whose parents did not attend college are placed into technical or vocational programs that impede their progress toward college. The students at *Our School* are better positioned for college because of their placement in an early college high school, with its emphasis on college-going. This, however, is no guarantee of their success.

Researcher: The faculty is discovering the barriers that students are dealing with that impede their progress toward college. Though they work to fulfill the school's mission each day, they are powerless to deal with what students are dealing with outside of school.

Ms. G.: We try to do the best we can. I go to a lot of the homes. What those kids have to transition from, leaving that home until they get here, are totally different environments—so, so different. They really have to make a change, mentally, emotionally, physically, from where they have come from to here.

Researcher: Learning to negotiate these different environments can be difficult for students. Lucey, Melody, and Walkerdine (2003) call this negotiation "border crossing." Each day these students cross borders of socioeconomic status and educational status; they live in two distinct worlds. These two settings are where two distinct scripts are being enacted, the family narrative and the institutional narrative; what Rubin and Berntsen (2003) call the "personal and cultural script."

Iliana: I'll be the first person in my family to go to college; that means a lot to my family.

Brennan: I am the first in my family to go to college. Sometimes it's hard for them to understand. My cousins think I will be taking advantage of my family by them paying for school and me not working as soon.

Researcher: Brennan's feelings of guilt are common among first-generation college students. Bui (2002) and Piorkowski (1983) report that it is difficult for first-generation college students to reconcile the conflict that their opportunities for college creates when the rest of their family is struggling financially.

Cody: None of my family went to college. My dad says…

Off-stage father voice: Your mom and I didn't have that, and we are happy. You don't need it either.

Researcher: This negative attitude toward college is but one type of the family narratives that students in *Our School* hear at home. Another narrative is one of support. Yet another is ambivalence.

Iliana: My mom didn't go to college because she had two kids. I was raised to be myself no matter what. My mom tells me…

Off-stage mother voice: Shine with your own light, not someone else's.

Cody: I really don't have anyone to talk to at home. I really can't go on about some subjects because most of the time my family does not find it interesting. My mom dropped out of high school. She doesn't know how to help me with work. She's just there saying do what you want. She doesn't know how to support me.

Iliana: I guess you could say I have good support. My mom had a child at 15. She wants to see one of her kids do something good. It didn't work out for my brother. My older sister has already screwed up.

Gabby: My parents don't know what college is. They don't know how to support me.

Researcher: Gabby's situation is not unique. The work of Horn and Nuñez (2000), Thayer (2000), and Vargas (2004) confirms that students whose parents did not attend college lack knowledge about college admissions, financial aid, and degree requirements, unlike some of their counterparts.

Brennan: My parents never went to college. They got married when my father was 18 and my mother was 16. They want me to have the life I want and not what they had. In the present economy, they know I'll need college.

Brittany: My mom went to college late in life. She said she didn't get the college experience. She struggled for a long time. My sister tells me every day that if she had this opportunity, she would run with it.

Brennan: Being the first in my family to go to college is really important; it means that I have broken the cycle. It makes me feel good to set a new standard. It's my dream and my family's dream too.

Iliana: My mom has six kids and goes to college online. She wants it to be easier for me than it was for her.

Brittany: My grandma said...

Off-stage voice: I failed that three times. Good luck. I don't think you can do it.

Cody: My mom told me...

Off-stage voice: I don't want you to take this offensively, but maybe you aren't cut out for a university; maybe you should think smaller.

Researcher: Astin and Osequera (2004) and Lamont and Lareau (1988) tell us that the families of many students like the ones in *Our School* simply lack the cultural capital related to college-going to pass on to their children. *Our School* hopes to be able to provide that cultural capital through its ties to the community college. Some researchers, such as Clark (1960, 1980) and Grubb (1989, 1991), however, question whether the community college has the institutional capital necessary to pass on to students for success. Students sometimes sense what others have passed on to them.

Cody: I have the troublemaker side in me from my dad and the potential side in me from my mom.

Researcher: The students in *Our School* use the metaphor of family to describe their relationships with the faculty and their peers. This is particularly noteworthy since many of these students have had negative experiences with school in the past, and since some come from homes with strained family relationships.

[*Lights come up on Mr. F., who is in his classroom pantomiming getting ready for the school day.*]

Researcher: This is Mr. F. He was in the Peace Corps. He saw the world, and brings that experience to his social studies class. He had just returned from a year in Africa before taking the job here at *Our School*. He is a father with three children of his own.

[*Lights come up on Ms. A., who enters with earphones in, listening to her iPod. She removes the earphones, takes off her jacket, and joins a group of other teachers who are now lighted. Some present her with wrapped packages, which she opens.*]

Researcher: This is Ms. A. The students love her. It seems like they relate to the young teachers. She's cool, knows the music they listen to, the movies they see. She incorporates these things into her lessons. She is from another state and is learning about college opportunities in this state herself as she exposes her students to the opportunities available to them. This morning the faculty is celebrating Ms. A.'s engagement and wedding.

Deal and Peterson (1999) tell us that it is important to have organizational rituals that connect people and communicate the core values of an organization. These experiences create cohesion and strengthen the metaphor of family that pervades *Our School*. The students haven't arrived yet. They ride buses from all across the district, so school begins a little later each day and ends early enough for them to ride the bus home from the traditional high school they would have attended.

Transportation is a barrier for many of these students. Most are not old enough to drive to school. Their parents are unable to bring them because of

Our School

work. Often they are unable to stay after school for tutoring or enrichment activities. Clubs must meet during the school day.

[*The Researcher weaves in and out of the group of teachers, unnoticed as he continues to introduce the remaining teachers to the audience.*]

Researcher: Mr. C. was hired to teach math earlier this year after teaching in England for the past year. He coaches cross country at another high school since *Our School* has no sports teams. His students are impressed that he ran a marathon this year.

Mrs. B. is the other English teacher. She works with ninth graders. She is nurturing, a mother figure in *Our School*. Her teaching experience includes an alternate school with a career focus and an arts magnet school. She has taught in both traditional middle schools and high schools. She understands these students, and they feel comfortable talking to her.

Mr. D. teaches science. His parents were first-generation college students, like many of the students he teaches.

Mr. D.: [*to Researcher, moving away from the group of teachers and toward the Researcher as he speaks*] When I grew up, both of my parents were first-generation college goers, so I guess that makes me a second-generation college student. Education could not have been more celebrated and more promoted in my home. I would be hard-pressed to find another family where education was valued more than mine. My older sister was a math major, and she was really gifted in math, but what that looked like was that she was doing math homework every night. That is a person that is gifted in math, not struggling with it. I knew early on what it looked like to be gifted in math. It looked like hard work every night. She majored in math; she is a programmer. I don't think a lot of these kids have ever had models like that.

Researcher: Have you ever shared that story with your students, Mr. D.?

Mr. D.: No. I guess I should.

Researcher: It appears that the math and science teachers at *Our School* are a little more detached from their students and interact with them mostly through course content, while the English teachers extend the work of the school counselor.

Mr. C.: That's something I hadn't thought about much until the past month or so. Next year I will certainly be spending the first couple of weeks working more on relationships and behaviors rather than on math.

Researcher: Mrs. G. is the guidance counselor. She is a first-generation college student and speaks of that openly when counseling students. She has just gotten to school. Gabby called; she missed the bus and didn't have a ride to school, so Mrs. G. left school to pick her up. She also paid Gabby's cell phone bill last month because she knew it was her only link to the school. Because the school is small, this kind of personal attention is possible. London (1989), however, suggests that dependence, or binding, can make independence more difficult.

Mrs. G.: [*to Gabby as they walk in together*] I did it, and you can do it too. It is possible, and don't let anyone tell you that you can't go to college, because you can. [*aside, to audience*] We are always focusing on college readiness skills. I meet with every sophomore student and their parent in their tenth-grade year. That is something that we have initiated this year. It has really seemed to hit home for these students.

Gabby: [*speaking to herself*] Wow! I am already a sophomore, and Ms. G. is doing my plan for what we are going to do, which college track I am going to be on, associate's in arts, associate's in science, because we are already in college. We are here. We are doing it.

[*Gabby exits stage left.*]

Mrs. G.: I think continuing to talk about college, meeting with them, talking about beyond community college and transferring is a huge part of the talk we go through here.

Researcher: Mr. E. is the newest teacher on the staff at *Our School*. Teaching is a second career for him. He has an engineering background and became a math teacher after his contracting business declined in the present economy.

Mr. E.: The students here want to please you and work hard for you.

Researcher: And they did work hard for him. This year 100% of his students were proficient on the state Algebra I exam, an accomplishment few seasoned math teachers across the district could boast. He is humble and down-to-earth. The students are fascinated that he is also an auctioneer. The teachers here have a unique opportunity to build upon the relationships they develop with students and to capitalize on that relationship in the classroom.

Austin: [*returns from stage left*] I like the staff here. They are the best teachers I have ever had. Before, I didn't see teachers as real. The teachers here are real people and are part of the family. I think we learn more because of that. Before, I wouldn't trust my teachers to tell them about my hardships. [*exits stage left*]

Researcher: You've met the principal already. She is away at a conference today.

[*The lights dim quickly and come up again to signal the passing of time.*]

Researcher: This is another day in *Our School*. The students are making presentations about the colleges they have been researching, and preparing for final exams.

Iliana: The teachers here baby us too much. I am ready for college classes.

Mr. C.: I had a conversation earlier this week with another teacher in which we were saying, our students still—a lot of our students still need a lot of progress in terms of approaching the classroom door as an opportunity, and not seeing teachers as the adversary in the sense that "they make me do stuff that I otherwise wouldn't choose to do, and that if I do the things that I would choose to do I would get in trouble with that authority figure." We're still working with probably the majority of our students to get them to approach this as a collaborative process rather than as an adversarial process.

Mrs. B.: I suspect the majority of them have parents who view work that way, that their boss is their adversary and the boss makes them do stuff and they do what they are made to do, rather than work is something where we are an organization that has a goal, and we are all contributing our part towards getting there.

Austin: I hated teachers before because they made me do work that I didn't like, and I back-talked teachers like I did my parents. I have decided to respect my teachers because they are trying to make my life better. I see myself as my own obstacle.

Researcher: One might question how Austin came to identify himself as the problem. Perhaps this has been reinforced at home or at school or both.

Mr. D: We talk a lot about college or university beyond the community college.

All teachers: [*in unison*] Not *if* you go to college, but *when* you go to college.

Mr. D: [continues] We want them to aspire, not just to get an associate's degree here, but to also take it further. They say they want to attend certain colleges sometimes for very naïve reasons. We have to really educate a lot of them with regard to not every university offers programs that they may be interested in. It is important to research them. I don't think they really understand how hard it is to get in to those programs.

Ms. A: They literally don't know. All of the sudden, when we turn on that motivation, the students are like, "I not only want to go to college. I want to go to the best one."

Mr. C: Both of my parents are college graduates, and also, my dad was a football coach who grew up in Mississippi, so he was a very big college sports fan. Between those two things, I came from, at a very early age, an appreciation for colleges. The thing that I have picked up is that a lot of our students, and I assume this is true of their families, don't have any understanding at all of the distinctions between prestige of colleges and what different schools offer, the different specialties that they might have.

Brennan: I thought colleges were about all the same. I thought people just went to classes and went home or to their apartment. I didn't know that people lived on campus. The only people I know who went to college went to a community college and they didn't live there. If I go to college…

All teachers: [*in unison*] Not *if* you go to college, but *when* you go to college.

Mr. F.: [*speaking to Mr. C.*] How many of these guys do you think are actually getting really prepared for college?

Researcher: A cutout of a student in cap and gown stands just inside the door labeled "Attributes of a Future-Ready Graduate." The life-size figure is labeled with qualities which successful students at this school should have:

[*Students call out these qualities in the same choral fashion as before.*]

Students: [*alternating, a slight pause between each*] strong team contributor…effective problem solver…creative/innovative thinker… proficient reader…critical thinker…curious researcher…relationship builder…knowledgeable global citizen…health-focused life long learner…effective communicator…capable technology user…financially literate citizen…self-directed… responsible worker…multilingual…literate consumer of media…skilled mathematician

Mr. C.: [*replying to Mr. F.*] They've got a long ways to go. Sometimes I think some of them just aren't college material, and I don't know what you can do about that, not everybody in this school is college material.

All teachers: [*in unison, except for Mr. C. and Mr. F.*] Not *if* you go to college, but *when* you go to college.

Mr. F.: I just hope we are not giving them a false impression, just because they are coming here. We need to be ready for that because just because they come here and the intention is for them to get a 2-year degree, not everybody is even 2-year degree material.

All teachers: [*in unison, except for Mr. C. and Mr. F.*] Not *if* you go to college, but *when* you go to college.

Mr. C.: We don't want to be just handing out 2-year degrees, not that we're handing them out; I mean, they still have to go through, to meet the requirements of the community college. It wouldn't look good if we are passing on to the community college for their fourth and fifth year, students who aren't capable of passing community college classes.

All teachers: [*in unison, except for Mr. C. and Mr. F.*] Not *if* you go to college, but *when* you go to college.

Mr. F.: We're new; it's hard to say what's going to happen. Are all these kids community college material? Are they 4-year college material? I don't know.

Iliana: My sister used to call home crying about how hard classes were. I think people overreact. College is not that hard. I thought it would be harder.

Ms. A.: I have a concern over the rigor in the community college courses. My English class is harder than their college classes. We expect more of them.

Gabby: I will come home to have my mother do my laundry. My cousins did that when they went to school.

Researcher: Ties to home are strong for first-generation college students. According to Schmidt (2003), they are more likely to attend a college closer to home or to commute to college. The first-generation college student struggles to maintain their connections to home while aspiring to a college education.

Gabby: Will I ever find my place? I found a pack, small but mighty. They care for their own; they leave no one behind; they are family. Could I belong in such a pack as this? They care for me; they accept me; they will always have my back. I have finally found my place.

Austin: I found out what I wanted to be here, and no one can stand in my way. I can be anything I set my mind to.

Cody: If you surround yourself with successful people, I think you will be more successful.

Researcher: Cody's instincts may be right. Researchers Lamont and Lareau (1988) believe that a person's habitus can be affected by the exposure to the habitus of others. Surrounding students with peers who have aspirations for college may have a positive effect.

Gabby: My life has been hard. I have been through a lot of hardships. In the end, I want everything to come out okay.

Brennan: My uncle said a wise guy learns from his mistakes, a wiser man learns from someone else's mistakes.

Mr. F.: The teachers here say they are learning a lot about teaching. I learned more this year than I learned in all my years of teaching. It's the best teaching experience I have ever had.

Austin: [*reading again from his novel*] "We play by their rules long enough, and it becomes our game."

[*Citation appears on the screen: Card, 1985, p. 167*]

Hector: We have a voice here. We can suggest something. At a regular high school they wouldn't listen to us.

Cody: I never even thought of college before I came here, but college doesn't seem like a big scary thing anymore.

Researcher: The students will soon learn that their principal has accepted a job at a school in another state and that Ms. A. will be relocating this summer after her wedding. She will help open another early college high school on a university campus in a nearby city.

[*Mrs. H. and Ms. A. turn and exit upstage; the lights dim as they exit, leaving the Researcher, Hector, and Brittany in the light*]

Hector: We can't predict how our lives will be; we can only make choices that determine how our lives will be.

Brittany: I'm not ready for everything yet. I am ready for the next step.

Hector: My story's not over.

[*lights out*]

Questions for Dialogue

1. What do you notice about the Researcher's use of language compared to the other characters? What values and conventions are represented? What meaning might you draw from them?
2. How does the metaphor of the early college high school as a family serve to both support and restrict students? What other metaphors may be useful?
3. In what ways does the private financial backing of early college high schools shape the school climate?
4. How can schools help students move beyond the labels they have been given, and support them in creating their own identities?
5. How can schools help students become the authors of their own life narratives?

Notes

1. Jobs for the Future prescribes specific methodologies in early college high schools receiving funding from the Bill and Melinda Gates Foundation. These methods encourage collaboration and are intended to engage reluctant learners.
2. The Development, Relief and Education for Alien Minors Act (DREAM Act) is proposed federal legislation that would allow students without legal status to pursue a college education.

3. One aspect of the 1994 North American Free Trade Agreement (NAFTA) is funding for the retraining of workers whose jobs have been lost to foreign competitors.

References

Abelson, R. (1996). Psychological status of the script concept. In M. J. Brosnan (Ed.), *Cognitive functions: Classic readings in representation and reasoning* (pp. 67–90). Dartford, UK: Greenwich University Press. (Original work published 1981).

Astin, A. W., & Osequera, L. (2004). The declining "equity" of American higher education. *The Review of Higher Education, 27*(3), 321–341.

Baxter Magolda, M. B. (2001). *Making their own way: Narratives for transforming higher education to promote self-authorship*. Sterling, VA: Stylus.

Berger, A., Adelman, N., & Cole, S. (2010). The early college high school initiative: An overview of five evaluation years. *Peabody Journal of Education, 85*, 333–347.

Bieber, J., & Worley, L. (2006). Conceptualizing the academic life: Graduate students' perspectives. *The Journal of Higher Education, 77*(6), 1009–1035.

Bui, K. T. (2002). First-generation college students at a four-year university: Background characteristics, reasons for pursing higher education, and first-year experiences. *College Student Journal, 36*(1), 3–12.

Card, S. (1985). *Ender's game*. New York: Tor Books.

Clark, B. R. (1960). The "cooling out" function in higher education. *American Journal of Sociology, 65*, 569–576.

Clark, B. R. (1980). The "cooling out" function revisited. In G. B. Vaughan (Ed.), *Questioning the community college role. New directions for community colleges no. 32* (pp. 15–31). San Francisco: Jossey-Bass.

Deal, T. E., & Peterson, K. D. (1999). *Shaping school culture: The heart of teacher leadership*. San Francisco: Jossey-Bass.

Edmunds, J. A., et al. (2010). Preparing students for college: The implementation and impact of the early college high school model. *Peabody Journal of Education, 85*, 348–368. doi: 10.1080/0161956X.2010.491702

Goldstein, T. (2002b). *Performed ethnography for representing other people's children in critical educational research*. Applied Theatre Researcher, 3(5), 1-11.

Grubb, W. N. (1989). The effects of differentiation on educational attainment: The case of community colleges. *Review of Higher Education, 12*, 349–374.

Grubb, W. N. (1991). The decline of community college transfer rates: Evidence from national longitudinal surveys. *Journal of Higher Education, 62*, 194–222.

Gullatt, Y., & Jan, W. (2003). *How do pre-collegiate academic outreach programs impact college-going among underrepresented students?* Washington, DC: Pathways to College Network Clearinghouse.

Hammond, W., & Steward, D. (Eds.). (2008). *Verbatim: Techniques in contemporary documentary theatre*. London: Oberon Books.

Horn, L., & Nuñez, A.-M. (2000). *Mapping the road to college: First-generation students' math track, planning strategies, and context of support*. Washington, DC: U.S. National Center for Education Statistics.

Jeffrey, B., & Troman, G. (2004). Time for ethnography. *British Educational Research Journal, 30*(4), 536–548.

Jobs for the Future. (2008). *Early College High School Initiativecore principles*. Boston: Jobs for the Future.

Kirst, M. W. (2004). The high school/college disconnect. *Education Leadership*, *62*(3), 51–55.
Lamont, M., & Lareau, A. (1988). Cultural capital: Allusions, gaps, and glissandos in recent theoretical developments. *Sociology Theory*, *6*, 153–168.
London, H. B. (1989). Breaking away: A study of college students and their families. *American Journal of Education*, *97*(2), 144–170.
Lucey, H., Melody, J., & Walkerdine, V. (2003). Uneasy hybrids: Psychosocial aspects of becoming educationally successful for working-class young women. *Gender and Education*, *15*(3), 285–299. doi: 10.1080/0954025032000103204
Mienczakowski, J. (1995). The theatre of ethnography: The reconstruction of ethnography into theatre with emancipatory potential. *Qualitative Inquiry*, *1*(3), 360–375.
Norris, J. (2009). *Playbuilding as qualitative research: A participatory arts-based approach*. Walnut Creek, CA: Left Coast Press.
Paget, D. (1997). Verbatim theatre: Oral history and documentary techniques. *New Theatre Quarterly*, *12*, 317–336.
Piorkowski, G. K. (1983). Survivor guilt in the university setting. *The Personnel and Guidance Journal*, *61*(10), 620–622.
Rubin, D., & Berntsen, D. (2003). Lifescripts help to maintain autobiographical memories of highly positive, but not highly negative, events. *Memory & Cognition*, *31*(1), 1–14.
Saldaña, J. (2003). Dramatizing data: A primer. *Qualitative Inquiry*, *9*(2), 218–236. doi: 10.1177/1077800402250932
Saldaña, J. (2010). *The coding manual for qualitative researchers*. Thousand Oaks, CA: Sage.
Schmidt, P. (2003). Academe's Hispanic future: The nation's largest minority group faces big obstacles in higher education, and colleges struggle to find the right ways to help. *Chronicle of Higher Education*, *50*(14), A8.
Smith, A. D. (1993). *Fires in the mirror: Crown Heights, Brooklyn, and other identities*. Garden City, NY: Anchor.
Steiner, C. (1990). *Scripts people live by: Transactional analysis of life scripts*. New York: Grove Press.
Striplin, J. J. (1999). *Facilitating transfer for first-generation community college students*. ERIC Digest, ED430627.
Thayer, P. B. (2000, May). Retaining first-generation and low-income students. *Opportunity Outlook*, 2–8.
Tierney, W. G. (2004). Academic triage: Challenges confronting college preparation programs. *Qualitative Inquiry*, *10*, 950–962.
Vargas, J. H. (2004). *College knowledge: Addressing information barriers to college*. Boston, MA: College Access Services, The Education Resources Institute.
Vargas, J. H., & Miller, M. S. (2011). Early college designs: An increasingly popular college-readiness strategy for school districts to reach more traditionally underserved students. *The School Administrator*, *6*(68), 18-25.
Wilder, T. (1960). *Our town*. New York: Harper.

Chapter 9

Queerer Than Queer!

Mark Vicars

Introduction

In 2010 the "National Anti-Gay/Lesbian Victimization Report" indicated that 45% of gay males and 20% of lesbians surveyed in the United States had experienced harassment and/or violence as a result of their actual or perceived sexual orientation during high school. In 2009 the Australian "National School Climate Survey" indicated that of 7,261 middle and high school students, nearly 9 out of 10 lesbian, gay, bisexual, and transgender (LGBT) students had experienced harassment at school in the past year, and nearly two thirds felt unsafe because of their sexual orientation. Nearly one third of LGBT students had skipped at least 1 day of school in the past month because of safety concerns.

Nearly every one of the 140 youths interviewed by Human Rights Watch (2001) described incidents of verbal or other nonphysical harassment of themselves or others in educational domains because of perceived sexual orientation. For many LGBT youth, relentless verbal abuse and other forms of harassment are all part of the normal daily routine, and it can come in the form of rumors, written notes, and harassment via text or the Internet, by peers who actively create a hostile climate.

As teachers, we need to put into practice a pedagogy that intervenes in institutional heterosexism—the overt or tacit bias against lesbians, gay men, or transgendered people in the belief that heterosexuality is superior to homosexuality. Heterosexism finds its most basic expression in educational communities that seldom have to move beyond the personal deficit model in attempting to meet the needs of lesbian and gay youth, and it is routinely expressed when the formal and informal curriculum fails to give any recognition to notions of other sexualities (McKenna & Vicars, 2013).

Equality and Diversity

Equality is about recognizing and respecting diversity and difference; it is not about giving certain groups "special treatment" or "extra rights." It's about treating everyone as an individual, with respect and consideration, and being aware of the impact that our words and actions can have on others and on society. It's about recognizing the impact that prejudice and discrimination have on people and taking positive and constructive steps to ensure that we do not perpetuate or promote negative attitudes, stereotypes, or damaging misconceptions about communities or individuals. Diversity is about embracing and celebrating the richness of society and ensuring that underrepresented communities have a stake in that society; it is about creating an environment that is positive about difference. Despite some advances in LGBT rights, homophobic, biphobic, and transphobic attitudes remain prevalent in our society. These discriminatory and oppressive attitudes and ideologies damage the lives of not only LGBT people, but the whole of society.

Religious and Cultural Issues

Public acceptance of homosexuality has increased in a number of ways in recent years. An understanding of homosexuality should be viewed within the cultural context of society. Issues typically faced by LGBT-identified people can be exacerbated or mitigated by their religious, cultural, or ethnic heritage. LGBT youth who come from certain cultural or religious backgrounds may have to face additional difficulties in that they may be forced to choose between their families and accepting themselves and living as openly LGBT.

As with social attitudes in general, religious attitudes toward homosexuality vary between and among religions and their adherents. Traditionalists among the world's major religions generally disapprove of homosexuality, and Abrahamic religions such as Judaism, Islam, and Christianity traditionally forbid sexual relations between people of the same sex, and teach that such behaviour is sinful. Religious authorities point to passages in the Qur'an, the Old Testament, and the New Testament for scriptural justification of these beliefs. Hinduism, Buddhism, Jainism, and Sikhism teachings regarding homosexuality are less clear; unlike in Western religions, homosexuality is rarely discussed.

What does the Bible say? Nowhere in scripture is reference made to the "condition" of homosexuality, only to homosexual acts. Often invoked is the story about the destruction of Sodom and Gomorrah, but this was not about homosexuality; it was about the sin of breaching sacred hospitality. Many passages from the Bible are often taken out of context, or interpreted without consideration for the culture of the time period in which they were written. Any interpretation of religious texts reflects the personal beliefs of the translators and the social beliefs of the time period in which they were translated.

Indeed, people and societies have utilized the Bible and other religious texts for their own ends. Perhaps the two most widely abused verses used to condemn homosexuality come from Leviticus: "You shall not lie with man as one lies with a women; this is an abomination" (Leviticus 18:22), and "If a man also lie with mankind as he lieth with a woman, both of them have committed an abomination; they should surely be put to death" (Leviticus 20:13). If Christians today insist on using this passage to condemn homosexuality, then surely they are also bound by the other rules and rituals described in Leviticus. Among other things, the Holiness Code of Leviticus prohibits:

- sexual intercourse during a women's menstrual cycle;
- tattoos;
- wearing certain types of jewelry;
- eating rare meat;
- wearing clothing made from blended textiles (e.g., cotton-polyester blends);
- cross-breeding livestock;
- sowing a field with mixed seed;
- eating or touching the dead flesh of pigs, rabbits, and some forms of seafood; and
- men cutting their hair or shaving their beards.

Jesus had nothing to say on the subject of homosexuality, and his absence of comment neither supports nor condemns it. The Bible says little about homosexual feelings and nothing about sexual orientation, as the concept of orientation dates from only the late nineteenth century. A number of homosexual relationships are described positively or neutrally in the Bible, and of the many hundreds of Jesus' instructions and prohibitions, few have a sexual component and none condemn homosexuality.

What does the Qur'an say? It is widely believed that homosexuality is forbidden in Islam. This perception is also embodied in Muslim laws to the extent that in some countries, homosexuality is a crime punishable by death (stoning). The word *homosexuality* does not actually exist in the Qur'an. The work of reformist scholars who have explored the issues of sexuality in Islam have developed viewpoints that challenge traditional ideas relating to sexuality. Movements of scholars, activists, and others who challenge the injustice and inequality that exists in Muslim laws and societies have been called "progressive Islam" or "reformist Islam." Reformists propose that shari'ah is merely an understanding of Islam that has been influenced by traditional customs and social values of the historical time in which it was formulated. Reformists believe that challenging shari'ah is therefore only challenging a particular understanding of Islam, rather than challenging Islam itself.

The assumptions made about homosexuality and Islam often are based on references to the story of Lut in the Qur'an. The story of Lut is not specifically about same-sex sexuality and/or same-sex relationships; it is about a people who are punished for committing several forms of unlawful (sexual) behaviour including widespread promiscuity, bestiality, paedophilia, and rape, as well as inhospitality towards guests, abuse of power, and intimidation. What do the media say? In western culture, gay men are often stereotyped as effeminate. Additional stereotypes of gay male identity include hypersexualization, extreme care in personal appearance, and knowledge or skills viewed as socially inappropriate for males (e.g., how to sew or decorate). Lesbians are often stereotyped as being overly masculine or as having typically "masculine" knowledge or skills. Bisexuals are often stereotyped as promiscuous, insincere, and/or still confused. There are a variety of ways that the media influences public attitudes toward LGBT people in terms of accurate and inaccurate forms of representation in newspapers and in television shows. Attitudes held by individuals toward lesbians, gay men, and bisexuals are often affected by social and cultural factors. Cultural theorists have noted how portrayals of homosexuality often center on stigmatized phenomena such as AIDS, paedophilia, and gender variance.

Questions for Dialogue

Where do you locate yourself in relation to the following discourses?

1. The Discourse of Innocence: used to maintain ignorance and not engage with these issues, denying the worlds/realities children are coming from—"it's a form of paedophilia"
2. The Discourse of Age-Appropriateness: "they're too young to know about sex and to understand sexuality"
3. The Discourse of Recruitment: "you'll make them gay"

4. The Discourse of Normalization: e.g., "that's what normal boys do", "it's not normal for children to grow up like that"
5. The Discourse of Justification: "[ethnic] parents will complain", "it's not relevant at our school"; "we don't have those families here"
6. The Discourse of Resignation: "we can't do anything about it", "our school's got enough to handle", "we'll lose our jobs", "it'll only incite more harassment for these kids from these homes", "we don't have time to learn new skills"
7. The Discourse of Controversy: "we don't want to alienate anyone", "it'll cause a stir in the school community", "we won't get staff consensus on this one"
8. The Discourse of Morality: "this is a moral issue, and our religious families will object"

Modeled after a conference presentation by Pallotta-Chiarolli, 2009.

Queer (in) the Curriculum

Schools shape identity, and they are the perfect setting for deconstructing the rigidities and inequalities that are centered on the binaries of the homo-hetero divide. Over the last few decades, the epistemic landscape around sexuality has been radically altered. Yet, the notion that sexuality is essentialist and biologically constructed, and that it can be considered from some external reference point—which is based on a preferred morality—remains unquestioned in educational domains.

It is increasingly important for educators to understand the emergence of a contemporary vocabulary that insists that rather than ignore, we celebrate differences in sexuality and sexual identities. Everyday identities, located and constructed through language, discursively reproduced in the process of social interaction, can provide educators with a powerful platform to intervene in injurious speech acts in educational domains (Vicars, 2006). Far too frequently, LGBT students in classrooms and school corridors experience a fractured sense of self that is reiteratively constituted through the authorizing, performative utterances of wounding words. By choosing to challenge initiatory transitive performative pejorative utterances toward lesbian, gay, or bisexual students, it is pedagogically possible to disrupt heteronorming processes.

Butler (1990) has written about the "heterosexual matrix"—a linguistically constructed worldview that reproduces itself by claiming gendered subjects as having an already implied desire for each other. The perlocutionary effects of the heterosexual matrix are, as Wright (2004) noted,

> ...[how] meanings, subjects and subjectivities are formed .... [C]hoices in language point to those discourses being drawn upon by writers and listeners, and to the ways in which they position themselves and others. Questions can be therefore asked about how language works to position speakers (and listeners) in relation to particular discourses and with what effects. (p. 20)

We should not assume that all students' identities are privileged and normative. As teachers, we should be both responsive and accountable to voicing the tacit entitlements in schools, and explicitly and determinedly including and celebrating the diversity of all lives and experiences into the teaching and classroom context.

Definitions Explained

The following section provides teachers with vocabulary to describe contemporary folk taxonomies of sexual identity. They pedagogically provoke insight to challenge the invisibility of gay and lesbian students in educational domains. Saying the L, G, B, T, Q, I words has to be the first weapon in our pedagogic arsenal to combat censorship and suppression. We urgently need to generate pedagogic occasions to question what is beyond the binary categories that constitute what is heterosexual and normalized or homosexual and disavowed. Conventional performance of the homo-hetero binaries in school communities would cast homophobic fear as central to the policing of the boundaries of what can and cannot be said.

The definitions below provide a starting point for thinking through what could happen when, as teachers, we start to decolonize the classroom space, routinely challenging the presumption of heterosexuality routinely embedded in our language, explicit/hidden curriculum, and pedagogies.

Biphobia: The irrational fear and intolerance of people who are bisexual.

Bisexual: A person who is attracted to two sexes or two genders, but not necessarily simultaneously or equally.

Coming out: Recognizing one's sexual orientation, gender identity, or sex identity, and being open about it with oneself and with others.

Discrimination: The act of showing partiality or prejudice; a prejudicial act.

Dominant culture: The cultural values, beliefs, and practices that are assumed to be the most common and influential within a given society.

FTM: Female-to-male transsexual.

Gay: Men attracted to men. Colloquially used as an umbrella term to include all LGBQ people.

Gender: (a) A socially constructed system of classification that ascribes qualities of masculinity and femininity to people. Gender characteristics can change over time, and vary between cultures. Words that refer to gender include *man*, *woman*, *transgender*, *masculine*, *feminine*, and *queer*; (b) One's sense of self as masculine or feminine, regardless of external genitalia. *Gender* is often conflated with *sex*, but this is inaccurate because *sex* refers to bodies and *gender* refers to personality characteristics.

Gender conformity: When your gender identity and sex "match" (i.e., fit social norms); for example, a male who is masculine and identifies as a man.

Gender identity: The gender that a person sees him- or herself as. This can include refusing to label oneself with a gender. Gender identity is also often conflated with sexual orientation, but this is inaccurate because gender identity does not cause sexual orientation; for example, a masculine woman is not necessarily a lesbian.

Gender-neutral language: Nondiscriminatory language to describe relationships—for example, *spouse* and *partner* are gender-neutral alternatives to the gender-specific words *husband*, *wife*, *boyfriend*, and *girlfriend*.

Gender queer: A person who redefines or plays with gender, or who refuses gender altogether; a label for people who bend/break the rules of gender and blur the boundaries.

Gender role: How "masculine" or "feminine" an individual acts. Societies commonly have norms regarding how males and females should behave, expecting people to have personality characteristics and/or act a certain way based on their biological sex.

Gender-variant / Gender nonconforming: Displaying gender traits that are not normatively associated with their biological sex. "Feminine" behavior or appearance in a male is gender-variant, as is "masculine" behavior or appearance in a female. Gender-variant behavior is culturally specific.

Hate crime: Hate crime legislation often defines a hate crime as a crime motivated by the actual or perceived race, color, religion, national origin, ethnicity, gender, disability, or sexual orientation of the victim.

Heterosexuality: Sexual, emotional, and/or romantic attraction to a sex other than your own; commonly thought of as attraction to the opposite sex.

Heterosexism: Assuming every person to be heterosexual, and therefore marginalizing persons who do not identify as heterosexual; also, believing heterosexuality to be superior to homosexuality and all other sexual orientations.

Heterosexual privilege: Benefits derived automatically by being (or being perceived as) heterosexual, which are denied to homosexuals, bisexuals, and queers.

Homophobia: The irrational fear and intolerance of people who are homosexual, or of homosexual feelings within one's self. It assumes that heterosexuality is superior.

Homosexuality: Sexual, emotional, and/or romantic attraction to the same sex.

Institutional oppression: Arrangement of a society used to benefit one group at the expense of another, through the use of language, media education, religion, economics, etc.

Internalized oppression: The process by which an oppressed person comes to believe, accept, or live out the inaccurate stereotypes and misinformation about their group.

Intersex: Intersexuality is a set of medical conditions that feature congenital anomaly of the reproductive and sexual system. That is, intersex people are born with "sex chromosomes," external genitalia, or internal reproductive systems that are not considered "standard" for either male or female. The existence of intersexuals shows that there are not two sexes only, and that our ways of thinking about sex (trying to force everyone to fit into either the male box or the female box) is socially constructed.

In the closet: Keeping one's sexual orientation and/or gender or sex identity a secret.

Invisible minority: A group whose minority status is not always immediately visible.

Lesbian: A woman attracted to women.

LGBTIQ: Lesbian, gay, bisexual, transgender, intersex, queer.

Marginalized: Excluded, ignored, or relegated to the outer edge of a group/society/community.

MSM: Men who have sex with men, but may not necessarily self-identify as gay.

MTF: Male-to-female transsexual.

Out, or Out of the closet: Refers to varying degrees of being open about one's sexual orientation and/or sex or gender identity.

Pansexual: A person who is fluid in sexual orientation and/or gender or sex identity.

Queer: (a) An umbrella term to refer to all LGBTQI people; (b) A political statement, as well as a sexual orientation, which advocates breaking binary thinking and seeing both sexual orientation and gender identity as potentially fluid; (c) A simple label to explain a complex set of sexual behaviors and desires; for example, a person who is attracted to multiple genders may identify as queer. Many older LGBT people feel the word *queer* has been hatefully used against them for too long, and are reluctant to embrace it.

Rainbow flag: The rainbow flag, or pride flag, was designed in 1978 by Gilbert Baker to designate the great diversity of the LGBTQI community.

Sex identity: The sex that a person sees him- or herself as. This can include refusing to label oneself with a sex.

Sexual minority: (a) members of sexual orientations or persons who engage in sexual activities that are not part of the mainstream; (b) members of sex groups that do not fall into the majority categories of male or female, such as intersexuals and transsexuals.

Sex: Refers to a person based on their anatomy (external genitalia, chromosomes, and internal reproductive system). Sex terms are *male*, *female*, *transsexual*, and *intersex*. Sex is biological, whereas social views of and experiences of sex are cultural.

Sexual orientation: The deep-seated direction of one's sexual (erotic) attraction. It is on a continuum and not a set of absolute categories. Sometimes referred to as "affection orientation" or "sexuality." Sexual orientation evolves through a multistage developmental process, and may change over time.

SRS: Sexual reassignment surgery; the surgery performed on transsexuals to make their bodies and their sex identities match.

Stereotype: An exaggerated oversimplified belief about an entire group of people, without regard for individual differences.

Straight: A person attracted to a gender other than his or her own; commonly thought of as attraction to the opposite gender.

Transgender: (Sometimes shortened to trans or TG) a person whose psychological self ("gender identity") differs from the social expectations for the physical sex he or she was born with. To understand this, one must understand the difference between biological sex, which is one's body (genitals, chromosomes), and social gender, which refers to levels of masculinity and femininity. Often, society conflates sex and gender, viewing them as the same thing, but gender and sex are not the same thing. Transgender persons' psychological selves ("gender identities") differ from the social expectations for the physical sex they were born with; for example, a female with a masculine gender identity who identifies as a man.

Transition: A complicated, multistep process that can take years as transsexuals align their anatomy with their sex identity; this process may ultimately include sex reassignment surgery (SRS).

Transphobia: Fear or hatred of transgender people, manifested in a number of ways, including violence, harassment, and discrimination.

Transsexual: A person who experiences a mismatch between the sex they were born as and the sex they identify as. A transsexual sometimes undergoes medical treatment to change his/her physical sex to match his/her sex identity through hormone treatments and/or surgery; not all transsexuals can have or desire surgery.

Transvestite/Cross dresser: A person who regularly or occasionally wears clothing socially assigned to a gender not his or her own, but usually is comfortable with his or her anatomy and does not wish to change it (i.e., they are not transsexuals). *Cross-dresser* is the preferred term for a man who enjoys or prefers women's clothing and social roles.

Providing and making space for other interpretative locations situates the notion of text-to-life/life-to-text (Cochran-Smith, 1984) as a pedagogical expression of a will to knowledge as we work with students to find a way to articulate tacit experiences in relation to psychological, sociocultural, and historical interpretations. The notion of a text-to-life "utterance" not only means elaborating a new story of self, but also authorizes positions from which to reflect on a subject or theme that is connected in some way with the psychic and emotional life of the teller. Suggestions for using the above language in the classroom context include having students explore:

- purpose(s) and motivations for the use of particular language;
- words and images and the referents they evoke;

- construction and representation of identities;
- absences and omissions in everyday discourses prompted by the curriculum/texts;
- identities suggested by and within the curriculum/text;
- how language privileges normative performances of identity; and
- the social and cultural realities of the curriculum/text.

In Other Words

Tierney and Lincoln (1997) have noted the use of narrative (or story) as a form of social inquiry. Susan Chase (cited in Lincoln & Denzin, 2003, pp. 273–296) gives convincing reasons why we ought to take narrative more seriously in our teaching and our research, arguing that life stories themselves embody the action and knowing that we need to study. The story, or what in literature is termed an *evocative narrative*, is the place where biography and fact can fracture epistemic violence and boundaries. Storytelling is the manner in which the boundaries of self and others are re-aligned. As Ellis and Bochner (1996) noted,

> The accessibility and readability of the text repositions the reader as a co-participant in the dialogue and thus rejects the orthodox view of the reader as a passive receiver of knowledge; the disclosure of hidden details of private life highlights emotional experience and thus challenges the rational actor model of social performance; the narrative text refuses the impulse to abstract and explain, stressing the journey over the explanation, and thus eclipses the scientific illusion of control and mastery; and the episodic portrayal of the ebb and flow of relationship dramatizes the motion of connected lives across the curve of time, and thus resists the standard practice of portraying social life and relationships as a snapshot. Evocative stories activate subjectivity and compel emotional response. (p.18)

This chapter utilizes evocative stories to show something of how being identified or identifiable as gay becomes reproduced as a deficit in educational domains. As an openly gay/queer male educator, I have increasingly realized how a gay identity is experienced in a very differently than other identities. Maybe it is the counter-narratives, in which meaning becomes embodied and performed, that draws me toward fugitive storied ways of knowing to methodologically, politically, and psychologically create a distance from normalized ways of being (Brain, 2010). Revisiting the interpretive locations of the everyday pedagogies of normalcy, throughout this chapter I have drawn on stories told to me throughout my career by former students and colleagues to challenge disciplinary epistemologies and dislocate normalizing discourses.

The autobiographical accounts aim to show how experience of a sexual self becomes "produced through discursive practices" (MacLure, 2003, p. 19); namely, how heterosexism and homophobia are routinely and performatively constituted in the everyday life of schools. Telling personal stories can revitalize classrooms and provide significant pedagogic opportunities to reflect on how wider sociocultural narratives intersect with individual lives. The performative stories in this chapter purposely position "sexuality at the point at which various systems that regulate the social...are openly displayed" (Probyn, 1996, p. 130). Methodologically, they are messy in their evocative recreation of peripheral life experiences. Yet, an often unspoken reality is that research, and teaching, is messy.

The pedagogical promise of performative narratives for generating and presenting data in social research draws on post-foundational research methodologies. Academic interest in post-foundational research methodologies has demonstrated the increasing value in considering the symbolic, situated world, as seen and told by participants in research projects. The performative narrations here invite critical consideration of how artistic praxis can transform existing social and material relations of research production by utilizing individuals' meaningful representations of themselves. Not only do such narratives interject transgressive subject matter into contemporary social discourse, they also disrupt forms of dominant ways of knowing. They show us, I suggest, how identities are intimately akin and connected to the stories that we tell of ourselves in the world; they are messy because they often evade fixation, and are, at best, but performative interpellations at play.

Performing the Page

To re-engage with the play of queer lives, I have employed a reflective, performative methodology that aims to show how intimacy or detachment from the social world forms a landscape through which understandings of self and other become mediated. In the following scenes, the embodied narratives are a form of not only world knowing, but also world making. The scenes afford a critical pedagogical space in classrooms for texts of identity to be critically examined within and alongside existing curriculum. Making possible and present opportunities for rereading and writing the world, the scenes follow the concept of transformative artful praxis as outlined by McKenna (2012):

- learning about self and others as experiential practice;
- collaborative inquiry and connectivity through artful engagement to build respectful and collective knowing/meaning-making;
- critical interrogation of assumptions and beliefs to recreate personal narratives that explore notions of identity;
- relational knowledge creation related to psychosocial wellness;
- exploration of tensions and anomalies, generating opportunities for integration;
- making present discussions of social justice, equity, respect, and mutuality;
- reflexive knowing selfhood, life-worlds;
- generating opportunities to co-create ways of respectful engagements and community building; and
- creative explorations that provide a depth of encounter with "otherness" as reparation of injustice.

Each scene could be used to invite the reader to reconsider what is institutionally and pedagogically required to transform curriculum frameworks so as to explicitly include sexuality in the following areas:

- empowerment;
- personal meaning;
- equality;
- respect;

- individual differences;
- cooperation/conflict resolution;
- community;
- diversity;
- contribution;
- authority;
- reconciliation;
- social justice; and
- responsibility and freedom.

Issues of cultural, legal, and social definitions specific to schooling in the western hemisphere have served to create the milieu within which our students live. Examination of these rituals in classrooms is urgently needed to redress the intense negative imagery associated with lesbian and gays in schools. Students have the basic fundamental need and right for a socially constructed and historical sense of "belonging" and positive affirmation. Excessive promotion of compulsory heterosexuality can lead these young people to inevitably shape their visibility and sense of belonging. As fringe dwellers, the lesbian and gay students are intensely aware that many others don't see any need to listen to their stories in school. There are limited opportunities for them to fight for the concerns of their sexuality and identity difference.

Whilst global political activism for gay and lesbian rights is largely moving forwards, this group is still living in a very marginal context. Schools seem to be the last place where change is occurring. LGBTQI students are required to perform their identity with shifting definitions of their sexualities being played out in the larger world, and yet, they come to school and experience the anxieties of denied identities. Their stories remain unexpressed because of social prohibitions in educational settings.

Act One

When I was 16 I told my father I was gay. "You had better go and tell your mother." As I entered the bedroom where she lay, her gnarled fingers misshapen through rheumatoid arthritis clutched the heating pad she used to alleviate the pain in her joints. Heavy curtains were blocking out the afternoon sun. She had been prescribed new anti-inflammatory drugs that had a side effect of drying up her tear ducts; twice daily a pipette containing synthetic "natural tears" would lubricate her eyes and keep them functioning.

"I've something to tell you,"

I inwardly flinched,
"I think I might be gay."

Why did I say "think"? There was no doubt; in my body, I knew.

"I haven't got a son; I've got two daughters. What have I done wrong? It is wrong; it's in the Bible…You'd better leave."

The silence between us irrevocably fractured. She turned her face away from where I stood and started to cry. The tears came quite freely now. I abandoned the melodrama that was being played out behind the net drapes of my parent's house and fled, not quite skirts billowing, to the end of the road to catch a bus to a friend's house. Her parents had been informed of this possible scenario and were willing to let me stay until I had got things sorted out. My plan was to move to London and find the life that I knew was out there waiting for me, but would not be found on the streets of this small northern town.

As I was drinking hot sweet tea and retelling the events that led to my outcast state, the telephone began to ring. "It's for you, it's your father," my friend's mother called through to the kitchen, where I was still in the process of thawing out from the reaction of my parents. If only I had kept my mouth shut. Nervously, I took hold of the receiver.

"We have been talking and I'm coming to pick you up."

He began with

"We should talk."

And then…
"Are you a queen?"

I had no idea what he was talking about but could detect from the tone of his voice that whatever it was I had better not be one. As I sat at that formica-topped kitchen table, the gathering place for every important family event I can ever recall, I tried hard to numb myself to the situation, to the disappointment etched on the faces of my parents.

My father stood by the door and waited for me to give him the answer he wanted—

No!

"How do you know that you are…?"

He avoided saying it.

"Have you had sex with a girl?"

"Yes."

I lied.

"Have you had sex with…"

Again, he couldn't bring himself to say it, to name me.

"No"

I lied.

This was the last time my sexuality was ever mentioned. It was tiptoed around like I had some terminal illness that if named would rear up and consume us all. The lesson I learnt from my initial revelation was one of how language and discourse "is always productive: It brings a situation into play, enunciates evaluations of the situations and extends action into the future" (Denzin, 1997, p. 37). Looking back, what went and remained unsaid is far more descriptive and meaningful to my interpretation of that situation. I knew through their silence that my parents were holding out for a reversal, for a change of mind. In giving voice to what lay on the inside, I had created myself as I wanted to be seen and heard. In their silence, they were unseating that creation and hoping for an erasure of its possible existence (Vicars, 2009).

Act Two

I remember the day my brother told me he was gay. I recall the conversation between us almost verbatim.... I came to learn that Steve had "come out" to my parents when he was 17. He was in year 11 or 12 at an "all boys" Catholic school. Steve turned to drugs around this time, and as I was only 7 years old, I was spending a lot of time at our neighbor's house. I have more "family memories" of their family than I do my own

The words *poof* and *faggot* were used a lot back in the mid-80s. Between my defense of homosexuality and general gossip, slowly word got around that I had a gay brother. I did not hold back when questioned about my brother, and almost dared people to say something negative in front of me. I was 12 years old, living with my parents and my sister. The year was 1984. I had just started high school and was having a little difficulty at the time finding my niche.

My type of "in your face" defiance continued for much of my teenage years, affecting my life in many ways. My education, friendships, family life, and relationships would all suffer somewhat due to my choosing to accept and embrace my brother's sexuality. It definitely hindered my relationship with my sister. Although we had never really been very close, we grew further apart as her outwardly negative reaction to Steve grew.

My brother had already been diagnosed HIV-positive in 1984. Dad finally realized that he could lose his son, and my sister's attitude was more of a "well, if you play with fire...." She pulled further away from the family, at least for the next 8 or so years.

I found it very difficult to focus at school in year 9. No teacher ever discussed my brother with me; even though they had been made aware of the circumstances by my mother. It seemed like I was the only person at school who had a gay brother, and as it was the early days of the AIDS virus, people seemed almost scared of me, like if they got too close, maybe they could catch it from me.

The lack of emotional support at school and my ongoing bad grades and attitude resulted in a joint decision by the school and myself; that I would be better off leaving school and getting a job. I was only 15 and had just completed year 9.

By 1987, my brother had a new relationship. John was also HIV positive and a big rights activist, fighting for AZT and opening a halfway house for HIV-positive people who did not have family support. I volunteered at the house, helping out in any way that I could. I was still not driving at that stage, so I would often have sleepovers at the house.

Around this time, I was writing an English essay on the topic of HIV/AIDS. We were encouraged to read our essays aloud in class and I was happy to do so, as I felt that my essay was of high quality. I stood there bravely as I knew my topic would be controversial. As I read my essay aloud, I could feel the tension in the room build. I continued on, proud of myself for knowing so much about my chosen topic. I could hear some sniggers around the room at certain bits, but I expected that. As I had only been at this school for a little while and had a small group of friends there who already knew about Steve, this was the first time that I had openly discussed him, his house, my friends, their illness, their fight for medication. I could feel myself starting to become angry at one boy in particular. As I finished my essay there was an uncomfortable silence. Even the teacher did not know what to say. I stood there waiting for feedback. I realized the teacher did not know how to respond, so I made my way back to my desk, shaking my head as the realization that I was totally on my own in my fight for HIV rights started to sink in. It was at this moment that one boy decided to say his piece: "What a load of shit. Only faggots get AIDS and they deserve it, so what is the big deal." My feet were rooted to the floor. I could not speak. He declared: "All people with AIDS should be put on their own island and left to do die." I lost it. I started screaming at him at the top of my voice. All I could think of was wanting to hurt him, as he had just hurt my brother, my friends, me. "I hope you get it from sharing your needles you f–ing pig." By now I was completely distraught. I was crying and angrier than I have ever been. I picked up the nearest chair and threw it at the boy. Finally, the teacher, who had been very quiet through all of this tumultuous argument, stepped in. He grabbed me and told me that my behavior was unacceptable, threatening me with detention and suspension. Again, the realization that I was on my own swamped me. I calmed down and turned to the teacher and said, "You don't need to report me. I'm out of here and I'm never coming back." I walked out of the classroom and without so much as a backward glance I left. I never did return, and I never heard from the school. Not so much as a phone call to see if I was okay or if I was returning. My education was over....

Act Three

SILENCE can be the deadliest weapon and safest shield.
It is what I turned to and what I did when cornered by identities I never wanted to claim. Retreating into SILENCE was a way to grin and bear it.

I heard my calling by age 7; they had a word for boys like me:

SISSY!

PANSY!

POOF!

I now had names for something that I had hardly ever thought of at all.

At age 11, I graduated to a new knowledge:

HOMO!

FREAK!

QUEER!

HATE

SHAME

REPRISAL.

I understood how my life got discounted each day.
I felt

SHY

CONFUSED

ALONE.

At 16, I asked what's a HOMO? And the anger and hurt that had not been given voice

PREVAILED

ACCUMULATED.

Spoken through a language of:

MEASUREMENT

NORMS and DEVIATION

that

ACCOUNTED FOR, EXPLAINED:

PATHOLOGIZED

~~SISSY!~~

~~PANSY! POOFTA~~

~~HOMO! FREAK!~~

I retreated into SILENCE.

Act Four

I would say that when he went to primary school, when he was 5, that is when it all started. We are an open family and Paul has always tended to say how he felt, which obviously caused problems. His first teacher would often say to us, "Paul doesn't mix very well; he would rather play with the girls than with boys." The school picked up on that immediately; it became an issue of concern for them that he was choosing to mix with girls more than with the boys. We were invited to school and asked questions as to why we thought he did this. The teachers asked us about what he did at home and what we did; said that we should try and encourage him to play with more boys' toys. As Paul got older the name-calling got progressively worse. He had always been a bit effeminate, and as he became more outspoken he would say to us that he was different, and we would ask, "in what way?" He said he didn't know, but told us, "I must be different because they are all having a go at me." We tried to be supportive. There was this one time when Paul had trouble with another student. The lad was calling him gay so we went into school because Paul was getting upset and would come home and cry. We went to say to the teachers, he is not gay, for the simple reason that if we had said he is then it would go about school and make matters worse. I actually approached the teachers on several occasions and said, "Do you have a problem if he is gay?" And they said, "Well...no we don't have a problem...but...." The next thing we knew, we had a social worker at our door and she wanted to know what had happened at school and what was happening at home. We told her about the name-calling, that sometimes he didn't want to go in the morning, how he would make himself sick, how he would come home crying, and how sometimes he would mess himself at school because he was afraid of going to the toilets.

Throughout Paul's primary education he went to three different schools; at the first school he attended it was suggested to us that he would benefit from a fresh start. That was when he was in year 3. In the second school, we removed him because of the bullying; that was when he was in year 5. When he started secondary school it wasn't long before he stopped going completely. He said he didn't want to go to school because of what he had gone through before. He started making himself sick, and point-blank refused to attend. The school sent us letters, and we went up to see the head to try and sort it out. We gave different reasons. We never said he was gay. But, eventually we were called in again, and this time the deputy head told us about the rumors that had been going around the school. I asked him outright if he had a problem if he was gay; he said, "No, but other pupils do," and that "if Paul lashed out, then there would be a situation and we can't have that." The school didn't feel that they could put measures in place to prevent that from occurring. It was constructed as Paul's and our problem, so we moved him to another school. However, it wasn't that long before it started all over again, and in the end I got sick of it and went to the school and said, "I haven't got a problem with it and I'm his Dad." We were then called to a meeting about his behavior, and they started by saying they were going to exclude him. The school principal asked us, "Are you aware that he has a problem with his sexuality?" We said, "We didn't have a problem." This particular teacher was getting in my nerves 'cos he was saying, "Well you don't know what your son is getting up to." And that's what did it. I said, "You do know that Paul is gay." It went quiet and nobody said anything, but when they did, they said, "No, we didn't know, but we were aware of something being out of joint, but we didn't really know." I said, "Well, you do now."

We had tried all sorts of different ways to deal with what had been going on, but we just never had the backup to fight it or have anybody to help us. At the end of the meeting, Paul was excluded. They kept bringing up his sexuality, and in the end I said, "Excuse me. You are talking about my son. Why does his sexuality matter so much to you?"

When he went to the next school, the headmaster made it clear that being religious, he held certain views, and at that point we knew we wouldn't be able to go to school. However, we did feel reassured: The school had a reputation for being strict, the discipline was good, and the headmaster assured us that in his school, bullying didn't happen. What we did say was that "Paul does have certain feminine ways," and were told not to worry about that, how that would pass when he matured and started to grow up. It was about 6 months later that the problems began again, when Paul started being more open. The teachers didn't like it, and he was taken to the headmaster, who told him, "We don't want discussions in a church school about your feelings towards the same sex; whatever opinions you have, you've got keep them to yourself." There were a lot of incidents at this school, which, to be fair, were dealt with. But when Paul was found in a gay chat room on the library computer, we as a family ended up going to see a counselor at the school's insistence. We knew Paul had been contacting gay groups; he used to ring the gay switchboard and he had made contact with two or three youth groups. Paul assured us that he hadn't been looking at pornography, and we believed him. Eventually, we were summoned to school by the head, who gave us two options: that Paul either be excluded or leave early in year 11. His younger brother by this point in time had started to become affected by the situation, getting called out at school because of the attention that his brother was receiving.

When Paul first said he wanted to go to college I was a bit apprehensive because of all that had gone on before. When we found out that his tutor was gay, it made us feel at ease, because if he had a problem, we thought this time it might be different. If there was a problem at college, we knew we could get on the phone and would be able to get through. It would be straightforward, and that was a good thing for us.

Reflections: Prejudice

Prejudice is something that is felt and expressed, and it refers to a negative or hostile attitude toward another social group. Discrimination refers to an unfavorable action, behavior, outcome, or treatment. The distinction is simple: Prejudice is a thought or attitude; discrimination is the expression of that thought or attitude. Prejudice and discrimination on the basis of sexual orientation can be defined as follows:

> Homophobia is a fear of and/or hostility toward gay people or homosexuality. Homophobia is often expressed visibly, audibly, and sometimes violently. Coined in the late 1960s by the psychologist George Weinberg, the term refers to an aversion to gay or homosexual people or their lifestyle or culture and behavior, or an act based on this aversion. Homophobia has typically been employed to describe individual's antigay attitudes and behaviors. Homophobia can take many forms, including:

Personal (internalized) homophobia: This is the individual's belief that lesbian, gay, and bisexual people are sinful, immoral, or inferior to heterosexuals, or incomplete as women or men. Such views are always learnt, and lesbian, gay, and bisexual people themselves may share them. In this case, the homophobia is internalized. When lesbian, gay, or bisexual persons internalize the belief that they are sinful, immoral, or inferior they may hide their sexuality, try to make it mean less to them, decrease their expectations of life, or engage in behaviors that are harmful to themselves and others.

Interpersonal homophobia: This is the dislike, fear, or hatred of people who are lesbian, gay, or bisexual. This dislike, fear, or hatred may be expressed through name-calling, verbal or physical harassment, or acts of discrimination. Interpersonal homophobia can be acted out through shunning, ostracism, or low-level harassment, or it can be manifested through verbal and physical assault.

Institutional homophobia: This refers to the many ways in which government, business, churches, and other organizations discriminate against people on the basis of their sexual orientation. These organizations set discriminatory policies, allocate resources unfairly, and/or maintain unwritten, discriminatory standards for the behavior of their members or constituents.

Cultural homophobia: This refers to social standards and norms that dictate that being heterosexual is better than being lesbian, gay, or bisexual. These standards and norms are reinforced every day in television shows, movies, and print advertisements in which virtually every character is heterosexual and every sexual and social relationship involves a female and a male. They also are reinforced by the assumption made by most adults that all children eventually will be attracted to and marry persons of the opposite sex. Often, heterosexuals do not realize that these standards exist, whereas lesbian, gay, and bisexual people are acutely aware of them. This results in lesbians, gays, and bisexuals feeling like outsiders in society.

You exhibit homophobic behaviors and attitudes when you:

- think you can "spot one";
- use words such as *poof, dyke, fag, gay,* or *lezzy* as an insult;
- think that a same-sex attracted friend is trying to "pick you up" if they are friendly toward you;
- do not support same-sex attracted friends when they break up with their partners;
- make unnecessary or rude comments about, or feeling repulsed by, public displays of affection between same-sex partners;
- feel that gay, lesbian, bisexual, and transgender people are too outspoken about civil rights;
- assume that everyone you meet is heterosexual;
- assume that a lesbian is just a woman who couldn't find a man, or that a lesbian is a woman who secretly wants to be a man;
- assume that a gay man is just a man who couldn't find a woman, or that a gay man is a man who secretly wants to be a woman;
- assume that bisexual people are confused, or want to "play the field"; and
- do not challenge a homophobic remark for fear of being labeled gay.

Prejudice toward gay people and homosexuality can be brought about by:

- negativity about types of sexual behavior and relationships that are neither procreative nor within marriage;
- having religious beliefs that disapprove of sex and/or homosexuality; and
- having little/no social contact with lesbian and gay people.

Questions for Dialogue

1. What is your stance as a teacher when considering LGBTQI students?
2. What would your school look like if there was zero tolerance of homophobia and heterosexism?
3. What could you do pedagogically to stop oppressive commentary?
4. What can you do to:

    - guarantee a safe environment for LGBTQI students?
    - actively protect targets?
    - affirm sexual difference?
    - enable positive classroom discussion of LGBTQI issues?
    - challenge homophobic jokes or comments?
    - review the curriculum to ensure that there is no casual or implied acceptance of homophobia?
    - ensure the curriculum provides opportunities to challenge learners to think about the implications of prejudice and discrimination?
    - employ a proactive approach to dealing with and addressing homophobia and discrimination in your curriculum area?
    - model appropriate behavior with regard to tackling and preventing homophobia and homophobic bullying?
    - challenge homophobia and explain why such behavior is unacceptable?
    - provide support to victims of homophobia?
    - react consistently, sensitively, and appropriately to homophobic incidents?
    - challenge the derisive use of language around gender and sexuality?
    - work on biases (remember, the problem is homophobia not homosexuality)?
    - combat heterosexism in your classroom by visibly including LGBTQI issues and people?

References

Australian "National School Climate Survey http://www.glsen.org/binary-data/GLSEN_ATTACHMENTS/file/000/001/1676-4.pdf

Brain, J. (2010). Anorexia as a subversive bodily act: Psychic incorporation or body narratives of the self? Retrieved from http://www.women.it/cyberarchive/files/brain.htm

Butler, J. (1990). *Gender Trouble: Feminism and the Subversion of* Identity. New York and London: Routledge.

Cochran-Smith, M. (1984). The making of a reader. Norwood, NJ: Ablex.

Denzin, N. K (1997). *Interpretive ethnography: Ethnographic practices for the 21st century.* Thousand Oaks, CA: Sage.

Ellis, C., & Bochner, A. P. (Eds.). (1996). *Composing ethnography: Alternative form of qualitative writing.* Walnut Creek, CA: AltaMira Press.

Human Rights Watch. (2001). *Hatred in the hallways: Violence and discrimination against lesbian, gay, bisexual, and transgender students in U.S. schools.* Washington, DC: Author. Retrieved from http://hrw.org/reports/2001/uslgbt/toc.htm

Lincoln, Y. S., & Denzin, N. K. (Eds.). (2003). *Turning points in qualitative research: Tying knots in a handkerchief.* New York: AltaMira Press.

MacLure, M. (2003). *Discourse in educational and social research.* Buckingham, UK: Open University Press.

McKenna, T. (2009). *Heteronormativity—workplace discrimination in Australian schools: Gay and lesbian teachers in Australia.* Saarbrücken, Germany: VDM Verlag.

McKenna, T. (2012, March). *Activism art in a social justice pedagogy.* Paper presented at Creative Arts in Education—International Trends conference, Victoria University, Melbourne, Australia.

National Gay and Lesbian Task Force, National Anti-Gay/Lesbian Victimization Report 1984. http://www.thetaskforce.org/reports_and_research/reports?title=1984&tid=2599

Pallotta-Chiarolli, M. (2009). *Bridging and bordering cultural, gender and sexual divides*, Paper presented at Bridging Divides: ensuring access, equity and quality in literacy and English education, National Conference for teachers of English and Literacy. Tasmania 9-12, July 2009, http://www.englishliteracyconference.com.au/index.php?id=62&year=09

Probyn, E. (1996). *Outside belongings.* New York: Routledge.

Tierney, W. G., & Lincoln, Y. S. (Eds.). (1997). *Representation and the text: Re-framing the narrative voice.* Albany: State University of New York Press.

Vicars, M. (2006). Who are you calling queer? Sticks and stones can break my bones but names will always hurt me. *British Educational Research Journal, 32*(3), 347–361.

Vicars, M. (2009). *Dissenting fictions; Investigating the literacy practices of gay men.* Saarbrücken, Germany: VDM Verlag.

McKenna, T., & Vicars, M. (2013). Sexualities—the ultimate outsiders—gay and lesbians queried? In T. McKenna, M. M. Vicars, & M. Cacciattolo (Eds.), *Engaging the disengaged* Cambridge, UK: Cambridge University Press.

Wright, J. (2004). Post-structural methodologies: The body, schooling, and health. In J. Evans, B. Davies, & J. Wright (Eds.), *Body knowledge and control: Studies in the sociology of physical education and health* (pp. 19–33). London: Routledge.

About the Contributors

Allison Daniel Anders, Ph.D., assistant professor in the Department of Educational Studies at the University of South Carolina, teaches courses in qualitative research methodologies, social justice and education, and sociology of education. She taught college courses in prison and served as an evaluator for North Carolina's Incarcerated Individuals Program. Her research interests include narratives of targeted youth.

James A. Brooks teaches English, Latin, and Photojournalism at West Wilkes High School in Millers Creek, NC, where he has taught for the past twenty-seven years. Dr. Brooks received his Bachelor's degree in English Education (1985), his Master's degree in Leadership and Higher Education (1997), and his Doctorate in Educational Leadership (2011) from Appalachian State University in Boone, NC. He is a National Board Certified Teacher (Adolescent/ Young Adult, English/Language Arts). Dr. Brooks' personal and professional interests include music, theatre and film. He is particularly interested in the experiences of first-generation college students. Dr. Brooks has been recognized for his work in the area of media literacy by the National Council of Teachers of English (NCTE) with the 2008 Media Literacy Award. In 2007 he received the prestigious National Education Association (NEA) Excellence in Teaching Award in Washington, DC. In 2009 he was named Outstanding North Carolina English Teacher by the North Carolina English Teachers Association and was recognized as a 2010 High School Teacher of Excellence by NCTE. In 2012, Dr. Brooks was inducted into the National Teacher Hall of Fame.

Anne McGill-Franzen is a Professor and Director of the Reading Center at the University of Tennessee. The focus of Anne's professional work has been struggling readers, including policy that supports or constrains teachers' efforts to support children at-risk. Besides her work with struggling learners, Anne is interested in exploring ways to use community knowledge to create meaning and purpose in school literacy curricula. Anne's research with low-achieving children has been published in many journals including *The Reading Teacher*, *Language Arts*, *Reading Research Quarterly*, *Educational Researcher*, *Learning Disabilities Quarterly*, *Elementary School Journal*, and the *Journal of Educational Research*. Anne serves on the Board of Directors of the National Reading Conference, a professional association of literacy researchers, and is a member of the Joint International Reading Association/National Institute of Child Health & Development Committee on Early Childhood Education. In addition, Anne is a Technical Consultant for the UNESCO funded project on the diagnostic teaching of reading in Kenya, Ghana, and Tanzania.

Kimberly J. Howard is a PhD candidate in the Social Foundations of Education program at the University of South Carolina. Her research interests include race, critical notions of geography and place, and uses of performance in the dissemination of research. She currently works as an English as a Second Language teacher in a South Carolina public school.

Katherine Evans is an Assistant Professor of Special Education in the Department of Education at Eastern Mennonite University where she teaches courses in learning theory and special education and supervises pre-service special education teachers. She holds a Ph.D. in Educational Psychology and Research, as well as a certificate in qualitative research. Her research interests include teacher development, restorative justice, and the intersection of race, disability, and school and classroom discipline practices. She has taught courses in educational psychology, and learning theory, and special education and was a middle and high school special educator for students identified as having learning, behavioral, and emotional challenges.

Rachael Gabriel is an Assistant Professor of Reading Education at the University of Connecticut. Rachael's career in education began as a middle school literacy teacher in an urban charter school. She has since worked as a literacy specialist, pursued a reading specialist certification and a Ph.D. in Education with a focus on literacy studies. She holds graduate certificates in both quantitative and qualitative research methods in education, and she is a former fellow of the Baker Center for Public Policy. As a researcher, Rachael has focused on teacher preparation, development and evaluation with a specific interest in related policy and a continued interest in literacy instruction, and disability studies. Her research most often lies at the intersections of these fields with issues of equity, access and social justice. She currently serves as the editor of the online journal *Catalyst: A social justice forum*.

About the Contributors

Rosa M. Jiménez is an Assistant Professor in the Mary Lou Fulton Teachers College, Division of Educational Leadership and Innovation at Arizona State University. She examines the education, alienation, and empowerment of immigrant youth, with a focus on Language Minority Students and Latina/o secondary students. Specifically, she interrogates the academic and critical literacy potential of culturally relevant and critical pedagogies. Her most recent research examined the applications of Community Cultural Wealth theory in family histories curricula with Latina/o English Learners in California. Dr. Jiménez has over ten years of experience working in K-12 public schools as a middle school social studies teacher, literacy coach and educational researcher.

Kafele J. Khalfani is currently an assistant director for residence life at the University of California, Riverside. He will be completing his second year of study in the doctor of education in educational leadership program at the University of Southern California. He holds a master of fine arts in screenwriting from Loyola Marymount University.

Jessica Nina Lester is an Assistant Professor of Educational Psychology at Washington State University. She began her career in education as a middle school math and science teacher. She has since worked as a special educator in the US and Colombia, South America. She holds a Ph.D. in Educational Psychology, with a focus on qualitative methodology and cultural studies in education. Her main research interests lie at the intersection of culture, psychological constructs (e.g., learning, motivation, emotions, etc.), and education, particularly as related to the education of targeted youth.

Renee Moran is currently pursuing her doctoral degree in the Department of Theory and Practice in Education with a focus on literacy studies at the University of Tennessee-Knoxville. Renee is a graduate teaching assistant at the University of Tennessee and is currently teaching Emergent Literacy in the Reading Specialist Program. Prior to beginning her doctoral work, Renee worked for eight years as an elementary classroom teacher primarily in kindergarten and first grade in both the North Carolina and California school systems. Renee's research interests include teacher evaluation and the implications of a performance pay model as well as critical discourse analysis.

Irina Okhremtchouk is an Assistant Professor in the Mary Lou Fulton Teachers College, Division of Teacher Preparation at Arizona State University, Tempe. Her research interests include classification/stratification practices for language minority students, school organization, school finance, and the assessment practices for pre-service teachers. In addition to her academic work and research activities, Dr. Okhremtchouk has over twelve years of experience working in 6-12 education settings as a schoolteacher, program coordinator, child advocate, and school board member.

Katharine Sprecher has a PhD in education with concentration in cultural studies of educational foundations, a master's degree in social and cultural anthropology, and a teaching credential with emphasis in cultural and linguistic diversity. She has worked as a teacher, tutor, and mentor in K-12+ urban schools and beyond. Her research interests include critical, local-global approaches to multicultural education and postcritical feminist research methods. Dr. Sprecher has written, directed, and performed creative works for community spaces in multiple cities. She recently completed work on a national study as research associate at The Center for the Study of Youth and Political Conflict at The University of Tennessee.

Amy E. Swain is a graduate student at the University of North Carolina at Chapel Hill. She is interested in alternative schools and the punitive culture of public schooling. She served as an evaluator for North Carolina's Incarcerated Individuals Program and teaches courses for pre-service teachers in the social foundations of education and in multi-cultural ways of knowing.

Mark Vicars is a Senior Lecturer in Literacy in the School of Education at Victoria University, Melbourne, Australia. Mark has worked as a literacy educator within the compulsory and post-compulsory sectors, in Japan, Korea, Thailand, Vietnam, Cambodia, England and Australia. In 2010, he was awarded the Australian Learning and Teaching Council Citation for pedagogical approaches that motivate, inspire and support socially disadvantaged and culturally diverse students to overcome barriers to learning and to experience and attain success. Mark has had his research published in international research journals and edited volumes. He is past president of the Australian Association for Qualitative Research (AQR).

Studies in the Postmodern Theory of Education

General Editor
Shirley R. Steinberg

Counterpoints publishes the most compelling and imaginative books being written in education today. Grounded on the theoretical advances in criticism, feminism, and postmodernism in the last two decades of the twentieth century, Counterpoints engages the meaning of these innovations in various forms of educational expression. Committed to the proposition that theoretical literature should be accessible to a variety of audiences, the series insists that its authors avoid esoteric and jargonistic languages that transform educational scholarship into an elite discourse for the initiated. Scholarly work matters only to the degree it affects consciousness and practice at multiple sites. Counterpoints' editorial policy is based on these principles and the ability of scholars to break new ground, to open new conversations, to go where educators have never gone before.

For additional information about this series or for the submission of manuscripts, please contact:

> Shirley R. Steinberg
> c/o Peter Lang Publishing, Inc.
> 29 Broadway, 18th floor
> New York, New York 10006

To order other books in this series, please contact our Customer Service Department:

> (800) 770-LANG (within the U.S.)
> (212) 647-7706 (outside the U.S.)
> (212) 647-7707 FAX

Or browse online by series:
> www.peterlang.com

www.ingramcontent.com/pod-product-compliance
Ingram Content Group UK Ltd.
Pitfield, Milton Keynes, MK11 3LW, UK
UKHW022238230426
12048UKWH00018BA/1333